Massing the Tropes

Massing the Tropes

The Metaphorical Construction of American Nuclear Strategy

RON HIRSCHBEIN

PRAEGER SECURITY INTERNATIONAL
Westport, Connecticut • London

Library of Congress Cataloging-in-Publication Data

Hirschbein, Ron, 1943–
  Massing the tropes: the metaphorical construction of American
nuclear strategy / by Ron Hirschbein.
      p.   cm.
  Includes bibliographical references and index.
  ISBN 0–275–96722–0
  1. Nuclear weapons—United States. 2. United States—Military policy. 3. Strategy—
Terminology. 4. Nuclear warfare—Terminology. I. Title.
  UA23.H5165   2005
  355.02′17′0973—dc22   2005020497

British Library Cataloguing in Publication Data is available.

Library of Congress Catalog Card Number: 2005020497
ISBN: 0–275–96722–0

First published in 2005

Praeger Security International, 88 Post Road West, Westport, CT 06881
An imprint of Greenwood Publishing Group, Inc.
www.praeger.com

Printed in the United States of America

The paper used in this book complies with the
Permanent Paper Standard issued by the National
Information Standards Organization (Z39.48–1984).

10 9 8 7 6 5 4 3 2 1

I do not ... imply that metaphors and figures of speech can be dispensed with in ordinary utterances, still less in the sciences: only that the danger of illicit reification—the mistaking of words for things, metaphors for realities—is even greater ... than is usually supposed.... To take such expressions so literally that it becomes natural to attribute to them causal properties, transcendent properties, demands for human sacrifice, is to be fatally deceived by myths.

—Isaiah Berlin, *Essays*

Contents

Introduction:
A Faith-Based Nuclear Strategy

The world of human aspiration is largely fictitious, and if we do not understand this we understand nothing about man.... The most astonishing thing of all, about man's fictions, is not that they have from prehistoric times hung like a flimsy canopy over his social world, but that he should have come to discover them at all. It is one of the most remarkable achievements of thought, of self-scrutiny, that the most anxiety-prone animal of all could come to *see through himself* and discover the fictional nature of his action world. Future historians will probably record it as one of the great, liberating breakthroughs of all time, and it happened in ours.

—Ernest Becker[1]

PRÉCIS

I asked my friend Mark what it was like to serve as a medic in Vietnam. His reply was memorable: "I had no metaphors, just reality." How much does it exaggerate to suggest that nuclear strategists suffer the opposite affliction—they have no reality, just metaphors? Conflating the literary with the literal, latter-day strategists put their faith in the "eternal wisdom" of the time-honored metaphors found in ancient texts. This study transforms this assertion into an argument. There are, of course, caveats.

Undoubtedly, obdurate realities such as the destruction of Hiroshima, the results of subsequent nuclear testing, and American vulnerability to nuclear attack inform strategizing. Bernard Brodie, an early strategist, recognized a salient fact—perhaps *the* salient fact—of the nuclear age: "Nuclear weapons exist, and they are incredibly destructive."[2] Nuclear strategy is a conceptual strategy—an invocation of resonant metaphors—for interpreting this fact. Of course, like most privileged interpretations, the prevailing account of nuclear weaponry has become official reality—an ontology that confuses metaphorical concepts with real things.

Accordingly, this study emphasizes another indisputable reality—a fact that *should* be a caveat informing all nuclear strategizing: There are no facts about nuclear war-fighting; indeed the "fact" that nuclear arsenals deter war is, at best, arguable. Strategists labor under a fortunate empirical deficit: No one has experienced a nuclear exchange between belligerents. As Brodie warned: "In the contest of thermonuclear war, everything is new and every military arm or weapon is essentially untested."[3] Strategic discourse cannot accurately reflect the reality of nuclear war-fighting—luckily, there is no reality to reflect! Strategic presuppositions and scenarios are faith-based, and yet strategists are not noted for excessive humility and tolerance for dissent. As Lawrence Freedman observes in his influential account of nuclear strategy:

The legion of uncertainties ought to have created a common humility—to be so much in the dark with so much at stake. Unfortunately the frustration with this predicament led many strategists to show astonishing confidence in their own nostrums, combined with vindictiveness against those who differed.[4]

Analysts such as Philip Green agree that such unalloyed confidence is hardly justified. Strategizing is not rocket science; on the contrary, it is a peculiar genre of science fiction.[5] Lamentably, the fictive element of strategic scenarios is seldom recognized by the strategists themselves or their constituents.

Lacking empirical data, strategists make a fateful leap of faith in their struggle to devise a conceptual strategy for rendering apocalyptic weapons intelligible and manageable: They invoke time-honored primary metaphors that liken the unfamiliar exigencies of the nuclear age to the familiar conceptual templates of the remembered past. These primary metaphors, as we shall see, are conceptualized in terms of diverse, often contesting, secondary metaphors. In short, the newest weapons are conceptualized and managed in terms of the oldest metaphors.

These arresting, primary metaphors are not merely cognitive maps that construct *what* is happening. They also serve—as we philosophers say—teleological and normative functions: These tropes indicate *why* an event is occurring and what *should* be done. In other words, strategic metaphors are not mere academic ruminations; on the contrary, they are performative: They guide long-term policy-making regarding the development, deployment, and detonation of nuclear weapons. More significantly, they prescribe behavior during times of crises—critical junctures when decision-makers choose between peace and war.

There is a striking parallel between dramatic changes in the ancient Greeks' metaphorical accounts of conflict and equally dramatic changes in the American conceptualization of nuclear weaponry. The influence of the ancient Greeks on latter-day strategy is difficult to overstate. Decisions about nuclear endeavors are made in the halls modeled after Greek architecture, and weapons are named after Greek gods. This much is obvious. Less obvious, but more telling, is the realization that the chronicle of American nuclear strategizing retells an ancient, metaphorical account of the causes of war and prospects for peace.

Initially, Greek bards invoked supernatural imagery—the machinations of the Olympian gods—to account for earthly conflicts such as the Trojan War. However, after a series of setbacks and military disasters, the gods no longer smiled upon Athens. Thucydides responded by rejecting supernatural imagery in favor of a naturalistic account of conflict, an account regarded as "eternal wisdom" by today's political realists: all-too-human perfidy, not Olympian mischief, explained Athenian trials and tribulations. Athenian disasters in Syracuse and momentous conflicts with the Persians set the stage for Thucydides' realpolitik. Chronicling the deeds of the clever and ruthless Athenians, "Thucydides' account explicitly disavowed archaic ideas about justice: the guide to life is intelligent calculation."[6] Such calculation was informed by presuppositions about the indelible features of human nature, not mytho-poetic fantasies about divine intrigues.

Likewise, during the early heroic days of American nuclear endeavors, those "present at creation" invoked supernatural metaphors (mostly the Judeo-Christian variety) to account for their noumenal experience—witnessing events that were "wholly other." This sense of awe soon turned to an exuberant millenarianism: American leaders had an exclusive franchise on the power that binds the cosmos—a power that could be put to good use, or so it seemed. When fate no longer smiled on the American nuclear enterprise—the Soviets got The Bomb in 1949—the latter-day strategic oeuvre invoked the naturalistic metaphors of the ancient historian. Unlike the supernatural metaphors, these naturalistic tropes that inform Thucydides' political realism—*balance of power, deterrence, crisis,* and *necessity*—are taken literally. These root metaphors (the quintessence of political realism) are deemed eternal laws of international relations operating behind the backs and against the will of decision-makers. Further, as we shall see, in constructing nuclear strategy these root metaphors are conceptualized—often tendentiously—in terms of contesting, secondary metaphors. For example, the venerable notion of balance of power is likened to secondary metaphors such as an antique laboratory scale or to homeostasis within the international body politic.

I hasten to add that the meaning read into these metaphors and the performances these meanings entail are context dependent. (One of my least controversial claims is that American strategists are not citizens of ancient Athens.) Time and place determine whether a metaphor's time has come and how the metaphor will be interpreted and enacted. True, the metaphors that inform latter-day strategizing are found in the works of Thucydides, but times have changed. Surely American strategists do not share the consciousness and sensibility of the ancient Greeks in toto—it is misleading to liken Henry Kissinger to Pericles. Stripped out of their classic context, these time-honored tropes acquire a distinctly American accent: Unlike the ancient tragedies and historical narratives, strategic scenarios generally have happy endings—thanks to the invocation of clever words and some technological deus ex machina.[7] (Could it be that happy ending stories are irresistible because life ends tragically?) The men who control the fate of the earth (by and large, it's a male endeavor) are strong in the Enlightenment faith in "linear progress, absolute truths, and rational planning." They share a conviction that would strike the ancient Greek tragedian as hopelessly naïve: According to faith-based nuclear strategy the world can be rationally ordered and ultimately controlled—somehow, all problems have solutions.[8]

Metaphors, then, are products of time and place. The metaphors that inform strategizing are the lingua franca of an identifiable group. Quakers do not break the silence by advocating the new weapons essential for a "robust deterrence." It is essential to identify the nature of the group that "talks the talk." Accordingly, it's crucial to properly identify the name of the collective responsible for the theory and practice of managing the nuclear arsenal.

WHAT'S IN A NAME?

> We live in a world of abstractions, of bureaus, and machines, of absolute ideas and of crude messianism.
>
> —Albert Camus[9]

What is the proper name of the collective that ponders the development, deployment, and detonation of nuclear weaponry? Only geniuses and madmen experience the world uniquely. For the rest of us (I include nuclear strategists here) the experience of the world is profoundly shaped—if not inexorably determined—by our culture and by our secondary collective affiliations (subcultures). In other words, experience per se, and the metaphors improvised to make experience intelligible and communicable, are social constructions. Even religious experience—putatively unmistakable revelations of the divine—doesn't speak for itself. Such experience is, to say the least, mediated by one's enculturation. Somewhere Bertrand Russell observes that the Virgin Mary appears to Catholics, not Hindus. Likewise, Catholics are not awestruck by revelations from Krishna.

Nuclear weapons were not created by scientists, engineers, and military men working independently. The Manhattan Project was the work of a tightly-knit, excessively controlled cabal enduring years of secrecy and isolation in the remote wilderness of New Mexico. This cult-like sodality sought to unleash an awesome cosmic force. The latter-day defense intellectuals working in think tanks and bureaus such as the Department of Defense are no longer desert dwellers, although they haven't completely abandoned the belief in magic; they too have a distinctive culture. They don't have much in common with Buddhists or those who work at the Bureau of Fish and Game. In order to uncover and interpret the metaphors that inform nuclear strategizing it is essential to understand the nature of this evolving nuclear culture. How shall it be defined?

An old but apt saying: Those who control the definition control the argument. Not surprisingly, diverse, often contradictory, definitions have been assigned—often tendentiously—to this nuclear culture. (These definitions may reveal more about the writer than the nuclear culture itself.) In any case, certain definitions mislead because they are static: To invoke Nietzsche's bad name, concepts with a history cannot be defined, they must be narrated. Unfortunately, the usual, one-dimensional definitions are ahistorical. They don't account for the evolving, paradoxical nature of a movement that began as a desert cabal of scientific visionaries and evolved into an organization dominated by the most powerful figures in American society.

Critics of American nuclear endeavors, for example, depict a nuclear brotherhood, a perverse religion, or—worse yet—a "death cult."[10] As religious scholar James Aho explains:

The nuclear death cult ... [has] its initiation rites and cult masters, its succession of hiding the innermost altar where the power of life and death is wielded ... its secret twelve-digit codes ... [and] silent attendants who bear the mechanisms in attaché cases, perpetually hovering like angels of death at the right shoulders of the priests.[11]

True, the background, structure, and ideology of the Manhattan Project (as we shall see) had cult-like features. Supernatural metaphors and tales of Faust were invoked to interpret the wonder and terror of the Trinity Test. And given the risks involved in ventures subsequently dubbed "atomic diplomacy," "competition in risk-taking," or "games of chicken,"[12] it is understandable that some can't resist the temptation to invoke epithets such as "nuclear madness."[13] To state the case more cautiously, even a cursory glance at recent history suggests that it is premature to celebrate the triumph of reason in the collective life of the nuclear elite. Yet, contrary to some of the hyperbolic accounts, strategic decision-makers are not captives of a radioactive Jonestown. None of the distinguished psychiatrists who have studied strategic affairs conclude that nuclear strategists are psychopaths. Indeed, some studies suggest that the nuclear theologians and priests (a popular designation in the nuclear cult literature) fulfill the usual requirements for emotional well being: They derive satisfaction from their work (perhaps *too* much satisfaction) and personal life.[14] In any case, unlike many of the evanescent cults on the fringe of society, the nuclear brotherhood has survived and prospered.

At the other extreme, there are those who attribute the cunning of reason to strategic affairs. Strategizing about apocalyptic weaponry is seen as rather ordinary and readily comprehensible. Certain critics, of course, note the evil of such banality. However, the rationalists I have in mind champion American nuclear endeavors. Those involved in the theory and practice of managing the American arsenal are portrayed as calculating rational agents struggling to make the best of a dangerous situation. Others suggest that there is nothing odd or exotic about the bureaus and think tanks that devise scenarios for nuclear weapons: policy-making is understood as the organizational dynamics—the machinations—of an elite bureaucracy.[15]

Bureaucratic attributes are assigned to nuclear endeavors for good reason. There is evidence that what some regard as priesthood or cult is just another powerful, self-serving bureaucracy within the federal government. As former Pentagon official Richard Barnet explains: "National security managers have a personal investment in the health and aggrandizement of their own bureaucratic organizations. They equate the national interest and their organization's interest as a matter of course."[16] Accordingly, mundane factors such as bureaucratic rivalry, careerism, and profiteering are adduced to explain nuclear endeavors. Indeed, it is somewhat reassuring to learn that, like other bureaucrats, the national security managers are survivors.

To be sure, as Barnet suggests, the nuclear bureaucracy is ordinarily marked by the usual careerism and the jockeying for power and prestige typical of other well established organizations within the government. He goes so far as to intimate that it's all a game: Contrary to their overwrought public rhetoric, the members of the American team are not ideologues; they simply want to humble the competition. And yet, there is bad news: Unlike other bureaus such as the Social Security Administration, in extraordinary circumstances the bureaucracy advocates risking the destruction of itself and everything it cherishes. (As we shall see, such risks were hazarded in episodes such as the Cuban missile crisis.) Indeed, prominent strategists such as Leon Wieseltier don't sound much like the "organization man" when they excoriate those who believe that unilateral disarmament is preferable to extinction: "Unilateralism is a disgraceful notion produced by people who think so little of themselves that they believe in nothing except life."[17] It appears that nuclear risking-taking is routine. As Richard Betts concludes in his account of nuclear threats: "Presidents were unwilling to recognize nuclear combat as so unthinkable that they could not exploit its potential to secure international objectives."[18]

In any case, there are elements of truth in these contesting attempts at definition: The cult-like features of the nuclear brotherhood are evident in its origins and time in the wilderness in Los Alamos. Today, of course, the development and deployment of nuclear weapons are no secret, and the arsenal is managed by various bureaucracies within the federal government. There is something paradoxical in all this: On occasion the professionals who manage nuclear weapons behave like cultists who put their faith in magical powers of the cosmos and willingly risk everything for a glorious cause. Ordinarily, however, they behave like bureaucrats preoccupied with the continuity and growth of their organization. These paradoxical forces have not gone unnoticed by certain participants. Herbert York (a Manhattan Project physicist and first Director of the Livermore National Laboratory) quips that every nuclear era administration has made weapons and talked peace.[19] As playwright Friedrich Durrenmatt noted in *The Physicists* (a dramatization of the legacy of modern science), "He who exposes himself to the paradoxical exposes himself to reality."[20]

The collective mentality of those who manage nuclear weapons seems conflicted, if not paradoxical. Could it be that the strategic decision-making process is the outcome of the interplay of an evangelical zeal driven by preconceived visions of a secular millennium—a new American century, an imperium safeguarded by an array of nuclear weapons, and a prudent bureaucratic logic preoccupied with the continuity and success of long-established organizations? Strategists fantasize about weapons because of what Camus calls "crude messianism." The more evangelical strategists remain strong in the faith that the atom can work wonders in history. However, as Camus also recognized, the world of the atom is also a realm of bureaus. Those who strategize about apocalyptic weapons talk peace because, like the rest of us, they normally want to survive and prosper.

Strategic thinking seems to be informed by a dialectic between such irrational exuberance and more earthbound, bureaucratic imperatives. At times, there is no antagonism between these contradictory forces. On the contrary, they can be synergistic: The development and deployment of new weaponry (e.g. "Star Wars" technology) continues because it is driven by millenarian aspirations (rendering the United States invulnerable to nuclear attack) and bureaucratic calculations (billion dollar profits for military contractors). In extraordinary situations, however, the dialectic can be destructive. As we shall see, President Kennedy's vacillation during the Cuban missile crisis reveals that decision-makers can be pulled in opposite directions by their crusading zeal to settle scores in an apocalyptic battle and by their pragmatic need to assure the continuity of their in-group and the nation as a whole.

This dialectic between irrational, millenarian enthusiasm and rational, organizational imperatives takes place within the minds and the bureaus of those who manage the nuclear arsenal. In searching for the proper name for the conflicted collective that manages nuclear weapons, I found that anthropologists of religions such as Anthony Wallace invoke a concept, an ideal type, that roughly fits the facts—ecclesiastical bureaucracy.[21] Following Nietzsche's dictum, the development of such an evolving organization has signature features that must be understood historically. Specifically, in order to better understand the stories early and latter-day strategists tell about nuclear weapons, it is important to appreciate the origins and context of their narrative—their legitimizing script. The plot follows Wallace's account of the emergence of ecclesiastical bureaucracies:

Prior to World War II, civilization began falling apart around prominent European physicists probing the secrets of the atom. Despite their prestige and assimilated status, many of these Jewish scientists were persecuted by the Nazis. As the world collapsed around them, atoms disintegrated in their laboratories—the center no longer held. These first nuclear evangelists, men such as Albert Einstein, Leo Szilard, and Edward Teller, knew what nuclear weapons meant in Nazi hands. Understandably, it appeared that only the incredible power of the atom in the right hands could prevent the destruction of civilization.

Despite the unprecedented Nazi peril, and their own agonizing dislocation, these refugee scientists did not abandon hope. They remained optimistic even as American authorities scoffed at the jeremiads of these impassioned refugees, men who embodied the Hollywood caricature of the eccentric German professor. They ventured to America to promulgate what Robert Jay Lifton calls a new religion, a creed called Nuclearism: "A secular religion, a total faith in which 'grace' even 'salvation' … are achieved through the power of a new technological deity."[22]

Their conversion experience was regrettable but understandable under the circumstances. Gentle scholars who loved children suddenly became the advocates and architects of weapons that could kill or mutilate all the world's children. Later, many of these scientists would express remorse and dedicate their lives to nuclear disarmament. (Many of their names are listed as founders of *The Bulletin of the Atomic Scientists*.) However, given the emerging Nazi peril, even lifelong pacifists such as Einstein reluctantly supported the development of American nuclear weapons. Szilard prevailed upon him to send a guided missive to Roosevelt. The document—along with reports from British Intelligence—persuaded the president that:

1. There was a real possibility of the Nazis developing a weapon that would determine the outcome of the war—the atomic bomb;
2. The United States must move secretly and decisively to build the first nuclear weapons in order to counter the Nazis, assure victory, and promote a peaceful postwar world.

The Manhattan Project had many of the signature features often associated with cults. Its participants were removed from familiar surroundings, subject to excessive controls, and isolated in a secret society surrounded by armed guards. Charismatic leaders such as Robert Oppenheimer and Leslie Groves imposed discipline and conformity, and promised salvation through the invocation of a newfound power—an uncanny cosmic force that would work wonders in history. Unlike other cults, the Manhattan Project *did* actually summon-up a mysterious cosmic force. (Nuclear fission liberated the force that binds the microcosm, while fusion calls forth the power that lights the firmament.) Supernatural metaphors were invoked to render the cosmic power and the cult's glorious cause intelligible and communicable.

Like other cults, the Los Alamos scientists and engineers embraced a Manichean worldview depicting an intrinsically evil, subhuman enemy—an "other" to be passionately despised and feared. (Reinhold Niebuhr rejected this view and suggested that World War II was a struggle between two types of sinners, the Axis Powers being the most heinous.) In any event, who could doubt that the Nazis came about as close as inhumanly possible to the Manichean account of evil? However, it is worth noting that by 1944 the campaign to demonize the Japanese and Germans began to abate. Perhaps decision-makers reasoned that the defeated Axis Powers would soon be allies in postwar campaigns against the Soviets.

Events almost inevitably conspire against cultist promises, even cults in high places. Germany surrendered before the bomb was ready, and whether the destruction of Hiroshima and Nagasaki encouraged the surrender of a Japan already vanquished by fire bombing is arguable. Surely no one expected the Japanese to triumph in August 1945. The short-lived, nuclear monopoly didn't usher in the millennium—a time of uncontested American power and prestige. On the contrary, Soviet hegemony expanded into Eastern Europe. Most significantly—despite American wishful thinking to the contrary—the Soviets mastered nuclear weaponry in 1949.

If a cult is to survive the betrayal of its promise and the demise of charismatic leadership, it must evolve into a bureaucratic phase. The process often begins with a nativistic stage in which the organization is purged of heretics. In a predictable Weberian manner, legitimacy supplants charismatic leadership. (As we shall see, deterrence became the legitimizing ideology.) Operational procedures are standardized and imposed without regard to consequence or person.

The transition from cultist mentality to organization man is most obvious in the construction—or deconstruction—of enemies. During the cultist phase, demonized enemies (such as the Japanese and Germans) evoke hot-blooded passion. Apparently, only weapons regarded in supernatural terms were suitable for these "unnatural" enemies. However, during the latter-day, cold-blooded bureaucratic phase, it's nothing personal: those targeted for destruction are mere statistics in systems analysis. The good news is that, during the Cold War, ordinary Soviet citizens were depicted as friends, captives of a cruel police state. The bad news is that, none the less, they were targeted for destruction.

This peculiar irony is the outcome of the legitimizing script that emerged during the bureaucratic consolidation of American nuclear endeavors. The script seems to function like some unspoken grammar or logic guiding strategic thinking. The script relates strategic metaphors in a sequential, irreversible order. In effect, it expresses *the* story, the privileged narrative, about American strategizing. This study dwells upon these latter-day metaphors because they guide policy-making and decision-making at critical junctures. Just as, during candid moments, veterans reveal that their war stories are largely fictive, perhaps we should expect nothing less—or more—from strategic storytelling about possible futures.

Given the metaphysic of political realism that informs strategizing, it is not surprising that these metaphors are construed as eternal laws of the international universe rather than mere figures of speech. The scenario (this favored strategic term has more gravitas than mere storytelling), or rather this study's interpretation of the story, goes something like this:

THE GRAND STRATEGIC SCENARIO

> Atomic weapons are useful because of the stories people tell about them.
> —John Canaday[23]

1. *The balance of power*—no longer called the balance of terror since terrorism gets bad press—is vague, ambiguous, and fictional (a characteristic shared by other strategic metaphors). The fiction begins with an incommensurate comparison between two distinctly different entities or domains. The notion of balance of power is not merely the clichéd comparison of apples and oranges—two kinds of fruit. It is a comparison between two qualitatively different domains: International relations are likened to an antique laboratory scale or to homeostasis within the body (body politic). For the most part strategists promote a balance that favors the *appearance* of American superiority. The more sophisticated strategists recognize that once the capacity for assured destruction is attained, actual superiority is meaningless; nevertheless—or so it is claimed—promulgating a perception (or misperception) of superiority is prudent: Manufacturing such a perception with the latest weapons complemented by a robust, declaratory strategy is also prudent: It deters enemy aggression and possibly other actions inimical to American interest. Better yet, the perception of such a favorable balance allows American elites to practice coercive diplomacy.

2. *Deterrence*—the quintessential expression of political realism. Strategists presuppose a worst-case scenario regarding adversaries and a best-case scenario about the efficacy of their weapons and the cleverness of their long-term planning and immediate tactical goals. It is a virtual truism in strategic discourse that

adversaries are acting aggressively rather than defensively. (Soviet hegemony over Eastern Europe was construed as an offensive move toward world domination—or minimally European domination—rather than a defensive buffer against possible aggression.) Accordingly, a survivable nuclear arsenal had to be deployed to deter aggression by thwarting Soviet intentions and capabilities. The ecclesiastical bureaucracy that manages the American arsenal—so it was argued—had to keep producing nuclear weapons so that they may never be used. Not surprisingly, deterrence is conceptualized in terms of a variety of contesting secondary metaphors as we shall see. For example, to paraphrase the Harvard Nuclear Study Group, deterrence is like a crystal ball: it enables enemies to foresee that they have everything to lose and nothing to gain if they pursue actions inimical to American vital interests (whatever they may be). There is considerable ambiguity as to what adversaries are to experience as they peer into the crystal ball. Some strategists liken adversaries to CPAs engaged in noonday commerce—rational actors reckoning cost/risk/benefit analysis, while others argue that adversaries experience inconsolable anxiety as they contemplate certain annihilation. Finally, it as been suggested that deterrence is "existential" (a more acceptable term than the "madman" notion of deterrence[24]): anxious adversaries don't know what to expect if they act in ways inimical to American interests.

3. A *crisis*—an incident likened to a variety of events beyond human control such as natural disasters or medical emergencies—occurs if deterrence fails. Decision-makers struggle to reestablish the status quo ante through words or weapons. Of course, given the ambiguity of deterrence and the enthusiasm for crises—a leader's defining moment—there is an almost irresistible temptation to construe a wide gamut of events as crises. (In his Farewell Address, Eisenhower warned of this temptation and urged his successors to define challenges as problems to be resolved patiently in due course, rather than as crises requiring urgent, often reckless action. Just as his warning about the military-industrial complex went unheeded, his advice about crises was ignored.)[25]

4. If words fail to resolve a crisis it is somehow *necessary* to resort to weapons— even nuclear weapons—to resolve the challenge. As Herman Kahn urges, it is necessary to entertain the unthinkable. It is crucial to explicate this overused metaphor invoked to absolve decision-makers of responsibility. But second guessing is essential since strategists fail to indicate what's meant by necessity. As we shall see, unlike the primary metaphors just cited, the meaning of such "necessity" is never spelled out with secondary metaphors; perhaps the meaning is supposed to be obvious. (Michael Walzer, however, goes into considerable detail to explicate the notion of necessity. He likens the notion to a supreme emergency: an imminent threat of unprecedented horror.) However, for the most part, in official discourse invoking "necessity" is an argument-stopping, rhetorical ploy much like terms such as "national security" or "un-American." The terms, of course, may be meaningful, even self-evident to those who share certain strategic scenarios.

I suspect that strategists deem the sequence of tropes just outlined as necessary and irreversible. Reflecting their political realist pedigree, strategists presuppose that the progression (or regression) of events is somehow natural and inevitable. What is most disturbing in an age of assured destruction is an unquestioned doctrine: The climax of certain crisis scripts somehow "requires" an American nuclear response. (To be sure, while the Cuban missile crisis gives us pause, no one knows whether this doctrinal demand would actually be fulfilled at a critical juncture; I, for one, am not eager to find out.) A variety of endgame scripts are proffered to assure a happy ending to nuclear war-fighting scenarios. (One person's happiness, of course, may be another's misery. Herman Kahn thought that thermonuclear war-fighting may be a war of necessity. But he reassured an anxious public that only about 20,000,000 Americans might perish in such an inevitable conflagration.) In any event, weapons and metaphors proliferate to represent such notions of surviving and prevailing in a nuclear war as both credible and tolerable.

A series of ancillary metaphors drawn from everyday life are invoked to reassure the reader that the nuclear war-fighting won't get out of hand. Ladders of escalation are difficult to climb—gravity is on our side; firebreaks prevent the nuclear brushfire from becoming a conflagration; or nuclear war-fighting is limited to surgical strikes in which targets are properly excised without killing the entire body politic. And collateral damage seems no worse than bad credit.

I am writing this book because I suspect that strategists are largely unaware of the ancient, metaphorical basis of this privileged narrative: a story—the official reality—that unfolds amid an evangelical faith in the precepts of modernity. Strategic tropes are not seen as mere figures of speech or even as heuristic models of international reality. They are afforded the canonical status of eternal wisdom. The writings of Thucydides, Machiavelli, and Hobbes are an obligatory catechism. Likewise, the precepts of modernity are not seen as wishful thinking in light of the folly and carnage of the twentieth century. On the contrary, it is virtually self-evident to the doves (speaking of metaphors) that nuclear weapons can be managed prudently and used to deter aggression. And the hawks remain strong in the faith that nuclear weapons can be put to good use in pursuit of national objectives.

No doubt strategic metaphors exert an attraction—some would say a fatal attraction—to both hawks and doves for a variety of reasons. Obviously strategists do not want to experience nuclear war-fighting, they much prefer daring stories about catastrophic conflict to the real thing. Strategic scenarios are a time-honored, robust, masculine genre, stories told and retold to each generation.[26]

ARE NUCLEAR ISSUES STILL RELEVANT?

We live in a state of terror because persuasion is no longer possible; because man has been wholly submerged in History; because he can no longer tap

that part of his nature, as real as the historical part, which he recaptures in
contemplating the beauty of ... human faces.

—Albert Camus[27]

The remainder of this study develops and explores this account of
nuclear strategizing. However, before turning to this task a question
suited for the remainder of this introduction arises: Aren't strategic
nuclear issues passé? Surely, the bipolar disorder known as the Cold
War is long gone and, with it, the threat of mutual annihilation. Indeed,
shouldn't we be totally preoccupied with the war on terrorism; doesn't
9/11 illustrate the newfound vulnerability of the American homeland?

In response to these rhetorical questions I suggest there is nothing new
about the vulnerability of the American homeland. The homeland was
de facto rendered defenseless when the Soviets acquired nuclear delivery
systems about 1956. The threat remains and is exacerbated by the lax command and control of the nuclear arsenal in the former Soviet Union and the
omnipresent danger of accidental nuclear war. And the danger persists on
this side of the Atlantic because the mere figures of speech invoked to manage the nuclear arsenal are misconstrued as tried-and-true textbook science.
Finally, George Kennan's jeremiad should not be taken lightly: Properly
managing a nuclear arsenal requires infallible individuals; mistakes cannot
be remedied or forgiven.[28] Due to a mixture of negligence, wishful thinking,
and preoccupation with terrorism, we are, to paraphrase Kundera, rigid
prisoners of rigid conceptions of what is important and what is not.

Concern about nuclear extinction waxes and wanes. While several
Manhattan Project physicists "present at creation" offered dark counsel
about a dangerous, if not catastrophic, nuclear arms race, the interlude
of the American nuclear monopoly was a time of millenarian enthusiasm.[29] Surely the exclusive American franchise on the "ultimate weapon"
would usher in a time of untold power and prosperity for the elect among
nations. And yet, even this brief, four-year interlude was marked by foreboding: Despite (or again because of?) the American nuclear monopoly,
the Soviets extended their hegemony throughout Eastern Europe; Maoists
triumphed in China; and anti-colonial movements flourished in places
such as Indochina. Dark counsel about a nuclear arms race was taken seriously after the Soviets detonated an atomic bomb over Siberia.

Strategic counsel became dark indeed: During the Cold War the Soviets
acquired the capacity to obliterate the United States—time and again we
were warned that "the Russians are coming!" Proposals for arms control,
let alone disarmament, were invariably met with the refrain, "What about
the Russians?" ("What about the Americans?" was seldom asked, at least
on this side of the Atlantic.) Strategists insisted that tens of thousands
of apocalyptic weapons must be developed and deployed to avoid their
detonation: somehow, nuclear war could only be averted if decision-makers

convinced themselves and their adversaries that they were prepared to use these weapons. (Depending upon one's perspective, strategizing is marked by remarkable paradoxes—or by glaring contradictions.) Despite (or actually because of) this harrowing predicament, proponents of deterrence (mutually assured destruction—MAD) attach a triumphant coda to their narrative: One does not enter into the communion of strategic discourse without reciting the blessings of deterrence. According to the strategic catechism, nuclear weapons have ushered in a truly astonishing age, a miracle surpassing the promise of Christianity—peace on earth *without* good will toward men.

My personal response to our nuclear peril is probably not unusual. During my childhood I acknowledged that my teachers were right about the frightening prospects of nuclear war, but it didn't matter. After all, they were also right about Alexander the Great and the Andromeda Galaxy: ancient history, distant stars, and nuclear war were far removed from my experience—such remote, seemingly academic concerns didn't go beyond the classroom. The "duck and cover" air raid drills added a touch of mirth, if not absurdity, to the situation: How could my desktop spare my scrawny body from a thermonuclear flash brighter than a thousand suns? At least the drills got me questioning authority.

The Cuban missile crisis interrupted my adolescent reverie: suddenly the threat of extinction seemed real. If an opportunistic friend is to be believed, he even used the crisis as a pretext of seduction: "Since the world is about to end anyway.... " With the advent of the Test Ban Treaty nuclear testing went underground, as did my nuclear fears. I put nuclear terror out of my mind, lest it drive me out of my mind. Adolescent concerns blotted out the threat of nuclear omnicide in hormonal haze.

The Reagan administration, however, reawakened my fears by publicly enunciating longstanding strategic doctrine with considerable bravado, and by deploying weapons in pursuit of the doctrine. Accordingly, my teaching and research became preoccupied with the nuclear arms race. My concern, however, was academic and analytic, bereft of appropriate affect, let alone outrage. My humanity expressed itself, however, in bouts of anxious insomnia when I took what was said to heart.

Recently, the authorship of an op-ed piece in the *Los Angeles Times* gave me more sleepless nights. I had read numerous pieces by Robert McNamara. In radically different venues, I had also read pieces by Helen Caldicott (a long-time peace activist and strident critic of American foreign policy). However, I had never seen—nor expected to see—a piece co-authored by these two. At first blush, such collaboration seems as likely as George W. Bush selecting Michael Moore as his running mate. Apparently, McNamara chose Caldicott as his newfound collaborator because he believes we confront a tragically neglected predicament, a grave threat that has exercised Caldicott for years: thousands of

American and Russian nuclear weapons on hair-trigger alert are managed by all-too-fallible men.

Evidently, as the former secretary of defense's apologia in texts and films[30] suggests, he has acquired what some call "retirement wisdom." Perhaps former high officials such as McNamara gain a fresh perspective as they dissociate themselves from the Pentagon subculture, reflect upon their careers, and (perhaps) seek absolution. In any event, upon retirement, many former political, military, and scientific advocates tell a different, and very disturbing, story about nuclear weapons.

McNamara would not be the first architect of American nuclear endeavors to have second thoughts upon retirement. His former speech writer, a nuclear strategist named Daniel Ellsberg, obviously had second thoughts when he released the *Pentagon Papers* and became an anti-nuclear activist. Herbert York, a Manhattan Project physicist authored a book titled *Race to Oblivion* (the title speaks for itself). And Dwight Eisenhower's Farewell Address contains an oft quoted—but never heeded—warning of the peril of the military-industrial complex. It is, to say the least, noteworthy that at this late date, McNamara experiences a sufficient sense of peril to join his former nemesis in warning that:

Of the 7,000 nuclear warheads, 2,500 are maintained on hair-trigger alert, ready for launching. In order to effectively retaliate, the commander of the Strategic Air Command has only three minutes to decide if a nuclear attack warning is valid. He has 10 minutes to find the president for a 30-second briefing on attack options.... A nearly identical situation prevails in Russia, except there the early warning system is decaying rapidly.[31]

The fears of McNamara and Caldicott are well founded. An American president may believe he has the prerogative to "ride out" a first strike and to assess the damage and plan a proper response. In reality, however, the system is geared toward launch on warning. Upon his retirement, Air Force General George Lee Butler, former chief of the Strategic Command, revealed that the nuclear command and control system is: "Structured to drive the president invariably toward a decision to launch under attack.... We never said publicly that we were committed to launch on warning under attack. Yet at the operational level it was never accepted that if the presidential decisions went to a certain tick of the clock, we would lose a major portion of our forces...."[32]

Not surprisingly, those who remain in the strategic brotherhood are conflicted. Psychologist Steven Kull's penetrating study, *Minds at War*, suggests that strategists are not of one mind.[33] As the author explains: "One mindset attends to significant changes engendered by nuclear weapons and supports the search for adaptive politics. The other mindset ignores or discounts the evidence of such change."[34] As realists, strategists proffer dark counsel and insist that a nuclear war would be an unparalleled disaster.

However, time and again, Kull notes a dramatic reversal as strategists evangelize about nuclear endeavors ushering in a triumphant America.

Granted, there is good reason to try to understand what these conflicted men are up to. But is strategic doctrine the place to look? Could it be that strategizing offers very good reasons for American nuclear endeavors thereby obfuscating the *real* reasons? A philosophic response is in order: yes and no. To paraphrase Kissinger, weapons come first; strategy comes later. Strategizing serves diverse functions—how could it be otherwise?—and surely ideological justification is one of them.

It would be naïve to suggest that nuclear endeavors are driven solely by impurely academic, abstract ideas and ideals. Surely the appropriate place must be given to factors such as vested economic interests, bureaucratic politics (especially competition between the armed services and national laboratories), and the gadget-mindedness of certain scientists and technicians.

Expressing what may be retirement wisdom, Marcus Raskin (former member of the Kennedy administration National Security Council) explains that the nuclear strategists' most important function "is to justify and extend the existence of their employers.... They know enough not to question their employers' right to exist. And so it is with most—if not all—defense specialists who are paid to justify violence."[35]

However, it is equally naïve to conclude that strategizing is merely an epiphenomena—a cosmetic to cover up naked profiteering, self-promotion, and technological obsessions. Even Marx and Engels, who recognized ideology as a cover-up for ruling class interests, emphasized that ideology acquires a life and history all its own, a separate existence that outlives the reasons for its origins.

The biases, presuppositions, and hypotheses (or is it wishful thinking?) that guides American decisions about the development, deployment, and detonation of nuclear weaponry did not emerge ex nihilo. As historian Gregg Herken explains:

Since 1945, American policy on nuclear weapons has been sometimes determined—and always influenced—by a small "nucleus" of civilian experts whose profession it has been to consider objectively the fearful prospect of nuclear war. Scientists, think-tank theorists, and cloistered academics have traditionally formed this elite fraternity of experts.[36]

For the most part, nuclear strategy has a life and body of its own because it expresses the conceptual system that informs the theory and practice of American foreign policy—political realism. As Annette Freyberg-Inan concludes in her study of political realism:

During the early years of the Cold War the foreign policy establishments in the United States ... entered into a symbiosis with realist scholarship that, in many cases, was to last until the present day.... Realist scholarship had a profound impact on U.S. diplomacy, as reflected in the works of George Marshall, George Kennan, and Henry Kissinger. Mary Maxwell points out that "this was the most dramatic instance of academic theory persuading the practitioners...." As John Garnett has observed, "American policy makers swallowed Realism hook, line and sinker."[37]

Sometimes philosophy becomes commonsense. Strategic tropes serve as a conduit to transmit the "everybody knows" truisms of Thucydides, Hobbes, and Morgenthau to American decision-makers.

AUTHORIAL STRATEGY

> We are all writers. The reason is that everyone has trouble accepting the fact that he will disappear unheard of and unnoticed in an indifferent universe and everybody wants to make himself into a universe of words before it's too late.
>
> —Milan Kundera[38]

Chapter 1: Realists Are from Mars/Idealists Are from Venus

Not surprisingly, strategists consider themselves realists who eschew figures of speech and other mythic-poetic effluvia. I attempt to show that by taking their arresting metaphors literally, realists fail to recognize that strategizing is a literary project. With Derrida I argue that since a nuclear war has not occurred strategists can only write about it. A more complete, authentic realism would recognize the power of the pen: Strategy is about improvising resonant stories (scenarios) based upon time-honored metaphors. It is also about authoring cryptic texts, interpreting deliberately ambiguous messages, and orchestrating and interpreting symbolic performances—displays in which appearance is everything.

Chapter 2: What's *the* Story?

Since, truth be known, there is no truth to be known about the outcome of nuclear war-fighting, strategic scenarios are only stories about preventing and fighting nuclear wars. Accordingly, this chapter attempts to define the strategic genre. Knowingly or unwittingly—despite occasional expressions of humility—strategists invoke the authorial strategy that makes it appear that they put forth the tried-and-true literature of well established disciplines. But clearly, the genre is not rocket science. I suggest that strategizing is what Raymond Aron calls "strategic fiction;" imagined scenarios informed by considerable wishful thinking.

Chapter 3: Newest Weapons/Oldest Metaphors

This chapter explores the *conceptual strategy* of those who make long-term recommendations and critical decisions about the development, deployment, and detonation of the American nuclear arsenal. The awe-some power and unprecedented peril posed by nuclear weapons fomented a crisis of comprehension. In order to render the unfamiliar, inchoate nuclear threat intelligible and manageable, American nuclear endeavors initially were likened to ancient supernatural images. To be sure, such imagery was not taken literally. However, when the Soviet threat exacer-bated American fears, naturalistic ancient Greek tropes were massed to get a handle on the situation. Perhaps in a desperate attempt to convince themselves that things were under control, these metaphors were taken literally.

Chapter 4:   Like Nothing Else

The early heroic days of American nuclear endeavors elicited a fearful symmetry: the hope and terror typical of religious conversion. Strategists invoked supernatural, Judeo-Christian metaphors that likened these endeavors to a great cosmic drama. To be sure, it is unlikely that the early strategists literally believed that they were "present at creation" or had experienced "the second coming." This "Golden Age" of nuclear endeavors ended when the Soviets acquired The Bomb. As the chapter concludes, the parallels between latter-day strategists and ancient Greek authors run deep. For a time the ancient playwrights invoked supernatural intervention to rescue Athenian statesmen from their folly. But no deus ex machina entered the international arena to rescue strategists from the peril posed by Soviet nuclear weapons.

Chapter 5:   The Balance of Power

Shortly before the Soviet explosion over Siberia, Brodie admonished that nuclear weapons should be seen as instruments of war, not a visita-tion from a wrathful deity. Massing the ancient tropes, strategists likened the American nuclear predicament to a primary metaphor: calibrating the balance of power. The balance of power itself was likened to secondary metaphors such as an antique laboratory scale or homeostasis within the international body politic. Although balance can be determined in labora-tories or by mathematical formulas, there is no way to definitively deter-mine what constitutes a nuclear balance of power. Indeed, in the Alice in Wonderland world of strategizing, the elusive *perception* of the balance of power becomes determinative. Strategists, in effect, recommend author-ing texts and orchestrating symbolic performances to communicate such perceptions. Semiotics replaces ordnance in determining the balance and its putative effects.

Chapter 6: Deterrence: Peace on Earth without Goodwill toward Men

The nuclear arsenal is likened to a deterrent and praised for preventing World War III and Soviet domination of Western Europe. Deterrence per se is likened to a host of rational and irrational forces—or some volatile mixture thereof. But despite these unsettled conceptual issues there is consensus that somehow deterrence works. I question this consensus by arguing that the elegiac praise of deterrence is overwrought, and a host of other factors could explain the absence of superpower conflict.

Chapter 7: What If They Gave a Crisis and Nobody Came?

According to the grand strategic narrative, crises—episodes when leaders decide between peace and war—occur when deterrence fails. However, as Nixon's indifference toward the failure of the American arsenal to deter the construction of a Soviet submarine base in Cuba illustrates, this is not always the case. And, as marked differences in crisis management suggest, crises are conceptualized and managed in terms of an array of secondary metaphors. Kennedy likened crises to existential dramas in which a would-be hero reveals his true character; he likened his challenges to those endured by Churchill and Chamberlain prior to World War II. In his wishful thinking, Nixon likened himself to great statesman such as Wilson and Churchill confronting world-historical events. In practice, his crises occurred when—like Willy Loman, the feckless salesman—he was not "well-liked" and was ridiculed. Finally, Dr. Kissinger likened crises to medical emergencies to be treated by the premier specialist of the day, someone knowledgeable and wise who could restore homeostasis in the international body-politic—namely Kissinger himself.

Chapter 8: Necessity: The Mother of Mayhem

"Necessity," one of the most overused terms in strategic discourse, is invoked to absolve decision-makers of responsibility for actions that are morally dubious or disastrous—supposedly, they have no choice. And yet, the same decision-makers take full responsibility for unlimited numbers of fortuitous events. Whereas other primary strategic metaphors are explicated in terms of secondary metaphors (the balance of power is likened to an antique scale) the notion of necessity is not explained with any secondary metaphors by decision-makers or strategists. The notion may simply be an argument-stopping, rhetorical device. Walzer, as we shall see, offers a keen analysis of the notion of necessity, but he bases his understanding of the notion on his reading of the moral law. Not surprisingly, however, others read the law differently, to say the least. This realization suggests that necessity is not prescribed by transcendent principles; it is part and parcel of an unthought, unquestioned script—as Isaiah Berlin argues. It appears that strategists improvise a tacit, preconscious narrative in which one act follows another.

I suspect—to understate the case—that mainstream international relations analysts in general, and strategists in particular, would question this take on nuclear strategizing. By and large strategists see themselves as political realists strong in the faith that they are (as we said in the Sixties) "telling it like it is." The world according to the political realists is not a realm of texts, stories, and metaphors; it is a domain of obdurate laws of international life and death, inexorable principles ignored at great peril. Strategists claim that, as political realists, they offer a sober assessment of reality unsullied by naïve ideals and sentimental moralizing, let alone by figures of speech. They eschew wishful thinking and face reality as it is to make the best of a dangerous situation. It is essential to confront this robust, manly view of things before any more talk of metaphors. To paraphrase a bestseller, realists think they are from Mars, while their critics are from Venus.

CHAPTER 1

Realists Are from Mars/Idealists Are from Venus

Clemenceau spoke in Parliament of "an old system [political realism] which appears discredited today, but to which I am not afraid of saying I am still faithful."

—Jonathan Schell[1]

Despite its theoretic and practical difficulties, political realism exerts a powerful, sometimes fatal, attraction. Realists relish the notion that they are virile thinkers who—unlike effete idealists—have the guts to face the world as it is. In the words of Hans Morgenthau (the "Dean of Political Realism"): "Idealist critics of realism cannot bear to look at the truth of politics straight in the face. Realism tries to understand the world as it really is rather than as people would like to see it. Those who resist the truths of political realism deceive themselves."[2] Resisting the intoxication of wishful thinking, realists offer a sober view of a deterministic political world of cruel, natural laws. But could it be that in the nuclear age, a peculiar and dangerous epoch in which appearance usually counts more than reality, political realism is outdated, wishful thinking?

Realists are enamored by what they deem the eternal wisdom of the ancients. Indebted to Thucydides' truisms, Hobbesian mechanistic thinking and Social Darwinism they conclude *homo homini lupus.* Unable to put these old verities aside, they are inattentive to the symbolic turn in international relations: a world of cryptic, dissembling texts and highly ambiguous, symbolic performances. A more authentic realism would stress that, more often than not, the texts intended for adversaries are not designed to communicate strategic realities or the political actor's intention; on the contrary, dissembling phrases are intended to bluff and deceive. Likewise, strategists must read between the lines in interpreting an adversary's declaratory policy and communiqués.

Nevertheless, the world according to political realism is transparent and uncomplicated: it's a jungle out there, and only the strong, clever, and unscrupulous survive: That's both the law of the jungle and the eternal law of politics. Reflecting upon the post-Cold War world, former CIA Director James Woolsey concludes: "True, the Soviet dragon has been slain, but we live now in a jungle filled with a bewildering variety of poisonous snakes, and in many ways the dragon was easier to keep track of."[3]

The jungle, of course, is no place for women, which is to say those who see the study of international relations as more of a soft, literary project rather than a hard science of cruel laws. No wonder feminists are among the critics of realism. Contrary to congenial realist stereotypes, like many other critics, feminists are not necessarily naïve idealists convinced that noble ideals can guide international relations, nor are they advocates of utopian schemes. On the contrary, they hit realism where it hurts: Some feminists view realist bravado as self-confessional—a strategy for valorizing one's masculinity. Taking a less personal approach, others see realism as a body of gender-specific, patriarchal assumptions reified as the natural order of things.[4] As political theorist Jim George concludes, political realism is stripped of anything connected with stereotypical feminine characteristics: "The omission of women is absolutely integral to the 'theoretic' identity of orthodox International Relations practice ... [It] privileges 'maleness' in its entire gendered splendor over a 'femaleness' that, by definition, is incapable of anything more than supportive insignificance."[5] However, certain feminists (well aware that "fear" and "insecurity" are overused, realist terms) hit below the belt by suggesting that realists doggedly cling to ancient truisms because they are insecure, easily threatened males, fearful of an uncertain, relativistic world in which the center no longer holds.[6]

Whether realists "talk the talk" because they are insecure about their masculinity must be left for others to ponder. Realist presuppositions are a more pressing concern. For the most part, realists subscribe to certain premises regarded as the facts of international life. To be sure, there are variations on the realist theme, but in its simplest expression—a form not unknown to strategists—realists liken the international realm to the Hobbesian state of nature. Accordingly, political realism is guided by three premises; it is worth noting that the premises are informed by a metaphor taken rather seriously—the multifaceted nation-state is likened to a solitary rational actor:

1. The international realm is composed of sovereign states that are not beholden to any higher authority.

2. Like individuals, nation-states are rational—*albeit selfish*—actors that set realistic goals and act accordingly.
3. And like individuals, nation-states struggle to survive and expand their power. (Power is generally understood as the capability of invoking military might to maintain and expand hegemony.) This will to power is seldom tempered by moral scruples.

While sovereign nation-states remain the principal players, times have changed: These days, there is but one superpower, and the terrorist diaspora threatens national monopolies on violence—nation-states are terribly jealous of their exclusive franchise on violence.

The second premise is decidedly problematic. Are decision-makers invariably rational actors who set realistic goals and act accordingly? They are in theory, but are they in practice? According to Thomas Schelling, the key premise of realism is "not just intelligent behavior, but ... behavior motivated by conscious calculation of advantage."[7] Beholden to economic theory and carefully controlled laboratory experiments in bargaining, Schelling and other strategists presuppose that decision-makers look back upon a familiar landscape, the realm of noonday commerce—an everyday world of cost/risk/benefit analysis. This presupposition is just that: a presupposition, a first principle that is not empirically derived. To be sure, ordinarily, political actors reality-test and act accordingly. They are sufficiently rational to get elected or to seize, power and to accomplish a variety of goals.

However, a mounting body of evidence suggests that this rationality is not durable, especially in the midst of a crisis—episodes in which actors hastily decide between peace and war. As Holsti, an analyst not unsympathetic to prevailing accounts of international relations, concludes:

The evidence suggests that policy making under circumstances of crisis-induced stress is likely to differ in a number of respects from decision-making processes in other situations. More important, to the extent that such differences exist they are likely to inhibit rather than facilitate effectiveness of those engaged in the complex task of making foreign policy choices.[8]

As historian Barbara Tuchman recognized, there is nothing new about irrationality in high places, especially in crisis situations. Her *March of Folly* spans events from Old Testament sagas to the Indochina War. She concludes that leaders often persist in pursuing failed, dangerous policies. Indeed, those who should have know better often persist in self-defeating actions—they redouble their efforts when they forget their goals.[9]

Accordingly, at the risk of betraying my gender, I want to show that the uncharted, post-Cold War jungle—to push the metaphor—is much more bewildering than Woolsey and other realists suspect. It is a virtual jungle in which appearance and dissembling take precedence over reality and

candid expression. Contrary to the realist wishful thinking, the virtual
jungle of our era is not a realm of natural laws amenable to the eternal
wisdom of political realism; it is a fictive, literary world in which mythic-
poetic figures of speech are often mistaken for reality.

The past is familiar territory for the realist: a time when reckoning
ordnance and personnel made sense. But the present is a foreign country
for the realist, for how does one calibrate the balance of power in an age
of assured destruction when appearance is everything and deterrence is
a dubious and dangerous experiment in applied psychology? Indeed, in
this postmodern, post-Freudian world, realists hazard confident claims
about the intentionality of leaders far removed from their personal and
professional lives. They might well benefit from the outdoor hermeneutics of cultural anthropologists such as Clifford Geertz, who observes:

We are all natives now, and everyone else not immediately one of us is an exotic.
What looked once to be a matter of finding out whether savages could distinguish
fact from fantasy now looks to be a matter of finding out how others across the sea
or down the corridor organize their significative world.[10]

Given the symbolic turn in international relations, perhaps allusions to
the jungle are inadequate, if not misleading. We don't inhabit a world of
unmistakable threats populated by individuals with transparent motives.
Unlike other animals, humans live in a highly symbolic world of language
games—and we're "it!" Strategists are authors and interpreters of cryptic
texts and symbolic performances. As Ernest Cassirer observed:

Physical reality seems to recede in proportion as man's symbolic activity advances.
Instead of dealing with things themselves man is in a sense constantly conversing
with himself. He has so enveloped himself in linguistic forms ... that he cannot
see or know anything except by the interposition of [an] artificial medium.[11]

Nuclear strategizing is about texts and language. This genre is studied in
libraries and archives, not laboratories or observatories. Strategy is about
semiotics—sending and receiving messages. (As McNamara explained
during the Cuban missile crisis, he was trying to send a message, not
start a war.) These messages are often designed to deceive rather than to
communicate accurately. Deception is the name of the game. Strategizing
is about illusion and bluffing, about reading meaning in and out of texts.
Like the Sorcerer's Apprentice, strategists search for the right words,
some magical incantation, to make everything right with the world.

A more authentic realism—attuned to these new unrealities—would
recognize that the political realists' tried (and occasionally true) signposts
and territories (be they classical or neo-realists) are seldom seen. It's as if
we find ourselves in a theater of the absurd after we have gone through

the looking glass and fallen into some Lewis Carroll fantasy. While nuclear war is not unthinkable for certain realists, it is unthinkable that chimeras such as the balance of power are fanciful concepts, not real things.

To be sure—before the metaphors gets completely out of hand—residues and artifacts of the jungle remain. (It is comforting, perhaps, for realists to know that there are still predatory "dragons": nation-states doing what comes naturally in the state of nature.) But truth be known, it's terribly easy to get lost in a world of appearances, a tangled, dark forest of virtual reality—and unreality. Having mixed, if not tortured, Woolsey's metaphor, I want to be more explicit about the evanescent appearances, the dissembling messages, and the puzzling performances that bedevil those who would navigate the post-Cold-War world. Mainstream analysts recognize that in the post 9/11 world, reality isn't what it used to be.

The efficacy of supposed realities such as balance of power and deterrence are, to say the least, in doubt. The radical change in international reality, however, occurred long before 9/11; it occurred on August 6, 1945, with the detonation of the atomic bomb over Hiroshima.

To be sure, early strategists such as Bernard Brodie wrote with power and clarity about the atomic age changing everything. And yet, much like Clemenceau, they clung to the doctrines of political realism that seemed discredited by events. Indeed, for Brodie, the nuclear age changed everything except his embrace of political realism. Summarizing Brodie's educational background and subsequent experience, Fred Kaplan explains that he transformed his notions of political realism "into an intellectual construction grounded in lessons about power that he had learned in his school days at Chicago and every day were reinforced in the halls he occupied at Yale. The product was a pair of essays ... [that articulated] the first conception of nuclear deterrence."[12] No wonder Einstein admonished that the nuclear age changed everything except our thinking.

I want to contrast the bad old days when realism was a somewhat useful guide to navigating international affairs and an antidote to wishful thinking for the new realities (or better, the reality of the new unrealities) of the post-Cold War nuclear age. In such an epoch when appearance displaces reality and apocalyptic weapons proliferate, political realism per se seems like a forlorn expression of wishful thinking. An admittedly simplified, but perhaps not wholly inaccurate, account of American history might reveal the need for a more authentic realism. Such a realism would be marked by humility, given the precariousness of our nuclear predicament and the realization that we know more about the atom than ourselves.

Political commentator Lewis Lapham recognizes the hubris that bedevils the theory and practice of political realism: "[Political Realism] reflects the proud belief that man, as the pinnacle of everything that exists, is capable of objectively describing, explaining and controlling everything that exists, and of possessing the one and only truth about the world."[13]

TOWARD AN AUTHENTIC REALISM

A true realism takes into account the whole of reality, dictates diplomatic-strategic conduct adapted not to the finished portrait of what international politics would be if statesmen were wise in their selfishness, but to the nature of the passions, the follies, the ideas and violence of the century.
—Raymond Aron[14]

Political analysts were once clear on the concept—the world made sense during those bad old days. Nation-states were the only players in the international arena, and their leaders had the decency to behave in a somewhat predictable Hobbesian manner: Usually "wise in their selfishness," personal and national survival were supreme values. Given the justifiable fear of predatory nation-states in a world of international anarchy, vulnerability was an idée fixe. However—with the exception of some unpleasant incidents in the nation's capital during the War of 1812—the American homeland was safeguarded by two vast oceans and by divine dispensation (or so many fervently believed).

Nevertheless, all was not well in the lands beyond American borders: As the Western frontier closed, American interests became global. And, as two world wars illustrate, the newfound concern with European politics was not purely academic.

A realist understanding of international politics gained hegemony in the halls of power as realpolitik articles of faith became truisms. It was obvious to all that aggressive states readily fill the power vacuum that besets an anarchistic, international environment devoid of countervailing forces. (Political realism abhors a vacuum.) In any event, the meaning of "power" was clear—military might. Powerful armies, not high ideals, tipped the balance of power in a nation's favor.

Such historical lessons could be gleaned since there was, to say the least, precedence for warfare between nation-states. To be sure, historical analogies could mislead: often the generals were "fighting the last war." (Those who can't *forget* the past are condemned to repeat it.) In any case, somewhere between the insanity of remembering everything and the idiocy of historical amnesia there were lessons to be drawn.

Finally, given the way of the world, surely superior military power and strategies informed by the proper lessons of history would insure national security by deterring enemy aggression. Worse case scenarios weren't so bad: if deterrence failed, victory was both intelligible and likely.

Since When Is Survival the *Summum Bonum?*

Times have changed. According to what will likely become received wisdom, 9/11 changed everything. Evidently a terrorist diaspora, not a nation-state, orchestrated the attack on the World Trade Center and the Pentagon. True, various nation-states are accused of aiding and abetting terrorism, but the new, unprecedented threat to national security comes from a network of loosely organized cells, not sovereign states. Understandably, due to nuclear proliferation and lax controls of fissionable material in the former Soviet Union, there is anxiety about "dirty" radiation bombs—even fission bombs—falling into the hands of groups such as Al Qaeda. No one thinks such fanatics can be deterred no matter how formidable the American arsenal. And, as the nineteen hijackers and assortment of worldwide suicide bombers make clear, personal survival is not necessarily the supreme value.

There is a smug tendency to assume that fanatics willing to kill the innocent and to die for a cause are exotic, intrinsically evil beings who surely are "not like us." We would like to think that we are as enlightened in our selfishness as the realists suggest. (Of course, our culture venerates martyrs who died for a glorious cause: remember the Alamo, Saints of the Church, or Masada? More disturbing, to paraphrase Bertrand Russell, for every innocent killed by rogue terrorists, a thousand have been killed by legitimate nation-states.) Nevertheless, we cling to the belief that, unlike our adversaries, we cherish innocent life. And even if the lives of others aren't always sacred, can there be any doubt that we are rational actors with the good sense to behave like CPAs engaged in noonday commerce? True, there may be impediments, but we do our best to perform a diligent cost/risk/benefit analysis in order to assure our survival.

Ordinarily this might be true. But, as we shall see, those world-historic dramas known as international crises do not always bring out the best in decision-makers. After investigating crises at other times and places, cultural anthropologist Victor Turner offers a conclusion that contradicts an unquestioned realist presupposition: "People will die for values that oppose their interest and promote interests that oppose their values."[15]

Fanatical Cold War rhetoric gives us pause. A variety of secular and sectarian ideologues proclaimed "better dead than red!" Of course such oaths may be just that—rhetoric. Hopefully, we shall never know. However, international crises afford an opportunity to test Turner's conclusion. As we shall see, these critical junctures, in effect, offer a window through which we witness what occurs when decision-makers decide between war or peace. The actions of the "best and the brightest" during the Cuban missile crisis suggest that Turner's aphorism does not merely apply to exotics. Apparently Kennedy and his closest confidants were willing to risk everything to compel the Soviets to withdraw their missiles from Cuba. Heeding the advice of Disraeli, they hoped for the best but expected the worst. Unlike some of the ideologues in the Reagan administration, they did not expect a nuclear springtime in the aftermath of thermonuclear war.

Finally, as political analyst Richard Betts concludes, such perilous "competition in risk-taking" was the rule, not the exception at critical junctures:

Although postwar policymakers have always wanted to avoid nuclear war, they have never made that aim their highest priority; if they had, they could have minimized the possibility by making policy declarations, military preparations, and diplomacy during crises consistent with the notion that nuclear weapons should be used for nothing but retaliation against nuclear attack. [Of course the rationality of retaliating *after* deterrence fails is questionable.] U.S. policy, however, has rested on the principles that there are interests for which the United States would make the first use of nuclear weapons rather than concede.[16]

Problems without Solutions

The voluminous accounts of 9/11 are in accord on one issue: The attack on the continental United States shattered the myth of American exceptionalism. Neither Providence nor vast seas and a military colossus safeguarded the homeland. Realist discourse doesn't begin to convey the newfound, inconsolable sense of vulnerability. The unnerving sense of helplessness is, perhaps, best expressed by humanists such as Mark Slouka: "Last year's attack [September 11, 2001] was so traumatic to us because it simultaneously exposed and challenged the myth of our own uniqueness. A myth, most visible, perhaps, in our age-old denial of death.... This was not a terrorist attack. This was an act of metaphysical trespass. Someone had some explaining to do."[17]

Therein lies the problem: Political realists are at a loss to explain. Power vacuums, real or imagined, matter not at all to the terrorist diaspora, and surely the balance of power (whatever that may be) favored the one superpower—the terrorists were unimpressed. To understate the case, American military might was no deterrent. And, as if to add insult to injury to the realist way of thinking, the terrorists were fanatical, sectarian idealists, not practitioners of realpolitik.

More daunting still from a realist—or any other—perspective, terrorism is a problem without a solution. Despite its acerbic pessimism, political realism buys into the quintessential belief of Enlightenment optimism: all problems have solutions. Since the Hobbesian state of nature resembles scenes from *Lord of the Flies,* the answer is to be found in a tacit social compact establishing absolute monarchy. Likewise, the worst nightmares of the nuclear age could be averted, or so the realist strategists promised, through a balance of terror. Unfortunately, as Wallace Shawn reminds us, terrorists cannot be terrified. He poses a plaintive question to the experts, the realists of the foreign policy establishment:

Dear foreign policy therapist. I want to be safe. I want safety. But I have a terrible problem.... I lost several thousand loved ones to a horrible crime. I feel an overwhelming need to apprehend and punish those who committed this unbearably cruel act, but they designed their crime in such a diabolical fashion that I cannot do so, because they arranged to be killed themselves while committing the crime, and they are now all dead.[18]

But, contrary to popular misperceptions, there is nothing new about the problem of American vulnerability. To reiterate, the threat of nuclear terror has bedeviled the United States since 1956 when the Soviets acquired the capacity to deliver thermonuclear bombs.[19] However, it would be novel to suggest that then as now, terrorism—be it nuclear or conventional—is a problem without a solution. The unprecedented peril posed by nuclear weapons was to be solved by building more nuclear weapons: a strategy touted as deterrence—supposedly, the only realistic way of averting nuclear war. As I shall argue in subsequent chapters, the efficacy of deterrence is difficult to determine. Suffice it to say that it would be foolish to suggest that leaders don't have second thoughts about trying to impose their will on a nuclear-armed adversary.[20] Of course, to talk the talk, it would be equally foolish to suggest that deterrence is always "robust." Ever fearful that deterrence may fail, strategists proposed antiballistic missiles, evacuation routes, and fallout shelters so that America might survive and prevail in a nuclear exchange. But even if the latest incarnation of the Strategic Defense Initiative kept its promises (there are, to say the least, doubters) the homeland would remain vulnerable to cruise missiles, short-range, submarine launched missiles, and suitcase bombs and such. Ultimately there is no safety against a nuclear attack, and those unfortunate enough to survive will have—contrary to Herman Kahn's reassurances—horrific problems indeed: millions will perish, and starvation and disease will be rampant. And, since too many violence-prone Americans celebrate victories in spectator sports by rioting, it is not reassuring to imagine how they might respond to the spectacle of nuclear devastation. In any event, it is doubtful that the planned retaliation that will kill millions more who bore no responsibility for the attack will improve their plight.

Ever attentive to the role of lethal power in managing international disputes and settling scores, strategists (as we shall see) also advocated "extended deterrence": somehow the American nuclear arsenal could be used for coercive diplomacy to accomplish American objectives overseas. Once again, the conflicts of the post-Cold War world seem like problems without a solution, or at least a nuclear solution. Perhaps wars were once precipitated by predatory nation-states rushing in to fill the vacuum, as realists suggest. However, these days power vacuums—and other metaphors borrowed promiscuously from hard science—don't foment wars. Unlike the time when political realism had its uses, wars aren't about the construction of empires; they are about the *deconstruction* of hegemonic nation-states.

On almost every continent nations (peoples with impassioned collective identities) struggle to become states by dismantling existing regimes.

The recognition that balkanization is not limited to the Balkans is hardly news. What is less obvious is the irrelevance of nuclear weapons to influencing these events. According to the realist canon, decision-makers respond to fear, and what is more fearful than the power of nuclear weapons? Again, as we shall see, these weapons supposedly assured "extended deterrence": in the realist canon, not only did nuclear weaponry safeguard the American homeland, it also promoted American international goals. American nuclear might matters not at all to Serbs, Croats, Kurds, and Palestinians (to mention but a few) seeking statehood. Worse yet, for American interests, the American arsenal does not deter terrorist cells bent on undermining or destroying the American state.

Is the Pen Mightier Than the Sword?

The tragedy of 9/11 illustrates the deficiency in traditional, realist notions of power. At one time it was appropriate to think primarily in terms of military power: the size of armies and lethality of ordnance mattered. Looking at World War II, the realists got it right: The Nazis were not defeated by words appealing to their higher nature, as the idealists prayed, but by the superior force of arms. These days, the imbalance of power between the terrorist diaspora and the greatest military colossus in history is clear; in theory such an imbalance should be the ultimate deterrent. Unfortunately, deterrence is a useless concept in the war on terrorism; indeed, for some, the certain prospect of painful death is an incentive, not a deterrent. In any case, it is unlikely that increased military spending will defeat groups such as Al Qaeda.

But there is nothing new about the dramatic changes in the notion of power. The nuclear age indeed changed everything. However, the nature of the change is seldom recognized, particularly by the realists. To be sure, Hiroshima and Nagasaki bear witness to the fact that there is nothing fictive about the unprecedented destructive power of nuclear weapons. But unlike other advances in weaponry, these weapons were not detonated again in warfare (as of this writing).

This is not to suggest that strategists are indifferent toward these weapons, and that they have not tried to put them to good use. The diverse versions of deterrence have one thing in common: they depend upon appearances. In one straightforward version, somehow leaders must convince adversaries—and themselves—that the threat to use nuclear weapons is credible. Other versions are about keeping adversaries nervous and guessing through the use of ambiguous terms and dissembling phrases.

While deterrence is about preventing adversaries from having their way, compellence is about making adversaries retreat *after* they have had their way. There is no difficulty documenting cases in which these weapons have been used for such coercive, atomic diplomacy.[21] In both the practice of deterrence and compellence such threats are communicated in a world foreign to political realism, a realm of words and symbolic performances. No wonder, like the rest of us, realists are seen in the archives and libraries struggling to read between the lines.

This is a world of semiotics: studies of the construction, communication, and reception of meaning. It is also a world of hermeneutics: interpreting the meaning of ambiguous texts and performances. As Richard Betts suggests, decision-makers themselves may be unsure about their intentions and the meanings they try to communicate, especially in crisis situations.[22] He concludes that leaders obviously like to bluff, but they are often unclear as to their response if the bluff is called. Such an unsettling view is consonant with a Freudian perspective that argues that humans are generally driven by passion, not reason; accordingly, contrary to realist expectations, decision-makers are not reliably "wisely selfish." Self-deception, not the will to truth, is the signature feature of human existence. In short, "reading" human beings is, to say the least, problematic.

Perhaps decision-makers aren't as complicated as these ruminations suggest. But are they as *uncomplicated* as realists such as Morgenthau aver? According to the "Dean of Political Realism" a decision-maker may delude himself or herself into believing that they grasp their own true intentions, but only a well-trained political realist truly understands what makes a decision-maker tick. Apparently, the transparency of actual human intentions enables the realist to become a mind reader: "As disinterested observers we understand his [i.e. a decision-maker's] thoughts perhaps better than the actor of the political scene does himself."[23] This claim is rather audacious for (as we shall see) reflecting upon the Cuban missile crisis, Kennedy allowed that much of his decision-making was impenetrable, if not mysterious, even to himself.

In the midst of the crisis little time was spent discussing the obvious—the lethality of nuclear weapons. The crisis was a war of words in which Kennedy and his associates struggled to interpret the meaning of Khrushchev's communiqués and to author communiqués that somehow expressed their resolve. Even ostensive military actions such as the blockade were more about semiotics—sending messages—than military objectives. As McNamara urged, the blockade was about "sending a message," not starting a war. Finally, Kennedy and his associates credit themselves with moving toward a resolution of the crisis with a literary ploy rather than a military maneuver. Alluding to a Victorian Trollope novel in which an ingénue ignores a missive from a suitor that disappoints, the "best and the brightest" ignored a guided missive from Khrushchev they found distasteful and responded to one deemed more congenial.[24] Understanding momentous episodes such as the Cuban missile crisis are matters of literary exegesis, rather than the observation of the ancient eternal laws of politics.

The time is long overdue for realists to accommodate themselves to the stark ambiguities of international life, ambiguities that reach their apotheosis in the nuclear age when leaders deliberately send uncertain messages and stage symbolic performances—appearance is everything. More than ever, political actors have become suspicious interpreters, dissembling authors and impostors, and improvisers of cryptic texts and performances. And analysts, despite our physics envy, are not observers of the incontestable facts—let alone laws—of international life. We have become interpreters of official interpretations. Our interpretations can be on target, but there is no bull's eye—no "smoking gun," no conclusive proof of our account of things. Our interpretations are invariably incomplete and contested; no authoritative tribunal can valorize our take on the performances in the international arena.

Lessons of History?

Op-ed writers and political analysts alike search in vain for historical precedence for the terrorist assault on the United States. Analogies are drawn to Pearl Harbor or Hitler, but the more sophisticated writers quickly point out that—unlike terrorist cells—Japan and Germany are readily found on maps. There is some mention of various terrorist groups that flourished in the dim past, but again, the more sophisticated stress that that was then, and this is now. Unable to locate the source of terrorism in time and space, some writers talks of terrorism as some supernatural incarnation of ultimate evil.

As I've stressed, there is no precedence of nuclear war-fighting between belligerents. Those who came closest to such a conflagration by jousting on the abyss with Khrushchev have gleaned an overarching lesson from the experience: nuclear crises must be avoided. Not only was Eisenhower's farewell warning about the military-industrial complex ignored; it is equally disturbing that his admonition about international crises went unnoticed. He warned his successors to resist the temptation to construe challenges as crises demanding urgent resolution at great peril; he counseled them to interpret such challenges as problems to be negotiated privately and prudently in due course.[25]

No Substitute for Victory?

In the bygone world of political realism, the notion of victory—even total victory—was an intelligible, attainable goal. This was a world of boundaries and frontiers. The Allies could land in Normandy, liberate Paris, and eventually cross the Rhine to conquer Germany. It was also possible to defend one's forces and homeland: geopolitics, ordnance, and personnel made a difference.

In this postmodern, nuclear era none of this makes much difference. No borders or geographical obstacles can defend the armed forces, let alone the homeland. The notion of victory itself dissolves into meaninglessness. But what would victory mean in the war on terrorism or amid the terror of a nuclear war? Would victory be at hand even if the battleship Missouri cruised into the Persian Gulf tomorrow with Osama bin Laden onboard ready to meet all American demands? Truth be known, the United States will always be vulnerable to foreign and domestic enemies who could harm Americans at home or abroad.

Perhaps the foregoing account of the limitations of realism in understanding the post 9/11 world doesn't go far enough. It stops short of confronting the unprecedented, limitless terror posed by nuclear weapons in the post-World War II world. The notion of triumphant nuclear war-fighting seem like an oxymoron. Realists, in effect, offer a time-worn program for determining winners and losers. Relying upon the nation-state as the fundamental unit of analysis, realists think of victory in terms of the survival and flourishing of a nation-state. But in an age of assured destruction, a nuclear war destroys that nation-state as a functioning civilization. The retired, high-ranking officers at the Center for Defense Information see themselves as consummate realists when they insist that a nuclear war is a war without winners.

One of these officers, Rear Admiral Eugene Carroll, participated in NATO war games as a commander of U.S. forces. The game anticipated the smallest details—up to a point. The war-gamers began by presupposing that the Soviets were mobilizing, and the best intelligence revealed they were about to invade Western Europe. Following long-established operational procedures, NATO authorized the first use of tactical nuclear weapons to repulse a Soviet conventional attack; the proper codes and commands were released and verified. However, at this point the game abruptly stopped. The Admiral suggested that war-planners were in denial: they could not think of the unthinkable results of detonating 7,000 tactical nuclear weapons. In the former commander's words, "There were no metaphors for the ensuing paroxysm."[26]

A genuine realism would recognize that strategic "scenarios" are literally fictions, which is to say stories. It would examine the authorial strategy used to tell these stories and position these narratives in the appropriate genre. In order to get a handle on these stories it would move in for a closer look at the metaphors used to construct these narratives. A genuine realism would be particularly attentive to those dark spaces where the games ends as strategists run out of metaphors. This is the sort of realism that informs the next chapters.

CHAPTER 2

What's *the* Story?

Who is this that darkeneth counsel by words without knowledge?
—Job 38:2 (KJV)

American nuclear strategy begins with dark counsel and utters words
without knowledge—for strategists know not of nuclear war-fighting.
And yet, such counsel seldom forebodes a tragic saga. On the contrary,
dark counsel is an essential dramatic artifact in cautionary tales such as
the book of Job and in the scenarios of nuclear strategy. In these morality
plays, those who keep the faith amid trials and tribulations reap abundant
rewards. Happy ending stories are persistent and irresistible.

Nuclear strategy, to state the case with more formality, is best understood as a formulaic, derivative narrative—an old story. In the beginning
was the story, not the word: Words mean nothing apart from narrative.
While the role of narrative in rendering experience intelligible has long
been recognized in the humanities, political scientists have also come
to appreciate the role of narratives in the construction and execution of
policy. Harvard political scientists Richard Neustadt and Ernest May call
it the "Goldberg Rule":

Avram Goldberg, a scholar and gentleman who happens also to be the chief executive officer of Stop and Shop, a New England chain of ... stores ... exclaimed,
"When a manager comes to me, I don't ask him, 'What's the problem?' I say, 'Tell
me the story.' That way I find out what the problem really is."[1]

The Rule—with apologies to Bach, a "Goldberg Variation"—has also
been applied to making sense of nuclear endeavors. Writing in the *Bulletin*

of the Atomic Scientists Hugh Gusterson explains: "Weapons systems, treaties, and strategies seem right (or wrong) in the context of the stories we tell ourselves about them."[2] We've grown accustomed to the deployment of apocalyptic weapons. Like Camus' Stranger who kills an Arab for no reason at all, it's as if we can get used to anything. We survive emotionally due to psychological, not national, defenses—a syndrome psychiatrist Robert Jay Lifton aptly calls "psychic numbing."[3] However, a person unaccustomed to American nuclear endeavors might well ask a seemingly naïve question reiterated in this study: What's the story; what's the point of developing, deploying, and detonating nuclear weapons? What is *the* story—the metanarrative—told and retold about nuclear endeavors? What sort of genre is strategic storytelling?

I claim that, like other cautionary tales, strategic storytelling is metaphorical: The saga of the nuclear age is rendered intelligible and manageable by likening it to a sequence of familiar metaphorical narratives derived from the remembered past. This book is about these time-honored metaphorical constructions.

The story strategists tell is indeed derivative: it improvises the morality play scripted in the book of Job. There are, to be sure, differences between Job's vexations and the strategic corpus: God restricted His gamble with Satan to Job and his immediate family; the men who play God gamble for stakes far beyond the nuclear family. By and large, strategists are optimistic about the outcome of the gamble because they embrace the American civic faith.

DEFINING THE STRATEGIC GENRE

> It is one of the peculiar intellectual accomplishments of democracy that the concept of the insoluble becomes unfashionable—nay almost infamous. To lack a remedy is to lack the very license to discuss the disease.
>
> —H. L. Mencken[4]

The Ebullient Civic Faith

The conviction that all problems have solutions reflects the ebullient American spirit; however, this conviction has also been a faith to die for. The architects of the Vietnam War—many of whom were also the architects of latter-day nuclear strategy—initially believed that awesome American military technology coupled with an unwavering national resolve would enable them to prevail in Southeast Asia. They believed that they had devised a clever, winning strategy. However, the gradual escalation/ escalation dominance strategy that supposedly made Khrushchev blink first during the Cuban missile crisis failed to deter the nationalistic ambitions of the Vietnamese. Eventually American strategists came to recognize the reality of their predicament—the conflict was unwinnable. After years of bitter, frustrating experience, they withdrew from Vietnam because they grudgingly and painfully—albeit momentarily—abandoned the civic faith: Vietnam was a problem without a solution. Indeed, if but for a brief and dark moment, they came to realize that, in this postmodern epoch, venerable strategic notions such as "triumph" lack intelligibility. The tragic reality that the architects initially denied, but reluctantly accepted, was that the war could not be won because one could not persuasively explain what victory meant.

Lamentably, and perhaps tragically, American strategists repented of their backsliding, overcame the "Vietnam Syndrome," and recovered their faith in the American credo despite (or because of?) the stark realities of the nuclear age. (It must be unbearable for those charged with safeguarding the commonweal to accept the reality that the American homeland lies defenseless against nuclear attack. To reiterate, even if the latest incarnation of the Strategic Defense Initiative kept all its promises, a missile defense is useless against suitcase bombs, cruise missiles, and short-trajectory submarine launched missiles, to say nothing of small ships sailing surreptitiously into American ports.) Finally—and there is a strong sense of finality here—there is reason to doubt that scenarios about nuclear war fighting ("if deterrence fails") are stories with a happy ending. An escalating nuclear war would surely end civilization, if not life, as we know it. Scenarios narrating limited nuclear wars that somehow don't get out of hand don't inspire confidence.

Not surprisingly, debates about the prospects of limited nuclear warfighting are informed by metaphors, not war-fighting experience. Critics of limited war scenarios liken reality to a slippery slope: any use of nuclear weaponry plummets history into a black hole. Advocates of limited war-fighting liken reality to what I call a "sticky ascent": like some all-powerful gravity, the forces of prudence prevent higher levels of escalation as "cool heads prevail." The truth of the matter is, of course, that no one knows whether limited nuclear war will likely escalate. One can only hope that no one wants to find out!

Bereft of empirical data regarding nuclear war-fighting, strategists author a *literary discipline, a highly imaginative genre.* They improvise familiar, time-honored metaphors in order to talk and write about something as unfamiliar and horrifying as nuclear war. They do so because, as Richard Feynman, a Manhattan project physicist, laments: "[My colleagues have an] utterly vain desire to see the terrifying, ineffable world of nuclear weapons in terms of something familiar."[5]

Despite the fact that there are no facts regarding nuclear war-fighting, and perhaps *because* strategizing is rife with internecine disputes, strategists often posit their conclusions with supreme confidence. As political analyst Philip Green observes:

Almost all works encountered in the field seem invested with a tremendously authoritative air, an air that one associates with scholarly work in the most well-established and systematically researched disciplines.... The study of deterrence was not in any meaningful sense a discipline; and somehow all the authority produced policy proposals and arguments one felt absolutely no urge to agree with.[6]

In defining a discipline, it is tempting to begin with the easiest task—indicating what a discipline is *not*. Heeding the advice of Oscar Wilde I deal with temptation by giving in. Green aptly concludes that strategic studies are not a scientific discipline. Nevertheless, these studies *do* constitute a discipline, but, to be sure, it is more difficult to accomplish the underlying task of this study: revealing what strategizing is about. I intend to show that American nuclear strategizing is a literary genre informed by a formulaic authorial strategy and an ancient ensemble of derivative metaphorical constructions embedded in Enlightenment optimism. (Indeed, as we shall see, a prominent political analyst claims that the nuclear arms race has ushered in the best of all possible worlds.) The nature of the authorial strategy is clear; however, explicating the derivative metaphors—the main task of this study—is a more formidable task requiring several chapters.

What Strategizing Is *Not*

In the popular imagination, nuclear strategizing is associated with rocket science, a connection that strategists seldom renounce. And yet, during moments of self-reflection and candor even the redoubtable Herman Kahn recognizes that strategizing is faith-based:

Uncertainty is another significant new development of the nuclear age—the creation of weapons whose unknown effects may be more important, and more harmful, than the known ones. Except for Hiroshima, Nagasaki, and a limited number of nuclear tests, we have no recent or actual experience from which to make judgments ... especially on the scale (thousands of megatons) that would be involved in a major war.[7]

He underscores this insight by recounting a conversation between a seasoned general and a young defense analyst, an exchange that reveals what I call the strategic uncertainty principle. Taken aback by the young man's lack of deference, the general scoffed: "How can you, a young man who has never fired a gun in anger, have the temerity to argue with me on nuclear war....?" Kahn lauds the fledgling strategist's telling response: "It takes about ten nuclear wars to get a sense of the range of possibilities—indeed, this is a very minimal level of experience. Just out of curiosity, how many such wars have you actually fought or studied?"[8]

But despite this cautionary tale, Kahn writes with supreme confidence as he precisely quantifies much of his speculation. As Philip Green quips: "It is a constant habit of Kahn's to impeach his own assumptions—and what better authority?"[9] Indeed, scientific prediction and explanation cannot be scaffolded on a sampling size of zero—happily, the number of nuclear exchanges as of this writing. Nevertheless, Kahn's strategic imagination is seldom chastened by this realization.

Logical coherence is yet another nominal requirement of scientific discourse. Strategizing strikes some as a Scholastic endeavor because, like the Schoolmen, strategists are supposedly obsessed with the logical coherence of their speculation, but profoundly indifferent to whether their ruminations *correspond* to empirical reality. However, leading strategic practitioners proudly admit that their thinking is bereft of such coherence.

Strategizing, according to Edward Luttwak, revolves around paradoxical—if not contradictory—ancient proverbs such as *Si vis pacem, para bellum.* (If you want peace, prepare for war; of course the dictum if you want war prepare for war, is equally compelling.) In any case, paradox reaches its apotheosis in the centerpiece of the strategic faith—deterrence doctrine, *the* great mystery of the canon. As we shall see, influential strategists argue that more nuclear weapons must be built in order to avoid their use. Further, the threat to use these weapons must be credible: American decision-makers must convince themselves and their adversaries that these weapons will be used in order to avoid their use. As critics such as Jonathan Schell observe: "Salvation from extinction by nuclear weapons is to be found in the nuclear weapons themselves."[10]

Curiously, proponents of nuclear endeavors acknowledge Schell's claim but insist that strategizing is somehow entitled to a unique, contradictory logic all its own. As Luttwak stresses: *"The entire realm of strategy is pervaded by a paradoxical logic of its own,* standing against the ordinary linear logic by which we live in all other spheres of life."[11] This is not an indictment, nor is it an invitation for an excursion into the interstices of Hegelian dialectic. He simply asserts that there is something inherently and uniquely paradoxical about conflict, and accordingly "strategic practice can be freed from the systematically misleading influence of commonsense logic ... this offers the prospect of an eventual liberation from the false discipline of consistency and coherence."[12] Somehow, the strategic narrative floats in a mysterious quintessence remote from any facts, let alone the scrutiny of logic and commonsense.

True, social theorists such as Marx and Freud see contradictory impulses at the center of the human drama—or trauma; however, their theories are reasonably coherent, or at least they don't celebrate contradictions in their work. Likewise, many of the discoveries and theories of twentieth-century physics are counterintuitive if not paradoxical. Yet, it is difficult to imagine Einstein and Heisenberg celebrating their emancipation from consistency and coherence. To paraphrase Einstein, God doesn't play with dice—but strategists do!

Scientific discourse must also be unambiguous, if not mathematically precise. It understates the case to suggest that deterrence doctrine is ambiguous: Such ambiguity has great appeal since it enables strategists to read their favored (often contradictory) meanings into the doctrine. Indeed, ambiguity is often celebrated as a virtue. Just as Luttwak lauds the incoherence of deterrence doctrine, certain colleagues urge that effective deterrence is *necessarily* ambiguous: supposedly, adversaries are most effectively deterred when they are uncertain about the equivocal meaning of American doctrine and pronouncements. In an apocryphal tale, an exasperated Henry Kissinger reacts to Jesuitical disputes about deterrence doctrine by exclaiming, "What in God's name *is* deterrence?"

What is most telling, strategic discourse doesn't generate the testable, falsifiable claims that many see as the hallmark of science.[13] Consider the essential claim of deterrence doctrine: nuclear arsenals prevented war between the superpowers. How could this claim be tested, let alone falsified? It would be necessary to do what God can't do—rewrite history. Somehow, the experimenter would have to return to 1945, abolish nuclear weapons, and observe the world during the next 45 years of the international bipolar disorder. Funding for such a project would not come easily. Without such proof, along with viable plans to successfully wage a nuclear war while defending the continental United States against reprisals, nuclear strategizing cannot be called a success story.

Finally, it should be noted that such scientific inquiry is systematic, cumulative, and ultimately successful. However, as chroniclers of nuclear strategy such as Fred Kaplan and Lawrence Freedman show, strategic thought is cyclical: the well-worn doctrines of the past are often recycled by new generations. Indeed, as we shall see, Thucydides' accounts of ancient wars have attained the canonical status of eternal wisdom. It is as if astrophysics confronts the mysteries of black holes and anti-matter by resurrecting the Ptolemaic system.

What Strategizing *Is*

What, then, *is* strategizing about? Revisiting the works of Herman Kahn reveals that Raymond Aron is right; such works are indeed "strategic fictions"—products of an overactive imagination. His ruminations about "the unthinkable" are about recurrent nightmares and hopeful daydreams, not systematic observation and controlled experiment. Of course, Kahn doesn't see himself as a dreamer. But what, then, is he about?

Strategists conflate the literary with the literal. To be sure, the writing is often technical, erudite, and occasionally numerical. But erudition is not cognition. Strategic discourse is a literary project—although, as stylists, strategists leave something to be desired. What sort of genre is strategic literature? Despite partisan differences, nuclear strategists share a formulaic, de rigueur, authorial strategy, a strategy designed to give the texts the look and feel of science or (minimally) a well established discipline. This literary plan of attack—which begins with an obligatory professions of modesty— should result in extreme caution in strategic conjecturing, but it does not.

1. Imitating scientific modes of exposition, strategists effect a calm, detached style despite (or because of) their subject matter. However, their confident, assertive prose betrays their passion. Typically, authors like Kahn liken themselves to expert surgeons who, undaunted by blood and bile, do what needs to be done. Likewise, in his cold, Teutonic rationality, Dr. Kissinger would never be confused with Zorba the Greek. C. Wright Mills recognized this authorial strategy long ago when he observed: "It is a sophistication of tone rather than ideas. The disclosure of fact—set forth in a bright-faced or a deadpan manner—is the rule.... Their power to outrage, their power to clarify ... all that is blunted or destroyed."[14]

2. Authors begin with an obligatory jeremiad about the abject horror of nuclear war and reassure the reader that they have no enthusiasm for such conflict; indeed, they urge that everything possible must be done to prevent such a catastrophe. They express the hope that their writing makes a very modest contribution to such efforts due to their realism and moderation.

3. A lamentation follows about the irreversible loss of nuclear virginity. Just as lost virginity cannot be recovered, so it is impossible to recapture the lost innocence of the pre-nuclear age—nuclear weapons cannot be "disinvented." Accordingly, we must, in the words of the Harvard Nuclear Study Group, "learn to live with nuclear weapons."[15]

4. As we have seen, the strategic uncertainty principle is invoked. Kahn was neither the first nor the last to invoke the principle. To reiterate, almost fifty years have passed since Brodie warned: "In the contest of thermonuclear war, everything is new and every military arm or weapon is essentially untested."[16] More recently, authors such as Lawrence Freedman reiterate the principle: "The thankful lack of experience of nuclear warfare ... has rendered highly speculative all thoughts on the likely causes of nuclear war, its course, and its finale."[17]

5. At this point strategic discourse becomes—as Lewis Carroll might say— "curiouser and curiouser." Given their admonition about radical uncertainty, one might expect strategists to abide by Wittgenstein's dictum: "Of that we cannot speak we must remain silent." But strategists are not reticent, let alone silent. On the contrary, struggling to find their own voice after their obligatory litany of caveats, they pen voluminous prose. It is at once curious and disturbing that their unemotional, authoritative pronouncements are seldom tempered by angst and self-doubt. It is as if they make what Kierkegaard (the doleful Danish existentialist) would call "a leap of faith." Putting their foreboding and uncertainty aside, this perilous leap occurs without Kierkegaard's signature "fear and trembling."

6. In dealing with the competition, strategists usually rely on one of two tactics. The cautious represent themselves as "ultra-moderates" charting a reasonable and responsible course between extremists. The Harvard Nuclear Study Group, for example, eschewed hawks and doves and represented themselves as owls. However, the young and audacious challenge orthodoxy and are marginalized, if not reviled, unless their time has come, and the world is ready for new doctrine. Kissinger's early work on limited nuclear warfare provides an example.[18]

I share the strategists' jeremiads, lamentations, and confounding uncertainty—who wouldn't?[19] This book reflects my struggle to understand the leap of faith that enables strategists to ignore their self-professed sense of uncertainty that should temper their pronouncements. Perhaps, as John Stuart Mill averred, it's simply a human tendency to ignore one's better lights: "While everyone knows himself to be fallible, few think it necessary to take any precautions against their own fallibility."[20] Freedman is right: the strategic uncertainty principle is a polite convention, an affectation, not taken seriously. Strategists quickly abandon their prefatory modesty and humility in favor of confident pronouncements and vindictiveness aimed at those who dare to differ.

Perhaps Herman Kahn is the most telling case. Despite his professed uncertainty, Kahn can't resist the temptation to pontificate, especially in light of the competition—the American Catholic Bishops' Pastoral Letter denouncing many of his doctrines on nuclear war-fighting. Seeing himself as a higher authority, he dismisses the bishops' injunction that a nuclear war should never be fought since it violates just war doctrine. Kahn proclaims—virtually ex cathedra: "My views are almost certainly not *wrong* on any of the issues raised here (I have carefully restricted my comments so that I can make this remark quite reasonably), though others might not agree that they are entirely right."[21]

Kahn's vehemence in promulgating his dogmatic nuclear theology suggests a possibility articulated by political analysts such as Dvora Yanow: policy construction is not simply a goal-directed exercise in instrumental reason. On the contrary, it is also an *expressive* affirmation of a strategist's values and very identity: "Policies can be seen as stories through which a polity's members express, to themselves and to one another, as well as to more distant publics, their collective identity and values."[22] Perhaps, as Durkheim averred, all religion is ultimately the worship of one's group. Could it be that invoking cherished metaphors expresses a strategist's allegiance to a powerful, elite sodality? In any case, as we shall see, this neglected, self-confessional aspect of strategizing colors and shapes the narratives strategists read into their arresting, albeit ambiguous, ancient metaphors.

Not all strategists, of course, endorse Kahn's views. However, by and large, the strategic community shares his abiding faith in deterrence doctrine: the strategy that putatively prevented World War III.[23] Indeed, deterrence is the credo of the strategic faith, a canon embraced uncritically and enthusiastically. No one enters the community of strategic discourse without acknowledging nuclear weapons as a blessing in disguise—*the* deterrent that bestowed peace on earth without goodwill toward men. Apparently, designating a weapons system, or virtually any imaginative scenario, as a "deterrent" ends all argument about the probity of such endeavors.

Suggesting that a weapons system or a strategic doctrine (weapons usually come first!) is anything but a deterrent is not, of course, forbidden by law; however, such an insinuation violates the boundaries of strategic thought. As Noam Chomsky explains: "A propaganda system is more effective when its doctrines are insinuated rather than asserted, when it sets the boundaries for possible thought rather than simply imposing a clear and easily identifiable doctrine that one must parrot."[24]

The concept of deterrence covers a wide variety of virtues and sins: indeed, given the self-confessional aspect of strategizing, there are as many notions of deterrence as there are strategists. And yet, there is a common denominator asserted by Freedman despite his profession of uncertainty. He offers a paean to deterrence echoed by most of his colleagues. His faith rests upon two premises: nuclear weapons have existed since 1945; and no world war has occurred since that time.[25] Evidently discounting the strong possibility of a post hoc fallacy, he argues: "My fortunate generation has been allowed to grow up in relative peace. I have not been required to fight for my country nor make any sacrifices at all and so I have enjoyed the full benefits of peace. Our peace has been gained at least in part by the sobering prospect of the destructiveness that would in all probability follow its collapse."[26]

Strategizing, in sum, lacks a scientific foundation and it is bedeviled—as practitioners acknowledge on occasion—by radical uncertainty. Given this predicament, it would seem appropriate for strategists to question their unquestioned presuppositions, and to adopt what Rorty calls an ironic attitude toward their final vocabulary. The strategic narrative is bereft of irony. Ironists, in Rorty's words, have radical and persistent doubts about their final vocabulary; they realize that arguments phrased in their established vocabulary cannot resolve these doubts; and, recognizing the plurality of possible interpretations of their situation, they grant that their vocabulary may not be closer to reality than competing perspectives. In short, "The ironist spends her time worrying about the possibility that she has been initiated into the wrong tribe [or] taught to play the wrong language game."[27]

Strategists (to invoke Rorty's notion of "final vocabulary") are commonsense metaphysicians in that they uncritically and enthusiastically take statements formulated in their final vocabulary as self-evident guides to belief, value, and action: "The metaphysician ... does not question the platitudes which encapsulate the use of a given final vocabulary ... he analyzes old descriptions with the help of other old descriptions."[28]

The strategists' final vocabulary is old indeed—a moveable host of metaphors well known to the ancient Greeks. This ancient lexicon encapsulates a story, a saga that reached a turning point when ancient, supernatural metaphors were abandoned in favor of the naturalistic tropes of political realism. Accordingly, our exploration of strategic metaphors must start from the beginning. As political scientists John Herz urged long ago: "The term power, like so many others (balance, alignment, cold war, and so on), is a metaphor. The study of metaphor should be included in any realist approach to the study of international relations."[29]

CHAPTER 3

Newest Weapons/Oldest Metaphors

A nuclear war has not taken place: one can only talk and write about it.
—Jacques Derrida[1]

Derrida's uncharacteristically clear epigram offers a telling insight about nuclear strategy. As we've seen, strategists—those who plan the development, deployment, and detonation of nuclear weapons—labor under a fortunate empirical deficit. Happily, there are no facts to be drawn, no lessons of history to be revealed, about nonexistent nuclear war-fighting. True, wishful, post hoc conclusions are drawn about the efficacy of nuclear arsenals in deterring war: nuclear weapons have existed since 1945, and no world war has occurred since that time. It should be obvious that correlation does not necessarily mean causation.

All strategists really know is what Brodie knew at the onset of the nuclear age; it's worth reiterating: "Nuclear weapons exist, and they are incredibly destructive."[2] What else needs to be said? As the strategic literature reveals, strategists are convinced there is much more to be said: they talk and write voluminously about nuclear war. Bereft of reality they discourse in metaphors cobbled together to tell resonant stories—scenarios about preventing or fighting the next war. As we've seen, strategizing is dominated by political realists who apparently believe that their claims about avoiding and fighting nuclear wars do not require an empirical database since they are guided by the "eternal wisdom" of the ancients. The nuclear subculture, of course, has constructed its own, inimitable lexicon of metaphorical discourse—Nukespeak.

A NUKESPEAK PRIMER

Nukespeak is not the product of a concerted propaganda effort.... It is more subtle, more pervasive, and probably unconscious, though none the less effective for that.... What we must be recognized is that there are no "facts" or "arguments" in public discussion that are not selected, defined, or dressed up by the devious devices of human language.

—Paul Chilton[3]

Nukespeak is defined in terms of its functions. To the extent that it is an effective, dramatic language it enables the reader or listener to suspend disbelief. Enchanted by the language, we may come to believe that there is a viable defense against nuclear war. Or, if not, that it is possible to survive and prevail in a nuclear war. Nukespeak changes the dread of nuclear winter to cheerful thoughts of nuclear spring. As such, Nukespeak is an ideology, when ideology is understood as a set of concepts, an official version of reality that serves a special interest. Ideological language privileges the views of those who manage the weaponry while marginalizing the views of critics.

In addition to a dramatic ideology, Nukespeak calms the alarmed, deflects skepticism, and promotes a cult of expertise.[4] Its metaphors serve as euphemisms, acronyms (a veritable badge of expertise) and insistence upon inevitability—there is no other choice.[5]

NUKESPEAK METAPHORS

What then is truth? A movable host of metaphors.... Truths are illusions which we have forgotten are illusions.... To be truthful means to employ the usual metaphors.

—Nietzsche[6]

Words did not always come easily to those associated with nuclear weaponry. Most of those "present at creation" at the first nuclear test heeded Wittgenstein's dictum and remained silent. All one witness could utter is that the nuclear conflagration "beggared description." Indeed, the Trinity blast (reportedly witnessed as a flash by a blind child a hundred miles removed) ushered in an epoch that beggars description.

The nuclear threat was like nothing else. Apocalyptic weapons threatened the destruction of civilization: then as now, there was no viable defense.[7] Indeed, it's a misnomer to liken the nuclear threat to a war. Warfare presents the possibilities of viable defense, possible advantage, and exhilarating triumph. A full-scale nuclear exchange does not offer such salutary possibilities. These facts of death are obvious and well rehearsed. The mind-numbing, ultimate evil posed by the nuclear threat is less obvious. As a recent study argues, evil reaches its apotheosis when trust is destroyed.[8] The advent of apocalyptic weapons marks the mass destruction of trust. After the Soviets obtained nuclear weapons and reliable delivery systems (*circa* 1956) vast oceans and unparalleled military might could not be trusted to safeguard the homeland from nuclear attack. At times, the terror seemed more cosmic than terrestrial. Providence no longer smiled on American destiny: The very power that binds the microcosm and lights the firmament suddenly emerged as a mortal enemy threatening to swallow human history in a black hole. Not only was the present imperiled as never before, the human future was in doubt.

In any event, as the voluminous strategic literature illustrates, those who orchestrated American nuclear endeavors didn't remain speechless for long. But before strategists could speak, they confronted a formidable task: somehow they had to improvise a *conceptual strategy* for triumphing over their crisis of comprehension;[9] somehow, nuclear weapons had to be rendered intelligible and manageable, in concept if not in reality. Strategic thought and action are products of this conceptual strategy. Accordingly, in order to more fully understand the history and nature of American nuclear endeavors we must somehow gain access to the strategists' conceptual world.

In her popular article, "Nuclear Language and How We Learned to Pat the Bomb," Carol Cohn allows that she spent a year at a strategic think tank to discover "How *can* they think this way?" After she quickly learned the language, and began to "talk the talk," she confronted a more daunting question: "How can *I* think this way?.... Like the White Queen, I began to believe six impossible things before breakfast"[10]

This chapter, then, is about the conceptual strategy of those who make long-term recommendations and critical decisions about the development, deployment, and detonation of the nuclear arsenal. (I have in mind analysts at universities, war colleges, national laboratories, and think tanks; and decision-makers in agencies such as the Department of Defense, the Department of Energy, and the National Security Council.) I argue that, in order to tell their story, those who control the fate of the earth[11] liken the unfamiliar exigencies of the nuclear age to the familiar conceptual templates of the remembered past. What are the salient features of such constructions, and what role do they play in strategizing?

The Oldest Metaphors

The greatest thing by far is to be a master of metaphor. It is one thing that cannot be learned from others; it is also a sign of genius, since a good metaphor implies an eye for resemblance.

—Aristotle

The antiquity of strategic assumptions alone should call the strategic enterprise into question. Bruce Blair (Director of the Center for Defense

Information) is among the analysts who warn that the American strategic mindset is perilously outmoded: "Thousands of weapons remain on hair-trigger alert, and the United States ... plans and operates strategic forces as if the Cold War never ended."[12] I suspect that latter-day strategizing is considerably more outdated than Blair suggests. Strategizing is informed by a time-honored mindset much older than the Cold War, a paradigm crafted out of the same metaphors Thucydides invoked to understand ancient conflicts. It may not grossly exaggerate to suggest that the United States plans and operates strategic forces as if the Peloponnesian War never ended.

I am not the first to suggest that the legacy of the "Golden Age" of Athens is persistent and decidedly mixed. Political analysts Stephen Holmes' invocation of the dark side of the legacy applies to ancient strategic metaphors with painful clarity:

European society ... remain[s] in thrall to ... classical thinkers who are peripheral at best and positively pernicious when taken seriously as political or theoretical exemplars. "The principles of Greek politics become flagrant and despotic anach-ronisms when transported, even with the best of intentions, into the institutional context of modern society."[13]

What are these ancient metaphors, these despotic anachronisms that captivate strategic thought? It is no great revelation that those "present at creation" at the first nuclear blast likened the experience to ancient, super-natural metaphors. To be sure, these tropes were recognized for what they are—hoary figures of speech. It is unlikely that observers of the Trinity Test believed that they literally witnessed a genie being uncorked, let alone the wrath of Vishnu or Jehovah or the Second Coming of Christ.

However, the ancient Greek metaphors that guide latter-day strategizing—*balance of power, deterrence, crisis, and necessity*—are not construed as mere tropes, literary relics of a bygone era. These concepts are afforded the canonical status of changeless laws of international rela-tions. They are the principal focus of this study because they constitute what (to reiterate) Rorty calls a "final vocabulary," the strategist's final answer to the unprecedented exigencies of the nuclear age:

All human beings carry about a set of words which they employ to justify their actions, their beliefs, and their lives. These are the words in which we ... [express] our long-term projects, our deepest self-doubts and our highest hopes. They are the words in which we tell ... the story of our lives.[14]

To be sure, those opposed to American nuclear endeavors—the nuclear abolitionists—also have a final, metaphorical vocabulary. However, my efforts are concerned primarily with explicating these latter-day metaphors and accounting for their persistence. I intend to show that these ancient notions are indeed a final vocabulary, a litany of unrecognized and misleading metaphors. More disturbing, these ancient tropes conjure up imaginary images and scenarios that define our present predicament and script anticipated outcomes thereby constricting the range of options.

It is misleading, of course, to suggest that strategists put their faith solely in the wisdom of the ancients; modernity also plays a role. The latter-day strategic oeuvre, shares metaphors invoked by ancient Greek playwrights and historians *and* the dubious aspects of their evangelical faith in the precepts of modernity in which these assumptions are embedded. Strategic tropes are not seen as mere rhetorical flourishes or even as heuristic models of international reality: they are seen as the verities destined to guide long-term policymaking and choices at critical junctures. Likewise, the precepts of modernity are not seen as wishful thinking in light of the folly and carnage of the twentieth century.

Metaphors as Conceptual Strategy

What is at issue is not the truth or falsity of a metaphor but the perceptions and inferences that follow from it and the actions that are sanctioned by it.... We draw inferences, set goals, make commitments, and execute plans, all on the basis of how we in part structure our experience, consciously and unconsciously by means of metaphor.

—Lakoff and Johnson[15]

Generically, metaphors are analogies that compare seemingly unlike domains without using connectives such as "like" or "is." As Lakoff and Johnson stress in their classic work on the subject, *"The essence of metaphor is understanding and experiencing one kind of thing in terms of another."*[16] That these connectives are omitted may explain why certain metaphors are taken literally. Contrast the common comparison in the obvious analogy "Life is *like* a journey," with a metaphorical comparison often taken literally—"life *is* a journey." Likewise, certain strategic discourse unwittingly conceals its metaphorical origins. Metaphors are covert conceptual operations that transfer one domain's characteristics on to another's.

For example, within this discourse community it is not politically correct to modestly suggest that the international order *might* be likened to an antique, laboratory balance or an organism (the international body politic). It is obligatory to take the trope literally by asserting international relations *are* a mechanism (or an organism) that function properly when the correct balance (or homeostasis) is attained. As events illustrate, the "correct balance" generally implies American strategic superiority, or rather the *appearance* of superiority—actual superiority being a chimera in an age of assured destruction. Moreover, metaphors such as "balance of power" are comforting: they imply that the world is intelligible and manageable in that a correct balance can be calibrated and attained, and its salutary consequences enjoyed.

Metaphors are not parallels that compare the same kind of thing—apples to apples; they are concealed analogies that implicitly compare disparate domains by exaggerating similarities while concealing differences—laboratory balances are not commensurate with the behavior of nation-states. This is not to suggest that metaphors are necessarily misleading, let alone pernicious. Supposedly, the metaphorical comparison Newton drew between the moon falling to the horizon and apples falling to the ground inspired his universal notions of gravity. But even such incredibly fertile metaphors are not an unalloyed blessing. The Newtonian comparison of the cosmos to a machine—taken literally—stymied progress in physics.

Recognized as figures of speech, metaphors can be playful, even heuristic, inspiring novel insights and connections. However, reified as accounts of changeless reality, metaphors can be misleading, if not perilous. Analyzing the role of metaphors in the political context, Murray Edelman explains that, as representation of political reality:

> Each metaphor intensifies selected perceptions and ignores others, thereby helping one to concentrate upon desired consequences of favored public policies and helping one to ignore their unwanted, unthinkable ... aftermaths. Each metaphor can be a subtle way of highlighting what one believes and avoiding what one does not wish to face.[17]

The power of Edelman's insight will become evident if we go beyond formal definitions and anecdotes by examining the *functions* of metaphors in strategic thought and deed. Strategic discourse abounds with metaphors taken in a literary, not literal sense. These metaphors serve a playful role in various discourses. However, metaphors also play a deadly serious function in latter-day strategizing. This function warrants considerable analysis.

Strategic discourse abounds with playful metaphors, rhetorical ornaments not taken literally. As Cohn learned, "Talking about nuclear weapons is fun."[18] The literature takes us through the looking glass into a magic kingdom. Despite the strategists' calm detachment, it's a crazy world after all: In the macabre humor typical of the genre, strategic doctrine is likened to varieties of insanity such as MAD (mutually assured destruction) or NUTS (nuclear use theory). Of course, Tomorrowland's scenarios aren't entirely terrifying. For the faint of heart they also offer hope: ladders of escalation, firebreaks, level playing fields, and nuclear umbrellas (essential if one must serve under hawks, doves, or owls, for that matter). These weapons arrive in RVs (re-entry vehicles) and buses (bearers of multiple warheads). For mature audiences, the redoubtable Herman Kahn offers a pornography of violence, obscene scenarios in which a "nuclear wargasm" is provoked by the latest "penetration aids" as history reaches its climax.

Of course such jocular plays on words aren't all fun and games; a variety of authors detect a subtext, and evasion of the implications of dark counsel. As Kahn concludes, in the final analysis, the playful tropes serve a serious function—they may be the only viable defense against nuclear war, a psychological defense. Just as Freud revealed a disturbing, unconscious dimension of humor, Cohn concludes that humor in the nuclear family serves a serious if not indispensable function: "Language that ... is sexy and fun to use deflates the forces of mass destruction ... [and] makes it possible to be radically removed from the reality of what one is talking about, and from the realities one is creating through the discourse."[19]

However, the latter-day strategic metaphors that are the focus of this study—*balance of power, deterrence, crisis,* and *necessity*—are taken so seriously that they are construed as self-evident realities, not figures of speech. A genuinely realistic, strategic preamble would begin: "We hold these fictions to be self-evident."

The Function of Strategic Metaphors

The problem was what words to use to refer to the new thing, how to capture a new concept, but also how to conceal ... the horror that had been glimpsed by a few.

—Paul Chilton[20]

What Chilton aptly describes as a crisis of comprehension is not purely cerebral. Those "present at creation" endured a dark night of the soul that threatened cherished beliefs, values, and aspirations as never before. It was as if, to invoke Nietzsche, they stared into the abyss, and the abyss stared back. Cast into a world without a horizon, the first strategists endured what anthropologists call "liminality": a time between and betwixt metaphors when old metaphors are useless and new tropes are yet to be marshaled.[21] Historian John Canady expresses the liminal terror when he observes: "20th century physicists found that they had to deal with the terrifying experience of feeling the metaphorical ground shaking under their feet.... A terror associated with wordlessness, blank spaces on maps, the unknown."[22]

It is widely recognized that certain metaphors are not mere rhetorical ornaments—they also serve as figures of thought, or at least of imagination. Strategic metaphors masquerading (to mix metaphors) as facts of life—obdurate features of international relations—serve cognitive, teleological, and normative functions: they shape the understanding, emotion, and actions of both authors and readers. In the daunting ambiguity of the international realm, the facts seldom speak for themselves. Metaphors, in effect, are strategies for controlling interpretation: They privilege official interpretations of reality and marginalize the competition.

In this cognitive capacity, metaphors such as "balance of power" putatively reveal what is occurring: In the strategic imagination, the international world is akin to an antique laboratory balance or an organism. Nuclear weapons are the heaviest ballast that tips the scale in a nation's favor or assures the robust health of the body politic.

Since tropes are figures of speech they cannot be proven true or false. Claims that a scale or an equation are in balance are amenable to proof. However, how can claims about a new weapons system upsetting the balance of power be confirmed or disconfirmed? For example, responding to the 1990 Iraqi invasion of Kuwait, some strategists claimed that the Iraqi annexation of Kuwait would upset the balance of power; others claimed that Israel, Turkey, Iran, and Saudi Arabia were sufficient countervailing powers. One would be hard pressed to devise methods to confirm, or to disconfirm, these contesting claims.

However, as we shall see when we go through the looking glass, strategists insist that *appearance* is everything. For example, during the Cuban missile crisis Kennedy and his closest advisors agreed that Soviet missiles in Cuba didn't upset the nuclear balance: The president allowed that the Soviets had enough weapons in place to wipe us out anyway. However, Kennedy and his confidants were concerned because the Cuban missiles might *appear* to upset the balance: But this realization simply defers the problem, for how can we be sure that a weapons system *appears* to tip the balance in an adversary's favor. No wonder strategizing seems like a venture through the looking glass.

Strategic metaphors, of course, do not merely indicate what is occurring: they serve a teleological purpose in that they reveal *why* an event is occurring. Like most icons, the balance of power figure represents a narrative—in this case, a cautionary tale drawn from the annals of antiquity and modernity. Both Thucydides and Hobbes taught that, undaunted by moral constraints, states seek power and ultimate hegemony.

Accordingly, the balance of power metaphor, as we shall is, is not merely descriptive; it also conveys an interpretive strategy. A nation's action is construed as an effort to redress the balance of power in its favor. Competing accounts are ruled out a priori. For example, during the Cold War, American decision-makers presupposed that the Soviets rapidly increased their nuclear arsenal to tip the balance of power in their favor. The possibility that the Soviet buildup was a response to domestic factors (such as the perceived humiliation of the Cuban missile crisis) was not entertained.

Finally, taken as a gestalt (which I suspect is the case amongst strategists) the metaphors explicated in this study are normative and performative. They narrate and prescribe *the* story about American policy. To reiterate, the sequence is as follows:

The *balance of power* prescribes a course of action: namely developing and deploying weaponry that will appear to tip the balance in America's favor.

The proper balance provides the blessings of *deterrence:* based upon rational calculation or abject fear (or some combination) potential adversaries have second thoughts about acting upon their intentions and capabilities.

A *crisis* occurs when deterrence fails. For example, American capability and declaratory policy failed to dissuade the Soviets from installing nuclear weapons in Cuba. In a situation construed as a crisis, decision-makers attempt to restore the status quo ante with words or weapons.

If words fail, it is *necessary*—as the narrative climaxes—to engage in nuclear combat. McNamara allows that if Khrushchev had rejected the Secret Deal it would have been necessary to attack Soviet installations in Cuba despite the likely outcome of thermonuclear war.

Literary critic John Canaday aptly suggests that these tropes woven into the strategic metanarrative serve several functions; of course whether the metaphorical constructs function as intended is another matter: ·

1. They attempt to connect the reader's experience to that of the author. Of course the reader's interpretation is guided by a priori notions of the domains bridged by metaphors. For example, The Bomb was likened to the creation of the world and to doomsday. Such images reveal more about authors and readers than about The Bomb itself.

2. Accordingly, metaphors may introduce meanings that defeat the author's purposes; doomsday weaponry might inspire fundamentalists and frighten the rest of us.

3. Therefore, a sophisticated author embeds metaphors in a tendentious context designed to limit and direct the reader's interpretation.

Of course, the author's interpretive strategies might fail. Or, even if they are successful, readers might delude themselves into believing that they truly understand what occurred.[23] In short, a hermeneutics of suspicion is justified in hazarding claims about what those "present at creation" *really* meant—they might be clueless themselves. We can, of course, discuss what the metaphors mean for us with more confidence. The story I tell about these metaphors is embedded in my interpretation of American nuclear endeavors. Interpreting metaphors is self-confessional: How could it be otherwise?

CHAPTER 4

Like Nothing Else

The atom had us bewitched. It was so gigantic, so terrible, so beyond the power of imagination to embrace that it seemed to be the ultimate fact. It would either destroy us all or it would bring about the millennium. It was the final secret of Nature, greater by far than man himself, and it was, it seemed, invulnerable to the ordinary processes of life.... Our obsession with the Atom led us to assign to it a separate and unique state in the world. So greatly did it seem to transcend the ordinary affairs of men that we shut it out of those affairs altogether; or rather, tried to create a separate world, a world of the Atom.

—David Lilienthal, first Chairman of the
Atomic Energy Commission[1]

How we interpret the world—and how we interpret other's interpretations of the world—is largely self-confessional. Our efforts to make sense of experience reveal much about our biography and group affiliations—often one and the same. What shall we make of the visions that appeared to the Christians, Jews, and unbelievers who witnessed the first atomic explosion along a trail the Spaniards called "The Journey of Death?"

We know of the earliest metaphorical accounts of nuclear endeavors through the reminiscences, polemics, jeremiads, and other writing emerging from the early heroic days of American nuclear endeavors. In general, the authors of these texts and their interpreters agree on this much: the Manhattan Project, culminating in the first nuclear explosion at the Trinity Test Site, was a noumenal experience. Theologian Rodolf Otto (credited with coining the term) explains that such experience calls forth: "A sense of awe, of fear and trembling, [it] is always part of the multifaceted experience. It begins to stir in the feeling of something uncanny, eerie, or weird.... Daemons and gods alike spring from this root."[2] No wonder, as Robert Lifton observes, the blast at Trinity—"brighter than a thousand suns"—converted the faithful to "nuclearism":

Men experiencing such an awesome event were likely to convert to *something*—to take on a survivor mission of some kind. And many did—either the mission of warning the world about the danger of this extraordinary new power, or the opposite mission of embracing the new power as something close to a deity.[3]

Interpreting the conversion experience and the metaphors improvised to render the experience intelligible and communicable is, however, problematic. The shock and awe of the Trinity Test left some speechless. We might also imagine that others blurted out the oft quoted metaphors without a second thought; perhaps clear meanings were only attached to these figures of speech ad hoc in retrospect. Few investigators, regardless of their contesting perspectives, take what their subjects say at face value. Marxists would not be tempted to take strategic pronouncements literally: such pronouncements would be considered an ideology to disguise or legitimize the strategist's privileged social location. Likewise, a Freudian might see strategy as a rationalization for unconscious impulses or a defense mechanism for quelling anxiety. Even the most unreconstructed positivist such as a Skinnerian psychologist would resist any temptation to take strategic pronouncements at face value: Such pronouncements would be deemed the outcome of biological imperatives and social conditioning. The daunting problematic of interpreting others' interpretations (in this case strategic metaphors) invites humility. The best we can ever hope for is to be on target, but no bull's eye. In short, a hermeneutics of suspicion is justified in explicating what those "present at creation" *really* meant—they might be clueless themselves.

That said, it seems reasonable to assume that meaning is context-dependent. Nuclear weapons were not created by scientists, engineers, and military men working independently. The Manhattan Project—to understate the case—was the work of a tight-knit group enduring years of secrecy and isolation in the remote wilderness of New Mexico. Words mean a great deal to such secret societies: they identify the group and the initiated, sanctify the glorious cause, and absolve the faithful of all that is dubious and destructive. As Freud recognized: "A group ... is subject to the truly magical power of words, they can evoke the most formidable tempests in the group mind."[4]

Accordingly, in order to get a handle on the supernatural metaphors that emerged from the early heroic period of nuclear endeavors, I have tried to understand the nature of the group affiliation of those who designed and detonated the first nuclear weapons. I suspect that the subculture that emerged became, in effect, an interpretive community: any attempt to understand the meaning of the emergent metaphors must take into account the nature of this community. As previously argued, this community has the signature features of an ecclesiastical bureaucracy.

"IT BEGGARED DESCRIPTION"

> The effects could well be called unprecedented, magnificent, beautiful, stupendous and terrifying. No man-made phenomenon of such tremendous power had ever occurred before. The lighting effect beggared description. The whole country was lighted by a searing light with the intensity many times that of the midday sun.... Thirty seconds after the explosion came first ... [followed by an] awesome roar which warned of doomsday and made us feel that we puny things were blasphemous to dare tamper with the forces heretofore reserved for The Almighty.
>
> —Thomas Farrell[5]

General Farrell's numinous prose highlighted General Leslie Groves' account of the Trinity Test, an authoritative report sent to Henry Stimson, Secretary of War. As Spencer R. Weart argues persuasively in *Nuclear Fear*, such imagery does not emerge ex nihilo; it's drawn from a cultural repertoire. As he explains: "The images we cherish have a greater role in history than has commonly been thought."[6] Like Carl Jung, Weart suggests that our seemingly extemporaneous, metaphorical appropriations of the world echo ancient archetypes.

The meaning of these archetypes, of course, is context-dependent: A monster etched on an ancient Chinese painting does not convey the same meaning as a jeremiad about the nuclear monster that arose from the Trinity Test Site. What is more significant, however, unlike the monsters of old that were usually either good or evil, the nuclear monster—and the other archetypes for that matter—were invariably represented paradoxically as both god-like forces for good *and* demonic forces for evil. Weart recognizes that these images are powerful and resonant precisely *because* they are contradictory—they unify opposites. Much can be read into such symbols. (Such representation is not unlike the all-loving fundamentalist God who is considerate enough to condemn critics of fundamentalism to eternal torment.)

In the Beginning

> It seems probable to me that God in the Beginning form'd matter in solid, massy [*sic*] hard, impenetrable, movable Particles ... so very hard, as never to wear or break in pieces; no ordinary power being able to divide what God Himself made one in His first creativity.
>
> —Isaac Newton[7]

At the dawn of the twentieth century the Newtonian worldview had long been considered the ultimate synthesis of scientific understanding. Both the physical and the social world seemed to be governed by a few simple laws accessible to any reasonably intelligent person. Newton was eulogized for discovering nothing less than the handiwork of the Divine Watchmaker.

It seemed unnatural, if not blasphemous, to question the eternal verities of Newton, for these verities seemed like nothing less than the sacred law of nature ordained by the Almighty. Canaday seems to intimate that such forbidden probing was likened to the primal oedipal crime: penetrating the secrets of Mother Nature.

Unlike the unfortunate, mythic king, the irreverent physicists didn't blind themselves when they beheld the newfound secrets of nature. Likening themselves to bright, mischievous children or explorers of old, they pursued theories and experiments that undermined the venerable paradigm of classical physics. Mysterious rays were discovered beyond the spectrum of Newton's imagination. Perhaps it was Roentgen who first evoked the enchantment, awe, and dread of the new epoch when he inadvertently discovered seemingly occult rays that penetrated objects. He demonstrated that these ghostlike emissions could pass through the human body to reveal the death imagery of the skeletal structure. To convey his experience of the numinous he called such emissions "x-rays."[8] Paradoxically, the popular literature simultaneously extolled the discovery as a utopian dream come true and as the advent of death rays that would kill us all.

Then as now, Einstein became an icon of popular culture. He depicted an uncanny world that defied common sense: space bent, time dilated, but somehow the speed of light remained constant. Newton was preoccupied with force. His classical physics; ($F = ma$) revealed the results of accelerating mass. In an equation that came to symbolize the mystery and terror of our age ($E = mc^2$) Einstein foretold of annihilating mass: annihilating an infinitesimal quantity of mass would cause an explosion such that the world had never seen. After the destruction of Hiroshima and Nagasaki, Einstein's passion turned to preventing the annihilation of the human race.[9]

In 1919 physicist Ernest Rutherford turned the dream of the medieval alchemist into reality through the first transmutation of matter. Once again, the new scientific priesthood worked magic with mysterious rays. Some thought there was no limit to what the newfound energy could accomplish. The distinction between transmutation and transubstantiation was blurred: It was as if Rutherford conjured up a divine power that would always be with us. The *London Times* articulated a millenarian vision of an atomic-powered life of love and leisure: "Our descendants will be taking the energy out of an ounce or two of matter instead of a thousand tons of coal."[10]

The millenarian vision of heaven on earth is ancient, arresting, and virtually universal. It resonates through the Western heritage in the Book of Daniel and in Revelation. Diverse Enlightenment thinkers offered secular visions of beginning the world anew through science, industry, and revolutionary nationalism. And, for a time, the men who managed the nuclear arsenal were strong in the faith that nuclear weapons would usher in an American Century, a time of uncontested power and prosperity for the elect amongst nations.

Of course, as Weart stresses, the ancient millenarian narrative—improvised to get a handle on twentieth-century physics—is not a saga of instant, blissful fulfillment. It's a morality play in which the chosen must keep the faith and muster the courage to use a newfound cosmic power to vanquish evil. He puts the lesson succinctly: "Someday, and perhaps soon, before humanity could enjoy the Golden Age, the fire and bloodshed of Armageddon must come."[11] For example, in his prescient *The World Set Free*, written in 1913, H. G. Wells narrates such a tale. After a devastating world war fought with atomic bombs in mid-century, the survivors come to their senses and establish a peaceable world government.

And yet, there were those who warned: be afraid, be terribly afraid. World War I refuted Alfred Nobel's sunny optimism about the deterrent effect of the terrible explosive he invented. His reassurance that "my factories may make an end to war sooner than your congresses," somehow doesn't ring true.[12] In the aftermath of the war it occurred to many that weapons of mass destruction were manufactured to be used. No wonder, according to Weart, prior to 1914 two-thirds of fictional apocalypses had been due to natural causes; after 1914 two-thirds were caused by humans.[13] Evidently, at this time, Churchill was amongst the pessimists. He warned that the nuclear millennium might be catastrophic, not triumphant; history might not have a happy ending. He ruminated: "Might not a bomb no bigger than an orange be found to possess a secret power to . . . blast a township at a stroke?"[14]

At the ceremonies in which he and his wife were awarded the Nobel Prize for their experiments in radioactivity, Pierre Curie asked the right question:

We may ask ourselves if humanity had anything to gain by learning the secrets of nature; is it ripe enough to profit by them, or is this knowledge harmful? The example of Nobel's discoveries is characteristic: powerful explosives permitted men to perform admirable work. They are also a terrible means of destruction in the hands of the great criminals who lead the people toward war.[15]

As Weart indicates, popular culture reacted to the startling advances in twentieth-century physics with a menagerie of bizarre metaphors: radioactive monsters, utopian atom-powered cities, exploding planets, weird ray devices, and much else.[16] The luminaries of post-classical physics responded with a reenactment of Goethe's *Faust* at Niels Bohr's Copenhagen Institute. This was neither the first nor the last time that it was intimated that the men who made the nuclear age possible were dealing with Mephisto.

Canaday devotes considerable time to a filigreed and probing exegesis of the production. After translating salient passages from the German, he offers a take on the production most readers would likely share: "The Faust legend proves an effective medium for representing these scientists as servants of a driving desire to master the secrets of the natural world."[17] However, reading between the lines and deconstructing various passages, he teases out a variety of subtexts that may or may not reveal more about the consciousness and sensibilities of the architects of twentieth-century physics. (Canaday allows that he is not doing rocket science, or even humble social science for that matter.)

In any event, as Canaday suggests, the play could be merely a light-hearted diversion for cloistered men who spent much of their lives in intense contemplation. Nevertheless, he entertains the possibility that the play could be a rewriting of *Faust* in which Mephisto doesn't get the best of the scientists. What is clear, however, is that the physicists who participated in American nuclear endeavors (or made such efforts possible) had *Faust* on their minds. Could it be that, by the time some of these men were inducted into the secret society at Los Alamos, they had already sold their souls? In their minds, did the transaction exonerate them from personal responsibility? Consider the lamentation Edward Teller shared with Leo Szilard: "The things we are working on are so terrible that no amount of protesting or fiddling with politics will save our souls."[18]

A Time in the Wilderness

My point is not to portray the Los Alamites as monsters—indeed my experience suggests that the majority ... were exemplary human beings. I do mean to point out, however, that a particular, complex rhetorical dynamic was central to their ability to do their work *without* being monsters.
                                                                    —John Canaday[19]

The time in the wilderness marks the cultist phase of the ecclesiastical bureaucracy that would come to manage the American nuclear arsenal. Like other cults, it was guided by a Manichean narrative and inspired by the promise of seizing a newfound cosmic power. However, unlike all previous cults in high places, the narrative came as close as humanly possible to reality; the promise was kept in a flash brighter than a thousand suns at the Trinity Test Site.

The Manhattan Project casts the paradoxical nature of nuclear endeavors in stark relief. The rise of Nazism contradicted the cherished, Enlightenment faith that only the ignorant are wicked. To this day, we ask ourselves, "How could this happen?" Not only did German culture enjoy mass literacy, it produced outstanding advances in almost every venue of civilized life. How could the culture that produced Beethoven and Goethe produce Hitler and Himmler? Reflecting on the unalloyed evil of Nazism, theologian Paul Tillich lamented that "the terrible has already happened."

It is worth reiterating that those responding to the Nazi threat by developing the atomic bomb had no semblance to Hollywood caricatures of villains, let alone monsters. Indeed, a typecasting department would have put most of these refugee scientists in the roles of gentle, pleasantly eccentric academics—Mr. Chips with a German accent. There was nothing funny, however, about Nazi pathology. Fearful of nuclear weapons in Nazi hands, these distinguished refuge scientists fled Europe and came to America, and they desperately tried to convince American officials to build nuclear weapons. Like many of his foreign counterparts, Robert Oppenheimer, a brilliant physicist who embraced progressive politics and pacifist principles (the Hindu doctrine of nonviolence—*Ahimsa*). As his biographers suggest, he didn't sell his soul to Mephisto, but he did lease it to General Leslie Grove, the overbearing military director of the Manhattan Project.[20]

Recollecting his Los Alamos experience, physicist Victor Weisskopf reveals his own angels and demons:

Those eventful years at Los Alamos evoke two opposite feelings. On the one side, it was a heroic period of our lives, full of the most exciting problems and achievements ... On the other side we must be deeply aware of the results of our work—which was awesome enough at the time, when we saw the explosion in the desert, and murderous enough when it destroyed two Japanese cities.[21]

Unlike most of their countrymen, the Los Alamos physicists were conversant with the esoteric notions of space and time that informed Relativity Theory and Quantum Mechanics. And unlike most of their countrymen, those cloistered in the secret society in the high desert found their lives rigidly governed by ancient notions of the sacred and profane. Despite their sophisticated notions of space-time continua, the lived experience inside the closely guarded boundaries of Los Alamos unfolded within an antediluvian milieu of sacred space and time.

Robert Oppenheimer selected the site of the Manhattan Project, a place that evoked fond memories of boyhood adventures at the ranch his family once owned in these deserted highlands of the Southwest. His close friend Haaken Chevalier goes so far as to suggest Oppenheimer treasured the site as a sacred mountaintop, the destination of a religious pilgrimage. Chevalier reflected: "Man, in those supreme moments when he must face his destiny and make ultimate choices for good or evil, seeks out the high places. A mountaintop was selected as the birthplace of the Thing."[22]

Theologian Mircea Eliade's explication of the sacred and profane is useful in understanding the metaphors that inform such a milieu. Paraphrasing the saga of Abraham, he explains that mere mortals are profoundly humbled at sacred times and places; like the Patriarch they see themselves as lowly dust and ashes.[23] Time and again, the men of Los Alamos reveal that they were astonished, humbled, and terrified by the power of the atom—the fission process secreted in the holy of holies at Los Alamos.

Ordinarily the men of Los Alamos walked about in profane space: a commonsensical, homogenous, three-dimensional, Newtonian world in which the very notion of space per se was taken for granted—a space open to all. Unlike profane space, sacred space is a noumenal realm of ritual, consecrated objects, and a holy of holies. Sacred space encloses the fount of supernatural power and authority. As Eliade explains: "The man of archaic societies tends to live as much as possible *in* the sacred or in close proximity to consecrated objects. The tendency is perfectly understandable, because, for primitives as for the man of all premodern societies, the *sacred* is equivalent to a *power,* and, in the last analysis, to *reality.*"[24]

The space within Los Alamos was certainly not open to all; it was like no other. Just as Jesus chased the moneychangers out of His Father's sacred house, armed guard kept all but the faithful out of Los Alamos. Unlike profane space, the sacred space was heterogeneous: There was a holy of holies, a forbidden place, which no man dare enter. For this place, in the words of the Los Alamites, housed the "dragon"—the experimental fission process. The ancient Hebrews were warned not to touch the sacred ark lest they die; Uziah disobeyed and was struck dead. Two physicists met the same fate at the holy of holies, the Omega Assembly Unit. (Some commentators point out that "Omega" connotes the end of all things.) The hapless physicists died an excruciating death from radiation poisoning when they toyed recklessly with nuclear fission. In Los Alamos cant they dared to "tickle the dragon's tail."[25] Just as Uziah was struck down by an invisible God, the physicists were felled by invisible rays.

The sacred space encompassing the nuclear genie is a place for sacrifice. Just as Marie Curie died of leukemia induced by radiation poisoning, could it be that the deaths of the reckless scientists were viewed as sacrifices to the newfound nuclear deity? This was not the last time that obligatory sacrifice was essential to somehow placate the supernatural power of nuclear weapons. Alvin Weinberger, the first Director of the Oak Ridge National Laboratory, explains the necessity of those who sacrificed their lives in Hiroshima:

Could Hiroshima be sanctified were it simply a test in which no humans suffered? I think not. The 100,000 or so who died at Hiroshima will, in the long march of human history, be viewed as martyrs—they were sacrificed as it seems to be turning out, so that mankind can live in the shadow of the bomb.[26]

Weinberger goes on to suggest that that a savior sprung forth from future nuclear developments:

Edward Teller may have supplied the nearest thing to a Quick Technological Fix to the problem of war ... not because men's motivations have been changed, not because men have become more tolerant and understanding, but rather because the appeal to the primitive instinct of self-preservation has been intensified far beyond anything we could have imagined before the H-bomb was invented.[27]

Apparently, nuclear research and destruction are not merely "to die for": death by radiation or conflagration is likened to a sacrifice to the supernatural. No wonder anthropologist Ernest Becker suggested that primitive notions of sacrifice are decidedly less dangerous and more humane:

All he [the primitive] wanted to do, with the techniques of sacrifice, was to take possession of ... invisible forces and use them for the benefit of the community. He had no need for missile launchers and atomic reactors; sacrificial mounds served his purposes well.[28]

Outside of Los Alamos, the physicists and engineers lived in profane time like the rest of us. They gauged their work and appointments in profane, Newtonian time: The clock ran forward in precise, measurable increments. But clearly, the Manhattan Project was a unique time, an unforgettable time, in the participants' lives, a time relived many times in their memoirs and other recollections. Unlike profane time, the lived experience of sacred time is cyclical, what Eliade calls "the eternal return." Cast in this perspective, holidays, in effect, are a reenactment of the holy days of old; indeed, the Catholic Mass is a return to the Last Supper. The ceremony culminates in the transubstantiation when (according to Orthodoxy) the wine and bread literally become the blood and body of Christ. During the sacred time in the wilderness, the men who designed the newest weapons harkened back to the oldest, supernatural metaphors for good reason: dramatic, if not traumatic, changes occurred in their environment and activity.

The lives of the Los Alamos scientists were beset by contradiction and paradox. Not only were many of these men disposed to pacifism, as we've seen: they were accustomed to cosmopolitan environments, not the primitive isolation of the high desert. More significantly, these gifted scientists were generally antiauthoritarian types who ordinarily wouldn't suffer the insolence of a college dean, let alone the Draconian rules of a secret, military installation. As Canaday concludes, disoriented by their environment and confronting the prospects of developing weapons of unimagined horror, the scientific community:

Turned to literature for its metaphors ... to counterbalance the pervasive strangeness in their lives.... They read the Bible and the Bhagavad Gita ... and quoted John Donne's divine poems and legends of Faust.... Existing works of literature thus enable the Los Alamites to tell stories of their war and drastic consequences in terms of *narrative necessity* [italics mine]....[29]

As Canaday suggests, not only did these time-honored texts offer metaphors that subsumed contradictions, they exonerated the scientists of personal responsibility by positioning their actions in a seemingly inevitable script. Such narratives of necessity are the lingua franca of political realism, and, as we shall see, the sine qua non of nuclear strategizing.

Generally, they invoked the Judeo-Christian supernatural metaphors they learned as children to explain the astonishing and ineffable. For the most part, ancient Greek metaphors were invoked only after the advent of Soviet nuclear weapons, a time of bureaucratic consolidation when the gods no longer smiled upon American nuclear endeavors. There were, however, a few exceptions besides Oppenheimer's oft quoted reference to Hindu scripture. The creation of a new, fissionable element conjured up ancient Greek myths. Unlike the alchemists of old, the physicists found the philosopher's stone—the cyclotron in which heavy elements were bombarded by mysterious neutron beams. Richard Rhodes reveals the paradoxical symbolism in his magisterial study of the making of the bomb. Describing the arduous, secret manufacture of plutonium, he writes: "They dried the speck of matter God had not welcomed at creation.... Seaborg would name the element for Pluto, the Greek god of the underworld, a god of the earth's fertility but also the god of the dead: *plutonium.*"[30]

The names bestowed upon the bombs that destroyed Hiroshima and Nagasaki were also exceptional in that supernatural designations were eschewed in favor of "cute" domestic nomenclature. "Fat Man" and "Little Boy" sound like fast-food items, not weapons of mass destruction. This manner of speaking was, perhaps, the first hint of latter-day Nukespeak, a conceptual strategy for evading the reality of nuclear weaponry: "DefCon 1" (full-scale nuclear war-fighting) sounds like pest control, not the end of the world; "MIRV" sounds like a drinking buddy, not a weapon with ten separately targeted thermonuclear bombs; and surely it's preferable to deploy "Peacekeepers" rather than "MX missiles."

For the most part, however, supernatural metaphors were evoked to express the terrible secrets that emerged from Los Alamos. The first atomic explosion occurred in July 1945 at a test site Oppenheimer named Trinity. Not surprisingly, the reasons for Oppenheimer's designation are subject to considerable interpretation (or overinterpretation). James Aho, one of the interpreters, allows that Oppenheimer insisted that he had nothing special in mind when he suggested the Trinity designation for the test. The learned physicist allowed that "Trinity was just something suggested to me by ... [John Donne's Sonnets] which I happened to be reading at the time."[31]

To reiterate, those of us who hazard accounts of great events rarely take the actors' explanations at face value; Aho is no exception. Naturally, Aho is curious as to why Oppenheimer was reading the mordant ruminations of a seventeenth-century poet. Relying upon various biographical accounts, Aho claims that the physicist was distraught over the suicide a former lover, Jean Tatlock. He sought solace in the sonnets of John Donne, ruminations about the Christian doctrine of the Trinity. Donne, in Aho's view, was obsessed with death and the transmigration of souls—a source of comfort for Oppenheimer.

Canaday, a literary critic, reads considerably more into Oppenheimer's choice of concepts. As he suggests, what we make of these supernatural metaphors is up to us. But, as he aptly anticipates: "Unless we are passive recipients of these texts, they will inspire ... a mixture of revelation and discomfort comparable to that felt by the Los Alamites themselves."[32] Oppenheimer's erudite, literary allusions are far from comforting. Canaday's exegesis begins with lines from Donne's "Holy Sonnet":

> Batter my heart, three-personed God, for You
> As yet but knock, breathe, shine, and seek to mend.

According to Canaday, the sonnet exhorts the faithful to rid themselves of earthly perceptions so that they might attain transcendent unity with a higher power. Oppenheimer knew that recounting the first atomic test in mundane, somatic terms could not possibly capture the grandeur and horror of the event. Indeed, those present at creation did not merely report that they saw a blinding flash and experienced intense heat; they tried to capture the experience with supernatural allusions—and illusions. As Canaday explains: "The Los Alamites' use of religious language translated their somatic experience into symbolic entities according to literary conventions."[33]

The very structure of the sonnet, according to Canaday, is designed to scramble ordinary patterns of thought: "The poem employs convoluted, confusing, and contradictory forms of syntax."[34] As such, like the nuclear era itself, it shatters established forms of thought.

Canaday seems to suggest that the sonnet's rapturous masochism (something akin to a sacral version of Battered Wife Syndrome) resonated with Oppenheimer as he anticipated the epiphanic climax of his efforts and, in effect, three centuries of physics. For, as Canaday reminds us, the fateful sonnet asks the faithful to glory in the Trinity as they are battered, enslaved, and raped by the three-personed God.

The scores of supernatural metaphors improvised to account for the Trinity Test and its aftermath are also subject to diverse, sometimes contradictory, interpretations. Not surprisingly, both Aho and Canaday have much to say about Oppenheimer's oft quoted allusion to Hindu scripture in which Vishnu proclaims "I am death, who shatters worlds!" While intriguing, these interpretations are not central to our analysis. What is central is the realization that the dawn of the nuclear age was almost reflexively interpreted with supernatural metaphors.

Less known observers, for example, failed to heed warnings and were knocked to the ground by the blast. Some likened their experience to the miraculous conversion of Saul when he was knocked off his mule on the road to Damascus. Others allow that the blast reminded them of Christ's ascension into heaven or His Second Coming. Visions of hell and doomsday came to mind, but others retold Exodus sagas: they were intent on venturing out of the wilderness into the promised land of invincible American power.

Even Soviet adversaries could revel in the promised land of American popular culture—after they were vanquished. This vision is condensed in a 1951 issue of *Collier's* magazine. In this scenario, the widespread revolt threatens to destroy the Soviet empire. Fearful of losing their dominion over Eastern Europe, the Soviets invade Western Europe, but the onslaught is brought to a halt with NATO tactical nuclear weapons. The Soviets foolishly launch a losing nuclear war with the United States. The Kremlin apparatchiks surrender unconditionally. U.S. officials establish a provisional government in Moscow. However, despite the devastation, everything turns out for the best. Paraphrasing the article, historian Gregg Herken writes:

By 1960 ... "fashion-starved" Muscovites [are] jamming a newly constructed football stadium for the first showing of postwar styles from the West. A theater troupe composed of former Red Army officers is then performing *Bezdelniki I Zhenshchiny* (*Guys and Dolls*) at the Bolshoi.[35]

In short, after a nuclear holocaust cleanses the world of communism the blessings of American popular culture can be enjoyed by all; this is as close to heaven on earth as it gets. The fortunate survivors in the former Soviet Union are decked in American-style fashions, captivated by spectator sports, and humming tunes from Broadway musicals—everything is right with the world.

CHAPTER 5

The Balance of Power

[Strategic thinking] requires appraisal of the atomic bomb as an instrument of war—and hence of international politics—rather than the visitation of a wrathful deity.

—Bernard Brodie[1]

As the 1940s ended the gods no longer smiled upon nuclear endeavors. It was widely believed—or hoped—that America's exclusive franchise on nuclear weapons would work wonders in history. Surely any adversary would think twice about acting in ways inimical to American interests, real or imagined. And yet, atomic diplomacy was failing. China "fell," and national liberation struggles began in Western colonies in Asia and Africa. The Soviets supported these movements, and—more disturbing still—extended their hegemony into Eastern Europe and blockaded Berlin. In short, the Soviets seemed intractable despite (or because of?) the American nuclear monopoly. Much to his amazement and chagrin, Secretary of State James Byrnes found that the Soviets were "stubborn, obstinate, and they don't scare."[2]

Nevertheless, much of American leadership kept the faith—millenarian promises don't die easily. They couldn't believe that their newfound cosmic power was a liability, not an asset. Nuclear war-fighting was not unthinkable for American officials: a variety of scenarios were proffered but discarded due to lack of bombs, delivery systems, and humane concerns. However, the prospect of a Soviet atomic bomb *was* unthinkable. Experts on Soviet affairs warned that surrounding the former American ally with atomic bases would provoke a response in kind. Nevertheless, as late as 1947 an ever-confident General Groves exclaimed: "Why those people can't even make a jeep! . . . The Russians would need 15 or 20 years to develop an atomic bomb . . ."[3] In retrospect, as Chester Bernard (Truman's atomic policy advisor) would lament: "There was a brief, a most deadly illusion, that we could retain a monopoly of the facilities and the knowledge for the production of fissile material."[4]

In August 1949 the Soviets detonated an atomic bomb over Siberia. Supernatural metaphors about The Bomb and American destiny were shelved. Brodie's exhortation was taken seriously.

BUREAUCRATIC CONSOLIDATION

> One of the most profound consequences of the bureaucratic revolution was the coming to power of a national security elite remarkable for its cohesiveness, consistency, and above all, persistence. Nothing like it existed before in the United States, and outside the area of foreign affairs, its equivalent cannot be found.
>
> —Richard Barnet[5]

The Soviet bomb was not the only problem bedeviling those who managed the American arsenal. The nascent nuclear bureaucracy faced a more immediate, internal challenge: a problem more threatening to the continuity of the organization than the primitive, undeliverable Soviet bomb. Apostate scientists, prominent military men, and even political officials questioned the propriety of developing, deploying, and detonating nuclear weapons. The proposed development of the "Super" (the hydrogen bomb) was particularly disturbing. Defections and purges occurred within the nuclear elite as it underwent its transmutation from a desert cult to an elite bureaucracy within the halls of power.

Joseph Rotblat (a Manhattan Project physicist and subsequent Nobel Peace Prize winner) was among the first to defect. He returned to his native England after his unsettling conversation with General Groves during the midst of the project:

Groves said that, of course, the real purpose in making the bomb was to subdue the Soviets. . . . Until then I thought our work was to prevent a Nazi victory, and now I was told that the weapons we were preparing were intended for use against the people who were making extreme sacrifices for that very aim.[6]

Other scientists lost their enthusiasm for nuclear weapons in the air over Hiroshima. Szilard wrote impassioned pleas for peace, and a penitent Einstein confessed to Linus Pauling: "I made one great mistake in my life, when I signed the letter to President Roosevelt recommending that the atomic bomb be made."[7] Colleagues such as Fermi, Bohr, and Frank shared Einstein's regret. Oppenheimer joined his colleagues in pleading for prudence and arguing against the development of the H-bomb. These scientists warned of an impending arms race and cautioned decision-makers about relying upon these weapons to obtain a false sense of national security. Their pleas were ignored: opposition to building Super was seen as heresy. Oppenheimer was formally purged when he was stripped of his security clearance in 1953.

In their retirement wisdom, officers of the stature of MacArthur and Eisenhower warned of the folly of the arms race. When MacArthur admonished "there's no substitute for victory," evidently he didn't have nuclear war in mind. Late in life he spoke with power and clarity about the unprecedented peril posed by the nuclear age:

By the very triumph of scientific annihilation—the very success of invention—has destroyed the possibility of wars being a medium for the practical settlement of international differences. The enormous destruction to both sides of closely matched opponents makes it impossible for even a winner to translate it into anything but his own disaster.[8]

And in his moving, oft quoted Farewell Address, Eisenhower insisted that disarmament (not merely arms control) was imperative. As he counseled:

We must learn how to compose differences, not with arms, but with intellect and decent purposes. As one who has witnessed the horror and lingering sadness of war—as one who knows that another war could utterly destroy civilization ... I wish I could say tonight that a lasting peace is in sight.[9]

Henry Wallace, Truman's secretary of commerce, lost his job for questioning the propriety of ringing America's former ally with nuclear bases. He believed the Soviets might construe such action as preparation for intimidation, if not total war. How would it appear to us, he wondered, if the Soviets surrounded the United States with nuclear weapons?[10]

Wallace was not the only official apprehensive about cult-like devotion to nuclear weapons. David Lilienthal rhapsodized about the magic of the atom during the early, heroic period of nuclear endeavors: "No fairytale that I had read in utter rapture and enchantment as a child, no spy mystery, no horror story, can remotely compare."[11] However, his colleagues' uncritical, enthusiastic devotion to nuclear weapons gave him second thoughts. He argued against building the H-bomb; he too was ignored. He resigned from the Atomic Energy Commission and criticized his former colleagues for their obsession with technological fixes: "There might have been an opportunity to try something bold and imaginative entirely outside the weapons field to improve the prospects for peace, but our obsession with bigger bombs as a cure-all excluded serious consideration of such a possibility."[12]

Lilienthal was replaced by Lewis Strauss, a Wall Street banker. Most historians do not laud Strauss for his critical, self-reflective sensibility: "Strauss was never troubled by any feeling of doubt that many of the atomic scientists, including Oppenheimer, felt about the bomb. He despised the peace movement."[13]

With Oppenheimer's humiliation the purge was virtually complete. No longer would the emerging ecclesiastical bureaucracy suffer those plagued by self-doubt and moral inhibition. A simple, synoptic vision of the world guided those who remained. With the advent of NSC 68 (a secret National Security Council document designed to guide nuclear strategy) the anticommunist Cold War ideology became an article of faith. Paul Nitze, its principal architect, warned of the peril of keeping an open mind about the struggle between the United States and the Soviet Union: "A free society is vulnerable in that it is easy for people to lapse into excesses—the excesses of a permanently open mind wishfully waiting for evidence that evil design may become noble purpose."[14]

The defections and purges of some of the most sensitive critics of nuclear endeavors led, in effect, to a process of unnatural selection that left only the most zealous in charge of nuclear strategy. The true believers coalesced into a bureaucracy that devised legitimizing ideologies (notions of balance of power and deterrence doctrine) while entering into symbiotic relations with other elite organizations. (Eisenhower would refer to it as the military-industrial complex.) Nevertheless, the old ways and promises remained attractive, even intoxicating. The emerging bureaucracy underwent episodes of revivalism that resurrected the early, millenarian promises of the movement. Indeed, each new weapons system, be it the hydrogen bomb, guided missiles, or nuclear submarines, was touted as the winning weapon.

It is misleading, however, to conclude from the foregoing that the nuclear elite didn't evolve beyond its early cultist mentality. The transformation of the elite is evident from its construction—and deconstruction—of enemies. During the days of hot war, Germany and Japan were deemed rogue states—rightly so. Rational (or rationalized) models of interstate politics such as the balance of power meant nothing to monomaniacal fascist rulers. Axis leaders were demonized as were entire civilian populations. Indeed, the hatred and fear of the Nazi regime prompted pacifist scientists to design the most lethal weapon ever developed.

Times changed. The bipolar disorder known as the Cold War presented other symptoms. There was good news, at least from the point of view of mainstream strategists and decision-makers such as Henry Kissinger: The Soviet adversary was deemed a legitimate nation, not a rogue state. True, Soviet leaders were adversaries, but unlike the fanatics ruling the Axis Powers, the Soviets would listen to reason—or so it was hoped. More good news: Entire populations were no longer demonized. On the contrary, ordinary Soviet civilians were depicted as victims of cruel apparatchiks, friends crying out for liberation. Likewise, citizens of the Warsaw Pact were declared victims of captive nations by an act of Congress: These citizens were also friends. The bad news is that these "friends" were targeted for destruction by strategic planners—nothing personal. Such cold-blooded scenarios climaxing in the annihilation of millions of innocent victims became the hallmark of latter-day strategizing. In effect, the advent of the nuclear bureaucracy marked the apotheosis of the Weberian account of such organizations: Not only did the leaders of nation-states have a monopoly on violence, as consummate bureaucrats they made decisions without regard to person or consequences.

Since the Soviets were a legitimate, albeit aggressive, regime that listened to reason, they were (according to the nuclear canon) preoccupied with the balance of power. And so it came to pass that American strategists abandoned notions of supernatural good and evil and depicted Soviet leaders as rational actors whose ambitions could be deterred by fine tuning the balance of power. (Soviet leaders seemed to share the same belief about their American adversaries.) The fate of the earth depended upon—or so it was believed—attaining the proper balance of power. Everyone seemed to know what this fateful requirement meant until they were asked to define it. But not many realized or acknowledged that the notion of balance of power—the quintessential doctrine for managing the newest weapons—was an ancient, ambiguous figure of speech as old as the ancient Greeks.

Of course, as Morgenthau and his realist colleagues admonish, a concept shouldn't be dismissed solely due to its antiquity. The notion of balance of power is not problematic due to its antiquity. It's misleading because strategists fail to recognize that they are interpreters, not observers: they reason about the balance of power as if the notion is an observable thing rather than an overused metaphorical concept. Indeed, like most tropes, it can be neither clearly defined, measured, nor calibrated.

THE FIRST REVISIONIST HISTORIAN?

> I believe that the Athenians, because they had grown in power and terrified the Spartans, made war inevitable (*anankasai*).
>
> —Thucydides

The *Iliad*'s mythic/poetic account of the Trojan War is a tale of supernatural intrigue, sacrilege, and vengeful goddesses spurned by mere mortals. In the Homeric epoch, Zeus remains neutral and insists that Fate must decide the outcome. Understandably, Apollo intervenes against the Greeks when they sack his temple. And the Golden Apple crisis, of course, embroils mere mortals in Olympian jealousies. Paris, it may be recalled, is given the precarious task of giving the Golden Apple to the fairest among maidens. The goddesses enter a competition in risk-taking by promoting their favorite candidates. Aphrodite tempts Paris with Helen, and the young Trojan prince deals with temptation the only way he knows—by giving in. Spurned, Aphrodite's rival goddesses side with Paris' soon-to-be enemies, the Greeks.

By way of contrast, Thucydides' account of the war is not about miraculous powers or fateful curses bestowed by the gods and goddesses. In prose that delights any latter-day realist, the ancient historian insists the Agamemnon's victory was based upon overwhelming military might. In short, the balance of power was in his favor. In an oft quoted passage in the "Melian Dialogue" Thucydides' abandons the prevailing notion that interstate politics is a morality play in which a deus ex machina intervenes at the last moment to assure the triumph of justice. To paraphrase the ancient historian, the strong do what they have the power to do and the weak must accept the consequences.

Likewise, Thucydides' eschews supernatural intrigues to explain the Peloponnesian War. Athenian ascendancy destroyed the equilibrium that supposedly kept the peace between rival city-states. Freely translating the ancient historian's account into Nukespeak: the Spartans lost confidence in a robust, second-strike capacity that could ride out an Athenian first strike. What is especially noteworthy—at least for my purposes—the war, according to this first revisionist historian, was somehow necessary. This necessity had nothing to do with the ordinances and machinations of the gods; the necessity lay in human nature itself. (The trouble, dear Homer, is not in the gods; the trouble is in ourselves.)

Thucydides' revolutionary account of interstate politics became the conventional wisdom—a commonplace—even among religious thinkers. Augustine concluded that far removed from heaven, and closer to hell, earthly principalities will never be the exemplars of Christian love. Less pious thinkers such as Machiavelli and Hobbes relegated Thucydides' reflections to the status of natural laws: The strong try to dominate the weak when they do what comes naturally. Rousseau deemed the balance of power as natural law that determines the interstate power structure, regardless of human intention: "It [the balance of power] maintains itself without effort, in such a manner that if it sinks on one side, it reestablishes itself on the other."[15]

There is no need to overstate the obvious: The notion of balance of power has informed political thought for at least twenty-five centuries. Regardless of political stripe, international relations theorists would agree that it is difficult to overestimate Thucydides' impact on modern thought and policy formation. As Gregory Crane concludes:

[Thucydides] continues to influence students and practitioners of foreign affairs. Thucydides' explanation for the Peloponnesian War has been cited to support

the general thesis that war arises when power begins to shift. Thucydides provides the basis for the "balance of power" politics that Western diplomats from
Bismarck to Kissinger have explicitly pursued.[16]

DEFINING THE BALANCE OF POWER

> There is nothing among civil affairs more subject to error than forming a
> true and right valuation of the power and forces of an empire.
>
> —Francis Bacon[17]

In their struggle to bestow the imprimatur of science upon their endeavors, social scientists appropriate the conceptual apparatus of the hard
sciences. Newton's particle logic and Darwin's evolutionary theory are
popular metaphors. In the hard sciences these concepts refer to testable
things. In social inquiry, mechanistic models and Social Darwinism are
metaphors, not things: Interstate behavior is likened to physics (law-
governed matter in motion) or to biology (the struggle to survive and
reproduce). True, these metaphors may have heuristic value or they may
mislead; in any case, they shouldn't be taken literally.

Strategists appropriate the notion of balance from mathematics and
science. If I remember high school algebra correctly, it is possible to determine whether an equation is balanced: the results to the left and to the
right of the equal sign must be equal: ($a + b = c$; let "a" = 1 and "b" = 1;
the equation is balanced if "c" equals 2).

Having completed this exercise in higher mathematics, I turn to antique
laboratory scales: If I place a gram on the left side of the fulcrum the scale
will be in balance if a gram is placed on the right side. It is possible to
confirm—and to disconfirm—whether a scale is in equilibrium.

Likewise, the notion of chemical stability is verifiable. We can determine whether the chemical properties of a solution remain in dynamic
equilibrium or whether the solution explodes (instability). ("Dynamic
equilibrium" has considerable scientific gravitas; perhaps it should be
appropriated by Nukespeak.) In any case, the luxury of such confidence-
building verification does not await those who ruminate about the balance of power in interstate relations. A mathematician can demonstrate
that the equation just cited does not balance if $1 + 1 = 3$. By the same
token a scientist can demonstrate that unequal weights throw the scale
out of balance. But how can a strategist decisively demonstrate that a
new weapons system or strategy alters the balance of power? During
the Cuban missile crisis, for example, what would constitute proof that
Soviet missiles in Cuba upset the balance of power? What conceivable
proof could President Kennedy and his confidants have relied upon to
persuade the hawks (the Joint Chiefs) that the missiles did *not* alter the
military balance?

Since, like other primary strategic metaphors, the notion of balance of power is ambiguous, strategists are free to read their favored meanings into the trope. Such interpretation is not merely an academic exercise. On the contrary, secondary metaphorical interpretations of the balance of power are *performative:* To reiterate, they prescribe long-term policymaking and decisions at critical junctures.

Indeed, strategists are advocates of action, not quiet contentment, let alone resignation. True, expressing retirement wisdom, former strategists and decision-makers often counsel that the balance of power is properly calibrated and durable. In his last testimony before Congress, Admiral Rickover argued that the existing fleet of nuclear submarines met all the putative requirements for a proper balance of power. He warned that continually escalating the arms race would surely upset the balance and expressed the forlorn hope "that a more sagacious species would take our place."[18] Not surprisingly, however, as a member of the nuclear establishment he advocated more naval weapons systems to correct the balance of power.

Strategists are seldom content with the status quo; the argument de rigueur is that the balance of power is askew and must be corrected by implementing their favored strategy and deploying their favored weapons system. To be sure, strategists may be genuinely fearful that an unfavorable balance (whatever that may be) undermines American national security. But surely it is not inconceivable that the push to dramatically alter the balance of power is also motivated by careerism and profiteering. I know of no cases where a member of the armed services or a corporate executive asked Congress for more money due to interservice rivalry or the desire to profiteer. Correcting an unfavorable balance of power is the usual pretext.

Turning to those who take the balance of power seriously, pre-nuclear accounts of the balance of power almost invariably contained a subjective element. One can imagine a monarch observing a field of battle in which his troops are outnumbered tenfold. However, even then crude threats and posturing (by today's standards) were designed to alter perceptions of power. This subjective element of balance-of-power thinking reaches its apotheosis in the nuclear age.

Nuclear era accounts stress the subjective, psychological nature of the concept. As we've seen, before terrorism got bad press, strategists struggled to calibrate the balance in terms of the harrowing anxiety induced by nuclear threats—*the balance of terror.* These days, such references are not, to say the least, politically correct. Just as one no longer calls the Department of Defense the Department of War, these days no one enters the community of strategic discourse by writing filigreed ruminations about "the delicate balance of terror."

Pre-nuclear Concepts

One must be prepared for the experience of encountering, after twenty
pages of analysis of the balance of power, the candid admission that "We
have been using the term *balance* without defining it, as if everybody knew
what it meant. . . . It is not far from the truth to say that nobody knows what
it means."

—Inis Claude, Jr.[19]

Claude begins his insightful account of balance of power by suggesting that the concept is a truism, a self-evident notion that any analyst
worthy of *his* realist credentials should grasp intuitively: promiscu-
ous use of the term is proof positive of "he-manliness in the field of
international relations."[20] Apparently, we know it when we *don't* see it:
"Balance of power is a mere chimera—a creation of the politician's brain—
a phantasm, without form or tangible existence—a mere conjunction of
syllables, forming words which convey sound without meaning."[21] Most
analysts and strategist, however, embrace the notion of the balance of
power uncritically and enthusiastically.

Like most arresting metaphors that—metaphorically speaking—survive
the ravages of time, a vague, ambiguous trope such as the balance
of power is sufficiently elastic to cover a few virtues and many sins.
Accounts of the balance of power are largely self-confessional: They often
reveal more about the author's descriptive and normative visions of the
international world than the world itself.

A review of the literature reveals the diverse meanings, ontological
issues, and policy-relevant concerns that bedevil attempts to understand
pre-nuclear notions of the balance of power.

Terms such as equilibrium and stability are touted as salutary outcomes
of a satisfactory balance of power between nation-states. The notion of
power is itself problematic, and (as we shall see) it has undergone transmutation in the nuclear age. However, pre-nuclear notions of power
stressed military prowess along with a robust infrastructure to sustain
and project military might. In this sense, power is about coercion: The
capacity to compel adversaries to do what they otherwise would not do.

It is a commonplace that the balance of power is likened to an antique
laboratory scale. I also suspect that a scale in balance evokes a subtext:
images of Themis, the blindfolded goddess of justice who holds the scale.
Accordingly, it is just, if not patently fair, to preserve a terribly fragile
international order through covert threats and overt coercion. Of course, as
realists from Thucydides to Morgenthau have urged, it is not in the nature
of nations to play fair. Statesmen move irresistibly to tip the balance in their
favor. As Admiral Carroll, a former NATO commander and Pentagon plan-
ner, concluded, American planners strive for disequilibrium, unassailable

superiority in conventional and nuclear forces. Such striving, he believed, fomented the nuclear arms race.[22]

Given the equivocal meanings read into balance of power, Claude suggests the term might serve normative, rather than descriptive, functions. Evoking the balance of power may be a not-so-subtle reminder to be attentive to power politics; create and sustain equilibrium (if a dove) or disequilibrium (if a hawk). As he concludes: "Many writers have used the term balance of power not as a definable concept but as a *symbol* of realistic and prudent concern with the problem of power in international relations."[23]

Political realists, of course, laud such exhortations. However, idealists such as Woodrow Wilson disparage amoral power politics based upon the injunction that might makes right. Wilson's disparagement, however, went beyond moralizing. He blamed the catastrophe of World War I, to a considerable degree, on the machinations of power politics informed by the notion of balance of power, and argued for alliances based upon decent principles. As Claude suggests, Wilson should not be summarily dismissed as a utopian; he should be praised for recognizing the liabilities of thinking and acting in terms of notions such as balance of power.[24]

Not only is there disagreement about the meaning and morality of the concept of balance of power, there is controversy about how it works. (As we have seen above, there are those who doubt its efficacy in sustaining the peace.) Political analysts who do not entertain such doubts are divided into two camps as additional metaphors are brought into play: those who liken the balance of power to a natural law (or process) operating apart from human volition, and those who see the balance of power as the outcome of prudent statecraft. Although Morgenthau equivocates, it is reasonable to assume that he sees balance of power machinations as the natural, if not inevitable, outcome of international anarchy. Echoing Thucydides, he finds nothing more natural than states striving to assure their survival by matching or surpassing the power of rival states. True, natural laws can be ignored: but a heavy price is paid for ignoring gravity—or the balance of power.

In other words, human intervention cannot change the laws of politics, but it can change the outcome of international challenges. Acting in accord with these laws assures the best possible outcome; ignoring power politics often leads to disaster. This line of argument resembles laissez faire economic doctrine. A "hands-off" approach to economics (thanks to the workings of the "invisible hand") assures that robust competition will produce the highest quality goods at the lowest possible price. By way of analogy, robust—if not ruthless—competition between nation-states somehow assures that each state will do what comes naturally: struggling to assure their survival and prosperity as they grasp ever more power and prestige. Somehow states automatically recognize that their very survival is contingent upon an international balance of power in which no state or alliance can overwhelm another.

Kissinger is among the strategists who recognize that the nuclear age changed everything including, of course, traditional notions of balance of power. One would think that the notion is as obsolete as reckoning cavalry troops. This is not the case. Evidently, the notion is so venerable—and ambiguous—that strategists continue to read a variety of meanings into balance of power, or rather the perception (to invoke another overused term) of the balance of power.

The Balance of Power in the Nuclear Age

Throughout history, military power was considered the final recourse.... A state's strength could be measured by its ability to protect its population from attack. The nuclear age has destroyed this traditional measure. Increasing strength no longer necessarily confers the ability to protect the population.... Power no longer translates into influence.

—Henry Kissinger[25]

As Kissinger observes, prior to World War II territorial expansion translated into increased national power. There was something terribly tangible about an adversary army occupying conquered territory. However, in the present era nuclear weaponry—or rather the credible threat to *use* nuclear weaponry—is more significant than territorial expansion. As he suggests, China gained more power through the possession of nuclear weapons than it would have gained by conquering all of Southeast Asia. Likewise, a non-nuclear Soviet Union in control of Western Europe is less formidable than a nuclear armed Soviet Union within its borders.[26] However, as Kissinger emphasizes, the *meaning* of this significance is far from transparent.

Indeed, the nuclear era turns traditional thinking about the balance of power into paradox, if not absurdity. An otherwise weak nation with a few nuclear weapons suddenly becomes a formidable foe. (Consider the case of North Korea or Iran.) However, today's only superpower, the United States, gains little (and may actually lose influence) by developing and deploying additional nuclear weapons. And, to reiterate, by any measure the United States is more powerful than the terrorist diaspora; however, such power—to understate the case—does not deter the terrorist agenda. In the postmodern epoch, as Kissinger recognizes, there are no clear—let alone unassailable—definitions of notions such as equilibrium or superiority. The paradox is obvious, palpable: "As power has grown more awesome, it has also turned abstract, intangible, elusive."[27]

Such adroit analysis marks certain academic writing on the notion of the balance of power in the nuclear age. One would think that strategists have entered a period of "liminality": old metaphorical constructions of the balance of power no longer work and new ones are unavailable to take their place. Given the stakes, namely the nuclear threat, anthropologist Victor Turner's chilling account of liminality would seem to apply. Those who endure liminality are "detached from mundane life and characterized by ambiguous ideas, monstrous images, sacred symbols, ordeals, humiliations, esoteric and paradoxical instruction."[28]

This is no way for strategists—quintessential products of modernity—to live. The enormity of the responsibility and threat posed by apocalyptic weapons is too much to bear; somehow things had to be put back in balance. In public, strategists proclaimed that nothing had really changed: the balance of power could be reckoned by counting warheads and delivery systems. Despite his academic skepticism about the balance of power, Kissinger reassured a reluctant Congress that the Strategic Arms Limitation Treaty (SALT) tipped the balance in favor of the United States. Other advocates of SALT reassured Senator Henry Jackson (sometimes referred to as "the senator from Boeing") and his allies that any treaty with the Soviet Union would preserve nuclear parity—although they were (to say the least) unclear on the concept.[29]

There were those, of course, who saw invoking the balance of power as more than a public relations ploy. Albert Wohlstetter was determined to infuse the concept with a meaning, a gravitas, suitable for the nuclear age. Wohlstetter responded to the brief interlude of quietism when it appeared that a durable strategic equilibrium had been attained. During the second Eisenhower administration both the United States and the Soviet Union possessed long-range bombers and thermonuclear weapons. Oppenheimer likened the situation to a standoff in which two venomous scorpions would surely kill and devour one another if they fought. It seemed like the best of all possible nuclear worlds. Paradoxically, the credible threat of mutually assured destruction insured equilibrium. In Churchill's words, apocalyptic weapons on both sides of the Atlantic were a blessing in disguise. He observed that this peculiar nuclear family was: "Ushering in an age where safety will be the sturdy child of terror, and survival the twin brother of annihilation."[30]

Relying heavily on self-serving Air Force intelligence reports and scenarios, Wohlstetter rejected this Panglossian vision. (Critics charge that, like other vested interests, the Air Force overstated the Soviet threat to press for more extravagant funding.) His arguments were closely reasoned and coherent. However, as political analyst Fred Kaplan points out, Wohlstetter and his colleagues were not working with real data: "There was, of course, no real combat data for World War III, the cosmic 'nuclear exchange' that the systems analysts of RAND were examining."[31] In effect, their RAND corporation reports confused precision with accuracy.

Evidently, the surprise attack at Pearl Harbor made an indelible impression on Wohlstetter's thinking—it became an arresting analogy. He argued that, contrary to sanguine reassurances, the American nuclear arsenal was vulnerable to Soviet attack. What seemed like good news—the proximity of American bases to the Soviet Union—was also bad news: the bases were exquisitely vulnerable to a surprise Soviet attack. As Kaplan observes, his preoccupation with the Pearl Harbor analogy fomented "grisly scenarios about Soviet first-strikes and American weakness; it would provide the rationale for a host of new weapons and much else ... and it would serve as a powerful engine driving ... the nuclear arms race over the next quarter century and beyond."[32]

Such ruminations led to Wohlstetter's influential article in a 1959 issue of *Foreign Affairs*, a contribution to what he called "balance of terror theory." The title is telling indeed—"The Delicate Balance of Terror."[33] In this time before terrorism got bad press strategists likened the balance of power to terrifying the hearts and minds of Soviet leaders and citizens. (The Soviets returned the favor.)

The epistemological and normative concerns are obvious. How does one determine whether leaders and citizens in a foreign culture are sufficiently terrorized? Indeed, how is such sufficiency defined? True, it is presupposed that a survivable second-strike capacity will assure the destruction of Soviet society, but will this capacity be interpreted in ways favorable to American planners? Convincing an adversary that a retaliatory strike is credible might upset the balance of power by prompting an adversary to take defensive and offensive measures. Likewise, if the threat is not credible an adversary may have the incentive to act aggressively, thereby upsetting the balance of power. This is no ordinary matter of mundane interpretation: claims about the salutary consequences of terrorizing leaders far removed from one's personal and professional life do not inspire confidence.

Like other strategists of a positivist bent, Wohlstetter seems profoundly indifferent to certain moral concerns. He is not troubled by injunctions against killing the innocent. And strangely, he seems indifferent to a policy-relevant, utilitarian concern: what good would be served by annihilating tens of millions of defenseless Soviet citizens if deterrence fails?

This is not to suggest that he is totally indifferent to all matters of morality. He believes that it is morally imperative to have a survivable second-strike capacity to deter Soviet aggression, and—if deterrence fails—to retaliate by annihilating the Soviet Union. Not only are European SAC bases vulnerable, somehow he reckoned that the chances of ten American bombers surviving a Soviet sneak attack are a million to one.[34]

In Wohlstetter's view such worries about the delicate balance of terror breaking down are pressing concerns. The best laid plans might fail amid the collapse of the Soviet Union. And, as if to prove that strategists are not prescient, he presupposes that everybody knows that USSR would obviously strike first were their empire crumbling.[35]

Perhaps the enormity of the terrorism Wohlstetter advocates can be revealed through a mental experiment. Imagine that Osama Bin Laden issues a *fatwa* in which he reveals he would like the capacity to kill half the population of an American city of 900,000; however, blast resistant shelters may frustrate his ambition. Wohlstetter expressed similar concerns in his influential article. He lamented that low-payload, low accuracy systems such as Minuteman and Polaris "may be frustrated by blast resistant shelters." Ideally, American weapons of mass destruction should be able to kill half the population in a city of 900,000.[36]

Wohlstetter certainly didn't convince all his colleagues about the fragility of the American arsenal. Kenneth Waltz, for example claimed that "given the impossibility of one side destroying enough of the other side's missiles to make a retaliatory strike bearable, the balance of terror is indestructible."[37]

In any event, decision-makers did not enter such neo-Scholastic speculations. Whether they were convinced by Wohlstetter or not, righting the balance of power became a pretext for escalating the nuclear arms race. According to historian Gregg Herken, McNamara was only familiar with two pieces of nuclear strategy before assuming office: Kissinger's *Nuclear Weapons and Foreign Policy* and Wohlstetter's "Delicate Balance of Terror."[38] There is reason to believe that he found Wohlstetter unconvincing: he was aware—to put it charitably—that Kennedy's campaign rhetoric about a "missile gap" was inaccurate. Nevertheless, the Kennedy administration relied upon Wohlstetter's fears to "get the country moving again."

During the next decade, despite a strategic triad armed with 40,000 nuclear warheads, the Committee on the Present Danger pandered to fear of a Soviet sneak attack. Likewise, during the first Reagan administration a "window of vulnerability" opened: Surely we must put our house in order by slamming the metaphorical window shut with missile defense technology and forward-based Pershing missiles. Of course, to press the metaphor, the "house" has no roof—truth be known: there is no viable defense against a Soviet attack whether the metaphorical windows are opened or closed.

Escalating the nuclear arms race by developing and deploying higher numbers of more sophisticated weapons seemed like the only answer to the concerns of Wohlstetter and his colleagues. Such actions are not prima facie unreasonable if his premises are accepted. However, worries about the balance of terror became a pretext for patent absurdity: the follies of civil defense. Supposedly equilibrium, if not superiority, could be maintained if the American public were safeguarded from nuclear devastation.

The Fallout

[In the event of a nuclear attack] it would probably be a great help if large numbers of workers all lie down close together. This will effectively create a new ground surface, and people on the up-wind perimeter would then help to provide protection for the rest. The alternative of jumping into a body of water should also be considered.

—Livermore National Laboratory Proposal for
Surviving a Nuclear Attack[39]

It is difficult to tell whether this call for the workers of the world to unite—or jump in the lake—should be taken seriously. The civil defense proposals proffered to protect the public are at best black humor, and at worst, an insult to the public's intelligence. Phrased more charitably, perhaps the public should be reminded that not all problems have solutions, especially the problem of safeguarding America from nuclear attack.

Apparently, in response to Wohlstetter's concerns about inadequate civil defense, Herman Kahn offered a reassuring account of the aftermath of nuclear war-fighting. As Philip Green points out, Kahn bases much of his account on the effects of radioactive fallout.[40] Accordingly, Kahn envisages an elaborate program of fallout shelters both as a deterrent and as a strategy for survival if deterrence fails. Such shelters are essential for "successful" nuclear exchanges.

Kahn's reassurance about recovery says little about the consequences of the devastation of the American infrastructure. However, he seems confident that American survivors will be better off than their Soviet counterparts before the war: "[If] half of our residential space is destroyed, then, even if everyone survives, these survivors will be better housed than the average (very productive) Soviet citizen."[41]

Kahn is also aware of possible morale problems in the aftermath of a nuclear holocaust. After all, the destruction visited by such a calamity is enough to make you sick. However, he thinks all will be well when the all-American work ethic is encouraged by a little pep talk:

[A] high percentage of the population is going to become nauseated, and nausea is very catching. If one man vomits everybody vomits. Almost everyone is likely to think that he has received too much radiation. Morale may be so affected that many survivors may refuse to participate in constructive activities.... This situation would be quite different if radiation meters were distributed.... You look at the meter and say, "You have received only ten roentgens, why are you vomiting? Pull yourself together and get to work." [However, in various scenarios, Kahn anticipates survivors suffering doses of 250 roentgens, and that *is* enough to make you sick.][42]

Kahn also cautions that we shouldn't get terribly exercised by the prospect of a full-scale, thermonuclear attack on North America. Eventually, all will be right with the world. In a book praised by recent influential officials such as Brent Scowcroft and Donald Rumsfeld, Kahn invites us to consider:

The possibility—both menacing and perversely comforting—that even if 300 million people were killed in a nuclear war, there would still be more than 4 billion left alive.... And a power that attains significant strategic superiority is likely to survive the war, perhaps even "win" it by ... extending its hegemony—at least for a time—over much of the world.... Reconstruction will begin, life will continue, and most survivors will not envy the dead.[43]

In Kahn's view, recovery will eventually occur no matter what. However, recovery would be hastened by an elaborate fallout shelter program and other civil defense initiatives. But surely those who promoted the fallout shelter craze knew of the firestorms in Dresden and Tokyo, to say nothing of Hiroshima and Nagasaki. The shelters would serve as crematoria, and even survivors would endure long-lasting radioactivity without the amenities of civilization.

Civil defense entered a new phase (for a short time) when urban arterials were marked as evacuation routes. Prior to evacuating targeted cities, dutiful citizens were to board their pets and file change of address cards at post offices (the IRS would forward tax forms). Somehow citizens would have to escape coastal zones targeted by nuclear submarines in about six minutes. Those fortunate enough to inhabit inland cities would have up to thirty minutes for a leisurely commute out of Chicago or Atlanta.

It is, of course, difficult to determine which areas would be safe from nuclear blast, firestorms, and radiation. As the age of assured destruction dawned, a group of intrepid New Yorkers determined that Chico, California (a rural college town about a hundred miles from any major city) was the ideal locale. Soon after they arrived construction began on a Titan missile base just north of town—such is the cunning of nuclear history.

Not surprisingly, no expense has been spared constructing "doomsday" aircraft and well-stocked shelters for the governing elite. An elaborate retreat was established beneath a five-star resort in the hills of West Virginia. The balance of terror demanded a robust and durable command and control system for nuclear war-fighting:

It is one of America's deepest official secrets, a combination of classified escape plans, cleverly concealed bunkers, and Space Age communication systems that, in the event of a surprise nuclear attack, would enable the government to regroup to provide critical services to a stricken citizenry and organize an effective military reprisal against its attacker.[44]

Evidently, these plans apply only to 46 of the highest government officials. What of the rest of us? In order to reassure those of us who would be left out in the heat, the Livermore Lab was commissioned to devise proposals for "Worker Protection Alternative for a Nuclear Attack With 30 Minutes (or Less) Warning."[45] Among the recommendations:

• Rapid evacuation from ground zero (when this location can be reasonably predicted) is always very desirable.[46]

- Jump into a deep body of water and swim (at least 3 or 4 feet under the surface) for as long as possible, while periodically coming up for air.[47]
- Individuals can get into as tightly fitting depressions as [soon] as possible.[48]

The proposal authored by David Gregg got bad press. In a memo, he seems exercised because "there was a leak to the press describing my work as being ludicrous and obsurd [sic]. The water emersion [sic] protection measures, which was only one of a number of technically sound measures identified, was taken out of context . . . [it was] suggested that in the event of a nuclear attack "people should go jump in a lake.""[49]

He suspects that the bad press is due to the machinations of KGB agents:

My "global" analysis identifying civil defense as an extremely important measure that must be taken by the United States to compensate for the imballance [sic] of power that has been created by the Russian civil defense effort, leads me to conclude that by far the most important beneficiary of a weak FEMA would be Russia. . . . There is very little doubt that the KGB has carefully studied how to manipulate the U.S. press and thus public opinion.[50]

Since he and his efforts to create a credible civil defense have been severely damaged, he fears that the results may well be catastrophic:

The potential consequences of this condition could be almost immeasurable. It is entirely possible that the result will be that a Russian nuclear attack will take place that could have been prevented. Thus, the potential damage to the U.S. population is almost unbelievable.[51]

Somehow we have survived despite Wohlstetter's concerns about the delicate balance of terror and Mr. Gregg's damaged reputation. It is a truism, an unquestioned article of faith, that—whether by accident or design—the balance has been calibrated with sufficient accuracy to provide nuclear deterrence.

CHAPTER 6

Deterrence: Peace on Earth without Goodwill toward Men

The concept of deterrence retains its value as an emotive word sparking feelings of security and safety, but [it] has lost any precise meaning. Nuclear deterrence today means whatever the speaker wishes it to mean. It is a blank check.

—General K. D. Johnson[1]

There is no agreement as to exactly what deterrence is or how it works. However, within the strategic community and well beyond, there is consensus that it *has* worked miraculously well for whatever reason. These days, of course, there are serious doubts as to whether it is possible to deter future terrorist attacks on the American homeland. Nevertheless, it is an article of faith that nuclear arsenals are essential for deterring the ambitions of nation-states with intentions and capabilities of acting in ways inimical to vital American interests.

Cast in the perspective that informs this study, deterrence is a primary strategic metaphor: the development, deployment, and threatened detonation of nuclear weapons are likened to a deterrent—an incentive that gives adversaries second thoughts about enacting their reputedly aggressive designs. Like other primary metaphors, deterrence per se, as we shall see, is conceptualized in terms of a welter of conflicting secondary metaphors. Not surprisingly, as General Johnson recognized, it is difficult to define deterrence—let alone use it as an analytic tool—since such diverse, often contesting, secondary meanings are read into the concept. Curiously, this realization leads to a plausible generalization about deterrence: it's an equivocal, metaphorical notion that serves a vital, *unequivocal* ideological function in American nuclear endeavors: It legitimizes—if not sanctifies—the entire gamut of prevailing nuclear strategies and weapons systems. Deterrence has been invoked to justify virtually every strategy short of disarmament.

Accordingly, this chapter views the concept of deterrence with suspicion; I begin with a noncontroversial claim (at least within the strategic community) and conclude with an iconoclastic suggestion:

- The obvious is least controversial: Within the strategic community deterrence—whatever it may be—elicits elegiac praise for preventing a superpower conflagration and for tempering the ambitions of today's rogue nation-states. Deterrence is likened to a miracle.

- While members of the community liken the American arsenal to a deterrent—at least in public pronouncements—there is ongoing controversy regarding what I call secondary metaphors: the literature is replete with contesting views as to what deterrence is and how it functions.

- An argument central to my analysis is considerably more contentious: Deterrence is an ideology. It is a very good reason for American nuclear endeavors, but it's not the *real* reason. The intentions and deeds of American planners are often inconsistent with deterrence doctrine.

- The chapter concludes with a scandalous suggestion: it is fallacious to presuppose that nuclear deterrence was primarily responsible for preventing a superpower conflagration.

DETERRENCE: A BLESSING IN DISGUISE

> Our foreign policy ultimately turns on the deterrence power of the American nuclear umbrella—the rock on which the renaissance of the West since 1945 was built and the foundation of our security.
>
> —Eugene Rostow[2]

Acrimonious academic debate about what deterrence is and how it works is, perhaps, the very signature of nuclear strategizing. Nevertheless, there is awestruck consensus about its wondrous power. One is struck by the evangelical zeal that informs discussions of deterrence; Rostow and the others see nuclear deterrence as a Rock of Age: the sacred, unshakable foundation of American security. In mainstream discourse references to these weapons of mass destruction begin with invocations about the blessings of deterrence. Indeed, one does not enter the community of strategic discourse without paying homage to deterrence. These obligatory encomiums celebrate deterrence for ushering in a millennium surpassing chiliastic visions of redemption.

General Groves assured an anxious world that: "Once each great power came to possess a full atomic arsenal, major war is impossible. All that stands in the way of effective international control is the acceptance by all the world's leaders of this fact."[3]

After the detonation of the H-bomb, journalist William Laurence—a reporter in considerable favor amongst the nuclear elite—reassured an apprehensive public that: "The hydrogen bomb has made peace inevitable. It has achieved the realization of one of mankind's most cherished dreams."[4]

American leaders embraced such grandiose claims in their declaratory statements intended for public consumption. However, in private, plans emerged for atomic diplomacy intended to *compel* adversaries to act in ways inimical to their interests: even triumphant visions of nuclear warfighting were not unknown.[5] The acclaim of former Secretary of Defense Caspar Weinberger is echoed by other high officials, by influential academics, and by the strategic community as a whole:

What then has deterrence done? Again, I must stress that it has worked and that it is working today. There have been 37 years of peace in Europe. Despite the threat of the Soviet Army; despite the threat of the Soviet's nuclear weapons, Western Europe has avoided the scourge of nuclear fire. Deterrence, thus, is and remains our best hope of keeping the peace.[6]

Michael Mandelbaum, a former Harvard don and member of the Council on Foreign Relations updates Dr. Pangloss when he insists that the chronicle of the nuclear arms race "is the story of the evolution of the best of all possible worlds."[7] And Lawrence Freedman, often credited with authoring the definitive study of nuclear deterrence, concludes more modestly that he owes his good fortune to the nuclear arms race: "My fortunate generation has been allowed to grow up in relative peace ... I have not been required to fight for my country nor make any sacrifices at all and so I have enjoyed the full benefits of peace."[8]

There is no need to belabor the obvious by compounding examples: nuclear weapons are seen as a blessing in disguise. No matter what the circumstances, strategists proffer very good reasons for maintaining a nuclear arsenal. Indeed, it appears that members of the NRA will give up their guns long before American planners recycle their nuclear arsenal.

Despite radically changed circumstances and momentous developments—such as *perestroika* and the unexpected, peaceful demise of the Soviet Union—strategists insist that the United States must keep nuclear weapons on hair-trigger alert to deter any future Russian perfidy. And, of course, these days, even former European allies are not to be trusted; only a robust American nuclear arsenal can keep the peace. According to Lawrence Eagelburger, a former Pentagon official, "The lesson is simple: The U.S. presence [American nuclear and conventional weapons in Europe] is the best insurance against rivalries inherent in Europe's nation-state system."[9] (Others also liken deterrence to an insurance policy; one can only hope that we don't have to be dead in order to collect.)

Apparently, like the poor, a nuclear-armed NATO will always be with us to deter imagined future aggression. Manfred Worner, the former secretary general of NATO, suggests that the alliance is needed more than ever to prevent another world war in the post-Cold War world. He cautions that Russia could become the most formidable military power on the Eurasian continent. He argues that future Russian belligerence can only be deterred by modernizing strategic nuclear forces and by credibly threatening first use of these weapons in the event of Russian aggression.[10] Unlike their counterparts in the former Soviet Union, American leaders and their remaining allies have not gone from paranoia to *perestroika*.

Unlike most strategists, Kenneth Waltz argues that nuclear proliferation (albeit *gradual* proliferation) is a universal deterrent that should be lauded, not condemned.

Can't Have Too Much of a Good Thing?

> The likelihood of war decreases as deterrence and defensive capabilities increase. Nuclear weapons make wars hard to start. These statements hold for small as for big nuclear powers. Because they do, the gradual spread of nuclear weapons is more to be welcomed than feared.
>
> —Kenneth Waltz[11]

Kenneth Waltz and Scott Sagan debate the implications of deterrence doctrine in a compact, articulate work, *The Spread of Nuclear Weapons: A Debate*.[12] Waltz, the consummate neorealist, argues that the gradual spread of nuclear weapons will deter war amongst new nuclear states. After all, if nuclear weapons deterred a superpower conflagration, why wouldn't they also deter conflict between new nuclear states such as India and Pakistan? It is ethnocentric to think otherwise. According to Waltz, no leader—regardless of nationality—wants to hazard even a slight risk that his or her state will be annihilated in a retaliatory nuclear attack.

Like Thomas Schelling, Waltz subscribes to the view that minimal rationality is sufficient to deter war. True, ideologues in rogue nations may have bizarre beliefs, but—to invoke a favored analogy—just as they wouldn't step off the curb in front of fast-moving traffic, neither will they gamble on actions that risk the destruction of themselves and everything they cherish.

While Sagan is critical of Waltz's analysis, he begins with a seemingly obligatory invocation to deterrence; he presupposes that deterrence guided policy-making and that—more significantly—it worked: "We have lived with nuclear deterrence for half a century now. The two superpowers maintained a long peace throughout the Cold War, despite deep political hostilities, numerous crises, and a prolonged arms race."[13] Sagan obviously shares Waltz's enthusiasm for deterrence. He is critical of Waltz precisely because he argues that nuclear proliferation undermines deterrence by increasing the danger of war.

Like his co-author, Sagan believes that decision-makers try to act rationally; however, they are also captivated by the imperatives of their organizations. Rather than relying exclusively upon the rational actor model, Sagan invokes organizational theory. He fears that the culture of military organizations endemic to many new nuclear states will impede the minimalist rationality essential for deterrence. Indeed, he reminds us that realists such as Waltz admonish that while elites *should* act rationally they sometimes fail to do so at critical junctures: "[Realists urge] that states should follow the logic of balance-of-power politics but their whole enterprise was animated by a fear that the U.S. will fail to do so."[14] In short, realists were not preaching to the converted: he argues a fortiori that if mature nuclear nations are not reliable rational actors, we cannot be supremely confident of the rationality of new nuclear nations.

The authors share the position that there are three requirements for deterrence; their differences stand out in stark relief as they examine these requirements:

1. Deterrence requires a reliable, survivable second-strike force;
2. There can be no "launch-on-warning" strategy;
3. Reliable command and control of nuclear weapons are essential.

Both authors concur that the first requirement can be met. However, Sagan fears that without civilian checks and balances imposed upon military culture, new nuclear nations might resort to launch-on-warning. Indeed, as we've seen, the present situation between the United States and Russia is more daunting than Sagan allows. Despite (or because of) the civilian control of the nuclear arsenal, strategic weapons (according to Robert McNamara and General Lee Butler) remain on "hair-trigger alert." Understandably, Sagan is apprehensive about what might transpire in failed rogue states in which the military is out of control.

Moreover, even if military bravado is inhibited by civilian control, the possibility of tragic accident is omnipresent. Sagan discusses the accidents and miscalculations that bedevil the management of the American arsenal and plausibly suggests that proliferation magnifies the risk of such accidents.

It appears that American decision-makers concur with Sagan but are forced by events to resign themselves to Waltz's prediction: Other states will acquire nuclear weaponry whether American officials like it or not. But just what is this "deterrence" that it is so vital to preserve and extend?

DEFINING DETERRENCE: THE SECONDARY METAPHORS

There is scarcely a society without its major narratives which are recounted, repeated and ... recited in well-defined circumstances: things said once and preserved because it is suspected that behind them there is a secret treasure.
—Michel Foucault[15]

There is, of course, nothing new about the concept of deterrence. As we've seen, Thucydides told the deterrence story when he wrote of credible threats of military retaliation giving adversaries second thoughts about acting out their ambitions. Even the so-called hostage relation between nuclear adversaries was painfully well known among the ancients. However, in his *Absolute Weapon,* early strategist Bernard Brodie proffered an oft-quoted, generic definition of the intention of deterrence that most authors still find congenial:

The writer [Brodie] ... is not for the moment concerned about who will *win* the next war in which atomic bombs are used. Thus far the chief purpose of our military establishment has been to win wars. From now on its chief purpose must be to avert them. It can have almost no other useful purpose.[16]

As analysts such as Lawrence Freedman recognize, averting war (deterrence) is about sending messages.[17] Given the faith-based nature of strategizing, there is no consensus as to whether these messages about nuclear policy should be clear and distinct or deliberately ambiguous. Authoring, transmitting, and receiving messages, of course, transforms strategic thinking from a military science preoccupied with systematizing battlefield tactics and ordnance to a literary endeavor—the esoteric realm of semiotics. On occasion, strategists endure a pessimistic moment when they realize that much can be lost in the translation of even the most finely crafted message.

Not surprisingly, nuclear deterrence doctrine has not undergone significant changes since the time of Brodie. The quarrels continue as to the appropriate metaphors and messages, and the daunting questions remains: "How much is enough?" This idée fixe of strategic thinking refers both to the number and type of weapons in the American arsenal (vertical proliferation) and to the worldwide spread of nuclear weapons (horizontal proliferation). No wonder Lawrence Freedman allows in his *Evolution of Nuclear Strategy* that he regrets invoking "evolution" in the title. In writing the book he came to understand that strategy is cyclical. Contemporary "new" insights about deterrence were said yesterday.[18] Historians such as Gregg Herken concur:

For all the differences of style and substance that Kennedy, McNamara, and their advisers tried to draw between themselves and their predecessors ... [their] attitude toward nuclear weapons bore a remarkable resemblance to that of Eisenhower at the end of his second term.[19]

Freedman also reminds us that the epistemological status of nuclear strategizing per se has not changed. He argues that, given the fortunate lack of nuclear war-fighting experience and the radical unpredictability of leaders facing nuclear annihilation, "nuclear strategy" may be an oxymoron.[20]

As he explains: "The thankful lack of experience of nuclear warfare, since 1945, has rendered highly speculative all thoughts on the likely causes of nuclear war, its course and its finale.... How, when, and why to use these weapons remain matters for inference and conjecture."[21]

I share Freedman's view. In reviewing the literature one is tempted to paraphrase a comment attributed to Brahms. Remarking on a rival's music he quipped: What's new isn't good, and what's good isn't new. It appears that both champions and critics of deterrence presuppose that there is not much to add to the early literature.

Taking a closer view of efforts to define deterrence, a review of this literature suggests that the notion of deterrence, of course, is not totally meaningless. Understood, generically, in the broadest sense, it can be used as an analytic concept rather than an argument-stopping rhetorical move. Philip Green, for example, positions deterrence doctrine[22] between advocates of disarmament and advocates of nuclear war-fighting: Advocates of deterrence don't want to give up the weapons, but—with few exceptions—they're not enthusiastic about fighting nuclear wars.[23] (To reiterate, strategists prefer fantasizing about nuclear war rather than experiencing such a conflagration.)

To reiterate, deterrence is also differentiated from "compellence." The former is intended to *prevent* adversaries from acting upon their temptations. The latter is intended to force adversaries to reestablish the status quo ante *after* they have acted in ways inimical to American interest—the Cuban missile crisis is a prime example.

The metaphorical nature of deterrence is apparent. It has been likened to variety of cognitive and affective domains. Indeed, it is difficult to think of a concept that it has *not* been compared to. The following inventory of these secondary metaphors is far from exhaustive.

Rational Actor Metaphors

Some analysts liken deterrence to the icy-cold cost/risk/benefit analysis of intelligent, rational actors—CPAs engaged in noonday commerce or savvy game players. Those who believe that adversaries are rational actors governing legitimate states believe that adversaries are intelligent individuals who listen to reason. Glenn Snyder, for example (an early game theorist) likens deterrence to gaming with a matrix involving precise, numerical probabilities and calculations that entail clearly rational decisions.[24]

The matrices and formulas of probability theory lend an aura of scientific/mathematical rigor and legitimacy to game theory. However, by way of contrast, it's been said that the science begins with metaphor and ends with algebra. Game theory reverses the process: it begins with algebra (or probability theory) and ends in metaphor. For example: Newton likened the world to a machine and derived mathematical formulas from this paradigm. These formulas could be tested and proved—or more importantly, disproved—empirically. Game theorists start with mathematics and conclude by likening decision-making to zero-sum games or to Prisoners' Dilemma. The conclusion that decision-makers will behave as rational gamers in the most extreme situations in some "competition in risk-taking" expresses wishful thinking, not scientific analysis.

As political analyst Philip Green suggests, it is unlikely that the tumult of the real world has the decency to correspond to the unsullied models of decision-making proffered by game theorists who are inattentive to historical legacy, cultural context, and baffling idiosyncrasies. Green offers this gloss on game theory:

This is not mathematics; it's a morality play that shows the virtues of the U.S. risking it's destruction by initiating a limited nuclear war in Europe. To assert commensurability and calculability where they are entirely lacking is to make a hidden value judgment of the most egregious kind.[25]

However, there is no consensus even within the rational actor school. Other analysts liken deterrence to the primal rationality needed for survival. Thomas Schelling, for example, offers this minimalist view of rationality. As we've seen, Schelling (echoed by Kenneth Waltz) believes that even the intellectually feeble and the hot-blooded fanatical leaders of rogue states don't (to invoke further metaphors) jump in front of fast-moving trucks—or invite nuclear retaliation.

Marshalling the Tropes: Fear and Trembling

Others liken deterrence to psychologically grounded secondary metaphors such as impassioned fear—threats of certain death and catastrophic destruction. In the words of the redoubtable Herman Kahn, it's about terrorism: "Deterrence means dissuasion by terror ... there is a motivation to refrain from an action because of a fearful threat (explicit or implicit) or a warning of fearful consequences."[26] To complicate things further, even within a particular domain, there is usually more than one variety of deterrence. As Kahn argues, "Type II" deterrence is about first strike capabilities. (He stresses that a credible Type II capability requires a massive and reliable civil defense so that a sector of the population can "ride out" enemy retaliation.) Kahn reasons, to put it simply, that if a second-strike capability deters by sending the message "be afraid," a first-strike capability sends a more powerful message: "be *terribly* afraid."

In considering Kahn's views about civil defense, first-strike capabilities, and nuclear war-fighting as robust deterrents, a passage from Dostoevsky's *Underground Man* comes to mind:

Have you noticed that it is the most civilized gentlemen who have been the subtlest slaughterers, to whom the Attillas ... could not hold a candle....? Now we do think bloodshed abominable and yet we engage in this abomination, and with more energy than ever.[27]

Kahn, perhaps, offers a detailed and complex classification of deterrence doctrine. In addition to three types of deterrence, there are four variations within each type. There is a variety, of course, of deterrence scenarios, and considerable speculation about the benefits and liabilities of minimum deterrence, finite deterrence, and pure massive retaliation.[28] His schemata of deterrence doctrine reads like tables in the Ptolemaic system.

Other advocates of deterrence urge that Kahn got it wrong. They argue that deterrence is about—or *should* be about—instilling caution in an adversary's planning.[29] Despite the speculative nature of such experiments in applied psychology, advocates on both sides posit their views with considerable confidence.

Some strategists such as Daniel Ellsberg (to be sure, early in his career) thought that posturing as a madman is the best of all deterrents. In a lecture entitled "The Political Uses of Madness" he suggested that irrational nuclear threats might be the ideal ... tool.[30] McGeorge Bundy gave the notion more dignity and philosophic gravitas when he labeled the notion "existential deterrence."[31]

Such ruminations, apparently, can inspire rather odd and disturbing fantasies. According to Nixon confidant H. R. Haldeman, Nixon toyed with the notion of using what he called a "madman theory" to exact concessions from the Vietnamese and to deter their further plans:

We were walking along a foggy beach after a long day of speech writing. He [Nixon] said, "I call it the Madman theory, Bob. I want the North Vietnamese to believe I've reached the point where I might do anything to stop the war. We'll just slip the word to them that, for god's sake, you know Nixon is obsessed with Communism. We can't restrain him when he's angry—and he has his hand on the nuclear button—and Ho Chi Minh himself will be in Paris in two days begging for peace."[32]

To be sure, some analysts liken deterrence to all of the above; the anxiety fomented by fear of nuclear retaliation will somehow prompt adversaries to slow down and think rationally—cool heads will prevail. Of course, as Karl Deutsch observed long ago: "The theory of deterrence ... first proposes that we should frustrate our opponents by frightening them very badly and that we should rely on their cool-headed rationality for our survival."[33] While, as we've seen, Schelling likens deterrence to a minimalist notion of rationality, he is well aware that context determines meaning. What, then, is deterrence? Evidently, it all depends:

Whether deterrent threats lead to desperation, hostility, and panic, or to quiescence, confidence, and security probably depends on how the threats are arrived at and expressed, what demands accompany them, and the costs and risks of initiating violence or reacting to it.[34]

Miscellaneous Secondary Metaphors

Deterrence has been conceptualized in terms of a variety of secondary metaphors that conflate cognitive and affective domains while placing boundaries on the limits and demands of deterrence. Certain strategists urged that American planners must eschew Dulles's brinkmanship—the all or nothing approach—in favor of a flexible response to aggression, or to threats of aggression. However, deterrence doctrine itself is a "flexible conceptual response" to virtually every variety of strategic advocacy.

Internecine controversy about the nature of deterrence goes well beyond the ontological issues just mentioned. The scope and certainty of adequate deterrence are also contested. Some strategists claim that the *certainty* of an American response is the best deterrent; others favor *uncertainty* as the best approach—adversaries must be kept in the dark.

There was once considerable interservice rivalry regarding which branch of the military should be charged with providing deterrence. The Air Force claimed that a robust Strategic Air Command is the best deterrent while (not surprisingly) the Navy advocated a fleet of nuclear submarines. Could it be that the strategic triad exists so that each service can be a nuclear power in its own right? Likewise, military contractors ("defense contractors" in Nukespeak) advertise the virtues of competing deterrent weaponry in journals such as *Foreign Affairs.*

Invoking deterrence is a flexible conceptual response to virtually every question about the propriety of any strategy or weapons system. It is a versatile, all-purpose trope that serves as both a verb and a noun. Vulnerable first strike weapons, land-based missiles such as the MX, are called deterrents. It would seem that since these missiles would be destroyed in a first strike, their intended use *is* a first strike.[35] (The Reagan administration changed the name of this weapons system to "Peacekeeper," Apparently, they are equipped with ten thermonuclear "peaceheads"; American weapons are always defensive—adversary's weapons are a priori offensive.) Given the honorable and just connotation of deterrence, virtually any strategy or weapon is a deterrent—at least in the discourse intended for public consumption.

Efforts to define and operationalize deterrence lead to complications, not clarity. Due to the vagueness and ambiguity associated with metaphors such as deterrence, it is not surprising that strategists have long argued as to whether deterrence should be limited to safeguarding the American homeland or extended to Western Europe and beyond. There is debate as to whether deterrence should be finite—limited to retaliating with a limited nuclear war, or (in Herman Kahn's charming phrase) a "nuclear wargasm"—going all the way.

Finally, between and within each partisan school of deterrence doctrine, there is no consensus about "how much is enough?" Often expressing retirement wisdom, prominent policy-makers claim that a few invulnerable nuclear submarines should give an adversary second thoughts. Others claim that the appearance of a robust strategic triad is a stronger deterrent.

Finally, some claim that deterrence must be intentional. However, others suggest that it is virtually automatic: the salutary—albeit unintended—outcome of arms racing. Likening deterrence to the economic models of classical liberalism, deterrence is seen as something akin to the invisible hand in laissez faire economics: regardless of human intentions everything turns out right with the world.

In any event, the metaphors invoked to define deterrence are reified. These tropes are not understood as mere figures of speech; on the contrary, they are construed as obdurate features of international life rather than modest conceptual strategies for rendering the nuclear era intelligible and manageable. Typically, we are exhorted to believe in deterrence—as if our life depends upon it. Such exhortations suggest that deterrence plays an unequivocal, legitimizing ideological function.

DETERRENCE AS IDEOLOGY

> There will always be "good reasons," and good theories, for having and using nuclear weapons. That is what the strategy of nuclear deterrence is—a good reason.
>
> —General K. D. Johnson[36]

As the good general realizes, there are usually two reasons for things: very good reasons and the real reason. Indeed, deterrence is a very good reason for possessing a nuclear arsenal, but perhaps it is not the *real* reason. Cast in this perspective, deterrence doctrines serve an ideological function by rationalizing disastrous policy; mandating an obligatory, unifying discourse; bestowing the imprimatur of science; and sanctifying a Manichean worldview.

Deterrence as Ad Hoc Rationalization

The rise of the Soviet Union as a nuclear power seemed like an unmitigated disaster. As World War II came to a bloody climax Manhattan Project scientists, and several political and military leaders, warned that the Soviets would obtain nuclear weapons in a relatively short time. To be sure, the Soviets might have developed nuclear weaponry regardless of American policy. However, American bravado about its atomic monopoly, ringing its former ally with nuclear bases, and the use of atomic diplomacy did not make the Soviets more tractable. The Soviets were in no mood to embrace the Baruch Plan or other proposals for arms control. In any case, like their counterparts worldwide, American governing elites are not in the habit of acknowledging their mistakes or misjudgments.

The timing of the advent of deterrence doctrine reveals its ideological function. During what some call the Golden Age of Nuclear Weapons (the four-year interlude when American officials enjoyed an atomic monopoly) talk of deterrence was virtually unknown. As Solly Zuckerman, the former chief science advisor to the British government, reveals:

> During the twenty years or so that I was myself professionally involved in these matters, weapons came first and rationalization and policies followed.... In 1945 no one spoke about "deterrent strategy" or about any other kind of nuclear strategy. I doubt anyone ... had heard of Bernard Brodie. To those who took the decisions, the atomic, and later the hydrogen bombs were simply immensely powerful weapons ... nations just had to have.[37]

The Soviet threat meant unprecedented peril: for the first time the American homeland was defenseless. Even if most Soviet aircraft could be stopped, a few planes armed with thermonuclear bombs could destroy the United States as a civilization. Yet American nuclear endeavors were not discredited. On the contrary, strategists portrayed the advent of assured destruction as the outcome of the cunning of reason—a blessing in disguise. The credible threat of mutually assured destruction has ushered in the millennial dream of peace on earth.

Perhaps this much can be said for deterrence: no doubt, on occasion, it gives potential belligerents second thoughts about acting out their ambitions. However, deterrence doctrine serves another strategic function: it is an ad hoc ideology that legitimizes the existence and activity of nuclear strategists. Who could object to deterring an adversary from harming the American homeland? Just as the Department of War was changed to the Department of Defense, perhaps the latter should be changed to the "Department of Deterrence." Defense, after all may involve bloodshed; deterrence (supposedly) merely involves sending effective messages and staging compelling performances.

"Deterrence" as Obligatory Discourse

It appears that, just as it would be unthinkable for a Crusader not to invoke the name of God to justify his fantasies and deeds (*deo volente!*), it would be unthinkable not to invoke deterrence to justify any conceivable tactic, strategy, or weapons. By invoking this shibboleth, a decision-maker in effect tells himself and his audience that even though the forces of evil are armed with apocalyptic weapons, all is right with the world—the children of light have the weapons and resolve to hold the powers of darkness at bay.

Consider the pressure that can be brought to bear on the highest officials, even the president of the United States. In his first Star Wars speech (March, 1983) President Reagan maligned deterrence for threatening the destruction of Soviet civilians: he urged that by rendering nuclear weapons "impotent and obsolete" the Strategic Defense Initiative (SDI) would eliminate the need for deterrence. This pronouncement provoked outrage among those accustomed to invoking deterrence to justify their weapons systems and strategic scenarios. Evidently, the president was properly chastened. In his next Star War speech (March, 1988) the president dutifully proclaimed that SDI would "enhance deterrence."[38]

Like other Nukespeak terms, deterrence is an argument-stopping term that invites automatic assent. One can dispute the propriety of nuclear war-fighting; however, it seems prudent, if not virtuous, to deploy nuclear weapons to prevent such hostility in the first place. No wonder even triumphant war-fighting policies—the very antithesis of war-prevention—are called deterrents. Consider Secretary of Defense Caspar Weinberger's "Defense Guidelines" leaked to the press in 1984: "United States capabilities must prevail even under the conditions of a prolonged war.... The United States must prevail and be able to force the Soviet Union to seek earliest termination of hostilities on terms favorable to the United States."[39]

Accused of abandoning deterrence based upon mutually assured destruction (MAD) for nuclear use theories (NUTS), Weinberger subsequently issued a statement to major American papers and periodicals in which he explained that this policy had nothing to do with war-fighting, as his critics charged. The policy was simply designed to "enhance deterrence."[40]

While even filigreed attempts to define deterrence doctrine are wrought with ambiguity, the doctrine's rhetorical use is transparent. Like Nukespeak in general, and strategic metaphors in particular, the notion of deterrence is used promiscuously as an argument-stopping strategy. Who could condemn efforts to dissuade adversaries from acting out their wicked intentions? Even clearly offensive first-strike strategies are permissible because they are "deterrents."

Deterrence and Physics Envy

Of course, deterrence doctrine is not merely an obligatory shibboleth or a piece of rhetorical legerdemain. It represents a conceptual strategy designed to convince the strategists and their constituents that plans for the development, deployment, and detonation of nuclear weapons have nothing less than the imprimatur of science.

In authoring his nuclear strategy, for example, physicist Herman Kahn affects the style of his profession. Overall, his tone is detached and seemingly value-free. Just as an effective physician must deal with dreadful disease unaffected by blood and bile, so a strategist must deal with the reality of our nuclear predicament with a steady hand undaunted by fear and trembling. Nevertheless, he leavens his hard, cold analysis with attempts at humor. He explains that a bit of levity is not inappropriate: "Thermonuclear war is not a joke, but professional or serous discussion of thermonuclear war can include humor, at least in Europe and the United States."[41]

He acknowledges that the Japanese may be ill-prepared for his levity; nevertheless, they are filled with admiration for the destruction of Hiroshima and Nagasaki: "Contemporary Japanese accounts indicate that the use of the atomic bomb was not regarded as unfair. Indeed there was some feeling in Japan of admiration for the technically advanced nation that could produce such a miracle."[42]

Whether the Japanese marvel at the technological wizardry that set their cities afire is arguable. It is also arguable as to whether Kahn asks the rights questions, and to whether his response to the questions he asks confuses precision with accuracy.

Like most strategists, Kahn sees himself as a realist who knows that nuclear weapons cannot be "disinvented"—once lost, nuclear virginity cannot be regained. Accordingly, he expresses unthinkable thoughts about deterrence and nuclear war-fighting: both a deterrent in some contexts and a necessity if deterrence fails. Kahn draws rather sanguine conclusions from what he deems objective, scientific studies about the aftermath of nuclear war-fighting:

Despite a widespread belief to the contrary, objective studies indicate that even though the amount of human tragedy would be greatly increased in the postwar world, the increase would not preclude normal and happy lives for the majority of survivors and their descendants.[43]

As critics such as Philip Green have argued, the objectivity of such studies are actually, at best, a dubious conjecture: happily the United States hasn't experienced a nuclear war. Green aptly quotes Kahn's RAND colleague Albert Wohlstetter: "Of course we have no wartime operational data drawn from World War III, and hope we never will."[44] Nevertheless, Kahn quantifies his speculation about the aftermath of such a war when he calculates American deaths ranging between ten and sixty million. As Green concludes, this is not mathematics; it's a morality play that shows the virtues of risk taking and punishing the citizenry of the Soviet Union if necessary: "To assert commensurability and calculability where they entirely lack is to make a hidden value judgment of the most egregious kind." No wonder, to reiterate, Green regards Kahn's works as "prophetic science fiction."[45]

Manichean Worldview

In his retirement wisdom, former NATO commander Admiral Carroll warned that nuclear strategists promulgated a cartoon image of the Soviet

Union as the evil empire. He warned the pronouncements of both strategists and policymakers implied "The existence of a threatening horde poised and ready to overwhelm us all at the first hint that we are not prepared to obliterate them with nuclear weapons; nothing else stays their evil ways."[46]

Kahn, for example, believes that the irredeemable evil posed by the Soviet threat is worth eradicating. To paraphrase Kahn, he asks, what price should Americans be willing to pay to punish Soviet perfidy? Again, he urges that it is worth ten to sixty million American lives to preserve American national integrity. However—as Green stresses—Kahn reveals his Manichean worldview in the questions he never asks: how bad would life be in these United States under Soviet domination; and how many lives would be lost, and how long would it take for the U.S. to regain its national integrity?[47]

As Fred Iklé (a strategist and policymaker) suggests, deterrence doctrine also offers absolution. The "hostage relationship" between the superpowers (deterring war by, in effect, holding civilians "hostage" to the threat of nuclear terror) makes a virtue out of what strategists deem a necessity.

Strategic analysis works like a narcotic. It dulls our sense of moral outrage about the tragic confrontation of nuclear arsenals, primed ... to unleash widespread genocide.... Our method of preventing nuclear war rests on a form of warfare universally condemned since the Dark Ages—the mass killing of hostages.[48]

Given the unquestioned assumption about the wicked designs of the Soviet Union, perhaps Iklé had documents such as the Gaither Report ("Deterrence and Survival in the Nuclear Age") in mind. Written in the aftermath of Wohlstetter's anxiety about the frangibility of deterrence, the report urged spending fifty billion dollars to protect American nuclear installations and citizenry from a Soviet sneak attack. In addition—much to the satisfaction of the military and recipients of military contracts—the report recommended new generations of nuclear weapons systems. Eisenhower, evidently, was taken aback by the report's worst-case assumptions about the Soviets and best-case assumptions about technology and bellicose strategy. Reportedly, he remarked: "You just can't have this kind of war; there just aren't enough bulldozers to scrape the bodies off the streets."[49]

Schelling, in effect, added a postmodern gloss on the report when he stressed that the instability of deterrence is not caused by plans for a sneak attack (such plans—if they exist—are closely guarded secrets); it is *fear* of such plans that renders the stability of deterrence problematic. Giving us a glance of the "through the looking glass" world of strategizing he cited the fearful reasoning involved: "He thinks we think he'll attack; so he thinks we shall; so he will; so we must."[50]

Herman Kahn carries this a step further when he constructs a scenario that makes preventative nuclear war permissible—in the name of deterrence, of course. He invites us to imagine a nuclear explosion of unknown origins at a nuclear plant in South Carolina. The Soviets know they aren't responsible, but fear that they might be blamed by the Americans and therefore subject to nuclear retaliation. Aware of Soviet fears, American officials are apprehensive about a Soviet first strike—"use 'em or lose 'em!" To deter a Soviet first strike, American forces strike first. True, in this scenario, the Soviets were not responsible for the nuclear accident, but the accident provides a pretext for settling scores with the evil empire. No wonder Kahn was the model for Dr. Strangelove.

REGARDING DETERRENCE WITH SUSPICION

> Thermonuclear weapons were not developed to deter anyone, but to demonstrate United States military superiority, and because it seemed to be a sweet new device worth developing. It was only after the Soviet Union developed thermonuclear weapons that the theory of deterrence came into vogue on both sides.
>
> —E. P. Thompson[51]

The Best of Intentions

More than five decades have passed since Bernard Brodie described our nuclear predicament: "Nuclear weapons exist, and they are incredibly destructive." Thousands of new weapons were developed and deployed after he wrote those words; all this is indisputable. Within the community of strategic discourse, as we've seen, there is but one privileged—if not indisputable—interpretation of American nuclear endeavors (at least for public consumption): nuclear weapons are developed and deployed solely for deterrence.

The presupposition that deterrence is the overriding intention of American decision-makers is dubious because there is a real possibility that elite intentionality is neither transparent (even to decision-makers themselves), durable, nor unitary. And even if we find this view of intentionality overstated, and grant that intentions reveal themselves through deeds, the deeds of decision-makers suggest that deterrence is an ideological reconstruction of their activity, not an accurate description.

In this post-Freudian, postmodern world we've come to recognize that intentions are not always transparent, even to decision-makers themselves. We humbly recognize the difficulty in interpreting the intentions of princes and prelates of the past—the past, after all, "is a foreign country." So is the present. Those who manage nuclear weapons are as remote from our personal and professional lives as Charlemagne or Pope Urban III.

Further, it is difficult to think of a social scientist who would take social actors' account of their intentions at face value. In moments of candor even presidents—like the rest of us—express profound bafflement about their intentions. Reflecting upon his behavior during the Cuban missile crisis, President Kennedy allowed that:

The essence of ultimate decision remains impenetrable to the observer—often, indeed, to the decider himself.... There will always be dark and tangled stretches in the decision-making process—mysterious even to those who may be most intimately involved.[52]

Even if we grant that, on occasion, elite intentions are obvious, intentions are volatile, as events illustrate in crisis situations. Prior to the Cuban missile crisis, as we shall see, Kennedy was concerned with preventing nuclear war. During the crisis, however, he risked nuclear war in order to compel the Soviets to remove their nuclear weapons from Cuba.

And contrary to realist presuppositions that portray the nation-state as a unified, rational actor, actual decision-making is neither unified nor monolithic. It is common, but misleading, to speak of "American intentions." As episodes such as the Cuban missile crisis illustrate, elite circles are beset by conflicting intentions. These critical junctures bring contesting intentions into play within and among decision-makers. During the "dark and tangled stretches" of the crisis, Adlai Stevenson wanted to do everything possible to prevent a nuclear war. Maxwell Taylor (and the other "hawks") on the other hand, demanded an immediate war with the Soviets. Indeed, Curtis LeMay urged an attack on Cuba even *after* Khrushchev resolved the crisis by reestablishing the status quo ante. Finally, as I have argued, Kennedy himself was bedeviled by radically conflicting intentions: He wanted to be both a Churchill and a Chamberlain—he wound up being both.[53]

In sum, elite intentions cannot be explicated with much confidence, even by decision-makers themselves. While we may be able to cast a parting glimpse at momentary intentions—at least in retrospect—these intentions are transitory and often contradictory. However, even if we eschew such skepticism and presuppose that—despite what decision-makers say—their *deeds* reflect their actual intentions, examining their deeds strongly suggests the decision-makers act in ways inimical to deterrence.

Deeds v. Words

Official deeds seem incompatible with deterrence doctrine. If American decision-makers merely intended to deter putative Soviet ambitions, they would have halted the arms race when the requirements for deterrence were met or surpassed. They did not. Strategists presuppose a worst-case scenario and a best-case technological fix. Based upon these presuppositions, what are the requirements for robust deterrence—how much is enough?

It was agreed that deterring pernicious Soviet ambitions and capability required second-strike weapons capable of inflicting intolerable damage upon the Soviet Union. Such damage is construed as destruction that would convince Soviet leadership that they have everything to lose, and nothing to gain, by attacking Western Europe or North America. In his early writings, McGeorge Bundy argued that the requirements for deterrence were attained during the Eisenhower administration: "In the real world of real political leaders ... ten bombs on ten cities would be a disaster beyond history; and a hundred bombs on a hundred cities are unthinkable."[54]

Strategists insisted, of course, that retaliatory weapons must be survivable—able to "ride out" an enemy first strike. A weapon developed forty years ago—the nuclear submarine—fulfills this requirement. It is virtually undetectable and its missiles are unstoppable.[55] But how much damage must these weapons inflict in order to give the Soviets—or other adversaries—second thoughts? (Somehow, the requirements increased with the advent of every new weapons system!) Kissinger reiterates what he takes to be the operative requirements shared by American planners.

In 1965, Secretary of Defense Robert McNamara defined the "assured destruction" requirement as the capacity to destroy one-fourth to one-third of the Soviet population, and two-thirds of Soviet industry.... The requirement was lowered: in 1968 it was defined as one-fifth to one-fourth of the Soviet population and one-half of Soviet industry.[56]

As Admiral Rickover testified in his last appearance before Congress, all these requirements were met long ago with the advent of the nuclear submarine fleet. Indeed, if the destructive power of *one* Trident submarine armed with D-5 warheads (the capacity to visit thermonuclear incineration on 240 targets) doesn't give an adversary second thoughts about aggression nothing will.[57]

If deterrence was the name of the game, why wasn't the American arsenal limited to a small, but redundant, fleet of submarines? Why were vulnerable land-based missiles developed and deployed unless these weapons themselves were designed for war-fighting, not deterrence? And—to continue in this rhetorical line of questioning—could it be that the arms race had more to do with military contractors than the Soviet threat, real or imagined? Or, as Admiral Carroll suggested, each of the armed services wants to be a nuclear power in its own right?

If deterrence were the overriding intention of American decision-makers they would not fashion weapons and strategies designed for first-use in nuclear war-fighting scenarios. This is not the case. According to deterrence doctrine, nuclear weapons are second-strike, relatively inaccurate, retaliatory weapons designed to deter adversaries by inflicting massive, indiscriminate damage. The Reagan administration witnessed the advent of extraordinarily accurate weapons capable of destroying enemy silos and command and control systems. It is reasonable to assume that American planners did not intend to destroy empty silos or vacated Kremlin offices.

Relying upon declassified documents, Daniel Axelrod and Michio Kaku show that the development and deployment of such weapons are consonant with strategies recommended by military advisors and others during every administration from Truman to Bush. For example, during the Eisenhower administration General Ridgway expressed his alarm at the recommendations submitted by the Joint Chiefs:

The conclusion [of the Joint Chiefs] ... pointed unmistakably to the advocacy of the U.S. deliberately precipitating war with the U.S.S.R. in the near future.... I thought this was contrary to every principle upon which our Nation has been founded.[58]

Ridgway was likely responding to the recommendations for triumphant nuclear war-fighting put forth by his colleague, General Nathan Twining, Chairman of the Joint Chiefs of Staff. Twining recommended annihilating a wide array of military, industrial, government, and urban targets. In the words of National Security archivist William Burr, "Twining was following the Air Force tradition of searching for the 'Achilles heel' whose destruction would cause a society to break down and capitulate."[59]

Plans such as Twining's became policy in the Single Integrated Operational Plan (SIOP), the list of sites targeted with nuclear weapons. Many of the incarnations of the plan remain classified. However, the National Security Archive—after considerable struggle—was able to declassify certain telling documents under the Freedom of Information Act. According to the archivists, the SIOP 62 "frightened the devil out of Eisenhower." The war-plan mandated policies inimical to deterrence along with "overkill" targeting that went beyond the requirements for deterrence:

- First use of nuclear weapons if U.S. authorities suspected a Soviet attack.
- Such a preemptive attack would deliver over 3200 nuclear weapons on 1060 targets in the Soviet Union, Warsaw Pact nations, and China.
- Targets included nuclear weapons, command and control centers, and minimally 130 cities.
- Fallout from such a massive attack would likely harm Americans and their European allies.[60]

True, the nuclear bravado of the first Reagan administration was alarming. But the administration simply went public regarding many of the strategic

scenarios of previous administrations. President Carter's Presidential
Directive 59, for example, mandates the construction "of nuclear weapons
accurate enough to destroy silos and other vital targets."[61] The recommen-
dation of Reagan advisor Colin Gray was not comforting: "The United
States should plan to defeat the Soviet Union and to do so at a cost that
would not prohibit U.S. recovery."[62] Such objectives are incompatible with
deterrence doctrine.

And quite obviously, if deterrence were the overarching objective of
American officials, war-prevention would be their primary objective in policy formation and at critical junctures (these junctures are explored in the
next chapter). According to Ellsberg, virtually every administration risked
nuclear war in pursuit of various objectives: "Again and again, generally in
secret from the American public, the U.S. nuclear weapons have been used
in the precise way a gun is used when you point it at someone's head in
a direct confrontation, whether or not the trigger is pulled."[63] Mainstream
analysts such as Richard Betts concur. As he concludes:

> Presidents were unwilling to recognize nuclear combat as so unthinkable that they
> could not exploit its potential to secure international objectives, and they lacked
> absolute confidence that adversaries would settle on the terms demanded.... On
> balance, their strategy resembled Russian roulette more often than chess.[64]

Somewhere Kierkegaard wrote that the purity of the heart is to desire
one thing. Strategists are not pure of heart. Like the rest of us, they seem
conflicted and driven by mixed motives and metaphors. True, at times
war-prevention was a priority; at other times they entertained fantasies of
triumphant nuclear war-fighting. It is misleading to claim that American
nuclear endeavors are solely about deterrence. Corporate profiteering,
careerist ambitions, interservice rivalry, the fatal attraction of the latest
technology, and hegemonic designs are part of the equation.

WORKS IN PRACTICE BUT NOT IN THEORY

> It does not follow that war has been deterred solely by the nuclear threat.
> There are many, many other practical military, political and economic fac-
> tors which weigh against superpower conflict far more effectively than the
> incredible abstraction of nuclear deterrence.
>
> —Admiral Eugene Carroll[65]

Advocates of automatic deterrence are generally well aware of the
problematic nature of deterrence doctrine. They grant that strategists could
have more in mind than deterrence: first-strike weaponry, atomic diplomacy, and grave risks during crises suggest that avoiding nuclear war is
not reliably an overarching objective. Indeed, advocates of unintentional

(automatic) deterrence might agree that deterrence is an ideology driven by economic interests, bureaucratic imperatives, and interservice rivalry. Such admissions, however, are irrelevant from their point of view. They argue that the lack of a sturdy conceptual foundation misses the point. Moreover, it's a distraction to dwell upon triumphant strategic fantasies. Most significantly, they even grant that, on occasion, deterrence fails, precipitating crises in which "competition in risk-taking" heightens the risk of nuclear war. There is, nevertheless, but one salient point for advocates of automatic deterrence: unprecedented decades without a world war illustrate that, despite the worst of intentions and for whatever reasons, nuclear deterrence works.

To paraphrase one influential advocate of automatic deterrence: the superpowers have unintentionally created a "nuclear weapons regime" that preserves the peace. In other words, regardless of elite intentions and fantasies, deterrence is astonishingly viable. This interpretation is worthy of any eighteenth-century drawing room in which classical liberals argued that justice and prosperity are the unplanned outcome of the proper economic system. Specifically, just as the unintended consequences of laissez faire capitalism produce the best of all possible economies, laissez faire arms racing produces something even more wondrous—the best of all possible nuclear worlds. This salutary take on our nuclear predicament is based upon post hoc argumentation and unprovable, counterfactual claims.[66]

The deterrence literature bestows privileged, uncontested status on the following post hoc argument:

America has had a nuclear arsenal since 1945;
No war occurred between the U.S. and U.S.S.R. after 1945;
Therefore, the arsenal deterred war.

Otherwise sophisticated analysts overlook the obvious: correlation does not necessarily prove causation. I suspect that if it were argued that the nuclear arsenal prevented war between the U.S. and Canada, these analysts would urge that salient variables are being ignored: There is no history of warfare between these nations. The same argument can be made about the superpowers. With the exception of the American invasion of Siberia in 1919, there is no precedence for war between the United States and the Soviet Union (or Russia, for that matter). Since there *is* a history of war between the United States and Germany, Italy, and Japan, why not argue that the nuclear arsenal prevented conflict with these powers?

Advocates of unintentional deterrence rely upon counterfactual argumentation: If the American nuclear arsenal *had not* existed, war would have occurred between the superpowers. The status of counterfactual claims is controversial. They make sense in discussing law-like propositions.

For example, if I lament that if I *had not* fallen off the roof, I wouldn't have been hurt (gravity—it's the law!). The existence of gravity is demonstrated by controlled experiments. However, other complaints don't make sense: "I shouldn't have left the slot machine because I was about to win a million dollars." (Alas, no law mandates that I must win.) Likewise, no law mandates that nuclear arsenals somehow *must* deter nuclear war.

To have a flair for the obvious, the deterrent power of nuclear weapons has not been tested by controlled experiments. Indeed, what conceivable experiment could demonstrate that *without* the American arsenal the United States and Soviet Union would have been locked in mortal combat? Such an experiment would demand a feat beyond the power of God—but not ideologues—rewriting history. Worse yet, it would be difficult to get a sabbatical—let alone a grant—to build a time machine, return to 1945, remove nuclear weapons from the international arena, and witness the ensuing drama.

There are, of course, lesser standards of proof which might also be convincing. With Aristotle, we should only demand proof and precision appropriate to the inquiry. Positivist standards of verification elude us, but is there no circumstantial evidence that suggests the efficacy of nuclear weapons in deterring World War III? The evidence usually mentioned is the syllogism listed above: no world war has occurred during the reign of nuclear weaponry.

This argument, however, doesn't inspire confidence because it is undermined by other circumstantial evidence. If, for example, the period from 1917 to 1945 had been marked by frequent US–Soviet hostilities, and if these hostilities ceased with the advent of nuclear weapons, it would be reasonable to suspect that the arsenal was linked to war-prevention. This is not the case. Save for the 1919 episode, there is no record of hostilities during this period.

Indeed, there is as much reason to suspect that nuclear weapons are a provocation, not a deterrent. According to doctrinal teaching, deterrence should have attained its apotheosis during the American atomic monopoly. Given the monopoly and the credible threat to use nuclear weapons (the destruction of Hiroshima and Nagasaki), the Soviets should have been extremely reluctant to provoke the West. However, it's worth reiterating that this was the most adventurous period in Soviet foreign policy.

Given the ill-defined, highly speculative nature of deterrence doctrine, we can construct contradictory narratives about the ultimate questions posed by a nuclear arsenal. Depending upon our mood and biases, we can argue that the arsenal deters war or that it provokes war. We can give license to our imagination and agendas because attempts to liken the arsenal to a deterrent or to a provocation can be neither confirmed nor disconfirmed.

CHAPTER 7

What If They Gave a Crisis and Nobody Came?

> We are all prisoners of a rigid conception of what is important and what is not. We anxiously follow what we suppose to be important while what we suppose to be unimportant wages guerilla warfare behind our backs, transforming the world without our knowledge and eventually mounting a surprise attack on us.
>
> —Milan Kundera[1]

Just before the fall election the administration learned that—despite its warnings—it had been deceived by Soviet diplomats: U-2 reconnaissance revealed that the Soviets were secretly constructing a nuclear base in Cuba. Prominent advisors warned the president that the secret base posed a formidable threat to American national security. Soviet nuclear weapons were but ninety miles from the American shores. American officials told Soviet Ambassador Anatoly Dobrynin that they considered these weapons a "grave threat."

There was also a strong personal incentive for the president to liken Soviet actions to a crisis. The surreptitious construction of the nuclear base presented a near-perfect opportunity for him to vindicate himself from the charges of critics. It was seemingly an ideal time to prove that he was no appeaser; this was *his* chance to settle scores with the Soviets, Cubans—and his critics.

It was as if the Soviets were inviting President Richard Nixon to the gravest crisis of the nuclear age by secretly constructing a nuclear submarine base at Cienfuegos Bay in Cuba in 1970. Nixon declined the invitation. Nixon and Henry Kissinger (his National Security Advisor) shared the same dire perception of the threat: In Kissinger's words, the submarine base was a "quantum leap" in Soviet strategic capability

Nevertheless, according to Kissinger, the president was distracted by other matters, thought it unwise to have a crisis before the election, and had his heart set on visiting the Mediterranean to witness the Sixth Fleet fire its guns.[2] Accordingly, much to Kissinger's dismay, Nixon instructed his associates to make sure that no crisis occurred. The president vacationed in Europe as planned.

But Kissinger was exercised by the Soviet deception and construction of the base. He wanted to construct a crisis—albeit a confrontation dramatically different from Kennedy's 1962 "joust on the abyss." Before the president departed for the Mediterranean, Kissinger prevailed upon the president to allow him to meet secretly with Soviet Ambassador Anatoly Dobrynin. Initial and subsequent negotiations (following Nixon's return from his vacation) enabled the disputants to settle the matter secretly, quietly, and diplomatically: The Soviets dismantled the base. The prudent resolution of what might have become the gravest crisis of the nuclear age is all but forgotten, even among the participants themselves.

A MATTER OF INTERPRETATION

> Hopping back and forth between the whole conceived through parts ... and the parts conceived through the whole ... we seek to turn them, by a sort of intellectual perpetual motion, into explications of one another.... All this is the familiar trajectory of what Dilthey called the hermeneutic circle.... It is central to ethnographic interpretation, and thus to the penetration of other people's thought, as it is to literary, historical, philological, psychoanalytical, or biblical interpretation.
>
> —Clifford Geertz[3]

Decision-makers, like the rest of us, are interpreters. And, like the rest of us, they often misconstrue their cherished interpretations as a fixed, unchangeable reality. And, as Montaigne suggested long ago, those of us foolhardy enough to try to penetrate these texts are interpreters of interpretation: We are to be found in archives and libraries conducting literary projects.

Of course, most of what transpires in the international world is ignored—it couldn't be otherwise. No one can digest everything that happens. Given the ever-expanding resources for gathering information and data transmission at virtually the speed of light, Ernest Becker's observation is telling:

The man of knowledge in our time is bowed down under a burden he never imagined he would ever have: the overproduction of truth that cannot be consumed. For centuries man lived in the belief that truth was slim and elusive, and that once found the troubles of mankind would be over. And here we are in the closing decades of the 20th century, choking on truth.[4]

Most events that come to a decision-maker's attention are given low priority—put on the backburner so to speak. Critics may reject this low priority interpretation of an event and insist that it should be given high priority. Critics of the Bush administration, for example, urge that global warming, poverty, and inadequate health care should be high priority concerns. And even seemingly vital concerns may be glossed over. Richard Clark, formerly Bush's chief advisor on terrorism, writes that he quit out of frustration. Recalling that dreadful day he explains: "I had not been allowed to brief the President in January [2001] or since, not until today, September 11."[5]

Most attention-grabbing events are ambiguous: They can be reasonably interpreted in two or more ways. In other words, such events don't present themselves with prefigured meanings: meanings are read into them. Sometimes, as we've seen above, it's inconvenient to interpret an event as a crisis. In other instances it seems imprudent and needlessly provocative to interpret an event as a crisis. When the Soviets shot down the Korean airliner, for example, the Reagan administration interpreted the incident as a tragedy—nothing to be done. Likewise, when Iraqi artillery fired on an American ship during the Iran/Iraq war, Reagan interpreted the event as an accident, not an act of war—Hussein said he was sorry. Of course regime change in Granada was interpreted as a crisis demanding urgent action to restore the status quo ante. The interpretation of the president, the "interpreter-in-chief," becomes official reality.

To paraphrase the venerable Epictetus, it's not the world that is the source of our crises, but our *interpretation* of the world. Due to the fame and glory that accrue to successful crisis promotion and management there is considerable incentive for decision-makers to interpret putative failures in deterrence as a crisis.[6]

This chapter continues the explication of the grand strategic narrative: a seeming irreversible, sequential plot in which a crisis follows the failure of deterrence. Of course, what constitutes a failure of deterrence is arguable. Rather than entering the fray, I have selected case studies of episodes in Berlin, the Middle East, and Cuba in which most strategists agree that deterrence failed (or at least officials promoted the fear that deterrence failed). In many of these instances decision-makers interpreted events as a crisis; other episodes were interpreted as problems to be negotiated while minimizing the risk of nuclear war; and finally, certain episodes were ersatz "manufactured" crises promoted for domestic political reasons. But what is a crisis? As always, those who control the definition control the argument.

CRISIS AS METAPHOR

> Many historians have a rather vague and certainly varied sense of what
> "crisis" really means, for on examination, the impact of the word dissolves
> in ambiguity.
>
> —Randolph Starn[7]

Curiously, Kahn realizes that a crisis is conceptualized in terms of what I call secondary metaphors. A crisis begins on Rung 4 on the metaphorical ladder of escalation, and may escalate to Rung 20—just short of nuclear war-fighting. Such escalation can often be likened to a strike in which labor and management credibly threaten to harm one another. However, as the competition in risk-taking escalates, Kahn likens a crisis to a game of chicken in which drivers race toward one another at top speed; the first driver to avert a collision is "chicken," an object of ridicule.[8]

However, for Kahn, a crisis itself is a real event; something "out there" that happens to a decision-maker; there is nothing metaphorical about "crisis" per se. He defines a crisis as a convergence of events—a turning point in history—that necessitates an intense confrontation. Such confrontations are driven by a sense of urgency and bedeviled by a lack of reliable information and the uncertainty of the outcome.[9]

Kahn reveals the subjective experience of enduring a crisis, but he reifies the concept. As we've seen, two decision-makers might interpret the same event differently: Nixon ignored the Soviet submarines while Kissinger defined the situation as a "mini-crisis." And, it may be recalled, Kennedy interpreted what he regarded as a less threatening Soviet base in Cuba as a provocation somehow necessitating the grave threat of nuclear war. Contrary to the realist presupposition that any rational actor will posit similar accounts of comparable events, decision-makers and strategists alike respond to the world with diverse, often conflicting, interpretations. As we shall see, certain failures of deterrence are ignored, some are defined as problems, and others are deemed crises—a decidedly hazardous move in an age of assured destruction.

Some operative definitions are in order:

- A failure of deterrence is likened to a problem when there is consensus that it can be resolved slowly and patiently in due course without public bravado and competition in risk taking thereby increasing the danger of war. Eisenhower admonished his successors: "To meet ... [international challenges] successfully there is called for not so much the emotional and transitory sacrifices of crisis but rather those which enable us to carry forward ... the burdens of a prolonged and complex struggle."[10]

- A failure of deterrence is likened to a crisis when it is construed as a critical juncture demanding urgent action that dramatically increases the danger of war. Crisis managers try to restore the status quo ante with words or weapons.

- However, as Richard Betts aptly argues, the very nature of the status quo ante is a matter of interpretation. During the Cuban missile crisis, the Americans wanted to return Cuba to its former missile-free status; the Soviets wanted to return Cuba to its invasion-free status.[11] In any case, in the present context, a crisis marks the interlude when officials decide between peace and war.

Case studies of episodes in Berlin, the Middle East, and Cuba illustrate that international challenges can be interpreted as chronic problems to be resolved in due course or acute crises demanding urgent, perilous measures. These episodes also reveal the secondary metaphors brought into play in constructing crises.

CONFRONTATIONS INVOLVING BERLIN

> It seems silly for us to be facing an atomic war over a treaty preserving Berlin as the future capital of a reunited Germany when all of us know that Germany will probably never be reunited.
>
> —John F. Kennedy[12]

The Berlin Blockade

The 1948 Berlin Blockade episode was a failure of extended deterrence. Those with millenarian views of the American nuclear monopoly believed that the Soviets—or any other adversary—would not act in ways inimical to American interests. They were wrong: Not only did the Soviets extend their hegemony into Eastern Europe, they directly threatened American interests by blocking access to the Western sector of Berlin.

In his memoir Khrushchev expresses frustration—if not humiliation—with the Potsdam Agreement that divided Germany and Berlin itself into Western and Eastern bloc sectors. He believed that Stalin acquiesced to the agreement because the Soviets were a weaker power.[13] Of course the agreement was not wholly advantageous to the Western powers since Berlin became part of East Germany—a less than ideal arrangement for Western access to the city.

Evidently, in March 1948 the Soviets wanted to incorporate all of Berlin within their sphere of influence. They restricted access and by June all roads and rail services were blocked and electric power was cut. The United States responded with a massive airlift that supplied Berlin with essentials. The Soviets ended the blockade about ten months after it began; the episode presaged more dangerous confrontations that would begin a decade later.[14]

Although it appears that war was never seriously considered to regain access to Berlin, the episode is usually defined as a crisis, albeit a "low intensity" crisis.[15] However, as I define terms, it appears that Truman likened Soviet actions to a problem—an issue to be resolved in due course without resorting to war. In effect, he made a virtue out of what he regarded as a necessity. American conventional forces would be overwhelmed by the Red Army if they tried to end the blockade. True, Churchill and others urged an American nuclear attack, but the American nuclear weapons were not assembled and there were doubts about the capability of the B-29 fleet to penetrate Soviet airspace and to find appropriate targets.[16]

However, as in so many other confrontations, the choice was not simply between "fight or flight"; American decision-makers responded with posturing and oblique threats. B-29s were sent to Great Britain and Germany—within striking distance of the Soviet Union. None of the planes had nuclear weapons, and American planners had serious qualms about escalating the confrontation by sending these aircraft into Soviet airspace. Nevertheless, it can be argued that what the Soviets likely perceived as a nuclear threat provided further incentive to end the blockade. In any case, the Western powers regained access to Berlin, and the city remained partitioned in accord with the Potsdam Agreement.

The 1961 Ultimatum

According to Khrushchev, Stalin's resolution of the 1948 episode humiliated the Soviets and exacerbated the problem: "After Stalin's death we realized that the agreement which liquidated the blockade of West Berlin (1948–1949) was unfair."[17] As McGeorge Bundy (Kennedy's national security advisor) suggests, the Soviets probably wanted to expel the West from Berlin for a variety of reasons. Khrushchev agreed with Bundy that East German defections to the West embarrassed the Soviet regime and undermined the East Germany economy. However, Bundy posits other possible reasons not discussed by Khrushchev: undermining the Western alliance by humiliating the Americans, frustrating West German ambitions, and showing his Chinese critics that he wasn't appeasing the West.[18]

Bundy also suggests that the Soviets tried their hand at atomic diplomacy to compel Western forces to evacuate Berlin. By 1958 the Soviets possessed thermonuclear weapons along with intercontinental bombers. Evidently, Khrushchev hoped that American decision-makers would think twice about another confrontation over Berlin. As Bundy explains:

Khrushchev hoped that the nuclear strength achieved by the Soviet Union ... would persuade the West that it must come to terms.... In this way the Berlin crisis ... was a Soviet exercise in atomic diplomacy—an effort to use a new appearance of Soviet nuclear strength to force changes in the center of Europe.[19]

Khrushchev insisted that East Germany must be afforded the right to control its own borders: "The West was putting its own, very one-sided interpretation on the question of the GDR's [the German Democratic Republic, East Germany) right to control its own borders."[20] Khrushchev candidly allowed that defections into West Berlin along with the West Berliners' exploitation of the East Berlin economy created an economic and social disaster for his ally: "The resulting drain of workers was creating a simply disastrous situation.... Because prices were much lower in East Berlin, West Berliners were also buying up all sorts of products that were in wide demand."[21] Accordingly, Khrushchev argued that the GDR must be given the sovereign right of "border control."

In addition, beginning in 1958 Khrushchev insisted that all of Berlin must de facto become part of the Soviet bloc, thereby curtailing Western access. Confronted with these demands, Eisenhower displayed considerable finesse by defining the situation as a problem, an issue that could be negotiated at a future conference. (There is much to be said for deferring confrontations.) The hero of D-Day, of course, enjoyed considerable advantage in his diplomacy—he was beyond reproach. Unlike his successor, Eisenhower had no need to prove his heroism by alarming the American people with frequent crisis moves.

Kennedy enjoyed no such luxury; he lacked Eisenhower's reputation. Many career diplomats and military officers regarded the young president as inexperienced, and the fiasco at the Bay of Pigs reinforced this view. In the words of one observer of Kennedy's predicament:

President Kennedy looked around the table—it must have seemed to him that everybody who made him feel insecure was sitting there: all the admirals and generals, all the CIA people, none of whom liked him, and he knew that.... I'm sure he was worried about ... the charge that he was going to be a liberal, peace-nik type.[22]

Curiously, although Eisenhower—unlike Kennedy—avoided perilous crisis confrontations with the Soviets, Khrushchev expresses disdain for Eisenhower and affection for Kennedy. (This is puzzling given Khrushchev's churlish behavior at the Vienna meeting in June 1961.) He writes:

I had met Kennedy in Vienna. He impressed me as a better statesman than Eisenhower. Unlike Eisenhower, he had formulated opinions on every subject. I joked with him [JFK] that we [the USSR] had cast the deciding ballot in his election to the Presidency over that son-of-a-bitch Richard Nixon.... I explained that by waiting to release the U-2 pilot Gary Powers until after the American election we kept Nixon from being able to claim that he could deal with the Russians.[23]

Kennedy set out to prove himself—to make a name for himself. His two books search for exemplary crisis metaphors; indeed, these texts are sagas of mixed and competing metaphors. His narration seems self-confessional.

These didactic accounts of great men and their crises begin when aspiring statesmen—politicians called to greatness—are vexed with cruel, unexpected calamities by foes, foreign and domestic. But the ensuing crises are about more than selfless jousts with fearsome foes. They are about a more formidable struggle, an existential crisis: the defining turning point in one's life—the ultimate battle with the self.

For Kennedy, crises were not merely a concern, they were an obsession. Unfortunately, he never got the crises he wanted. The Bay of Pigs attempt to overthrow the Castro regime was an unmitigated failure. He seemed to have a personal crisis when he met with Khrushchev in Vienna shortly thereafter in June 1961. For three years the Soviet leader had hectored American leaders about access to Berlin. Kennedy was confident that his vigor and charisma would prevail in face-to-face diplomacy. However, in Bundy's "Memorandum of Conversation" we learn that the bumptious Russian peasant reminded the Boston Brahmin of the American nuclear bases in Iran and Turkey and intimated that the Soviets might reciprocate quid pro quo in Cuba.[24]

The focal point of discussion, however, was Berlin. By all accounts the American nuclear arsenal did not dissuade Khrushchev from issuing a strident ultimatum in 1961. On the second day of the summit Khrushchev gave the president the message: Berlin must be neutralized within six months. If the Western powers do not cooperate, Moscow will sign a separate treaty with East Germany ending the Western occupation of Berlin.[25] The German leader, Walter Ulbricht, boasted that the treaty would empower him to hinder access to West Berlin and to close its airport. Kennedy insisted that there could be no compromise. In a vintage Khrushchev performance, the premier pounded the table and bellowed: "*I want peace. But if you want war, this is your problem.*" He reiterated that the treaty would indeed be signed—the West would be denied access to Berlin. In response, Kennedy lamented, "If that is true, it's going to be a cold winter."[26]

Both Khrushchev and Kennedy ruminated about risking nuclear war to preserve the status quo. As Ted Sorensen, a Kennedy confidant, explained: "He [Khrushchev] did not believe that Kennedy would start a nuclear war over traffic controls on the *autobahn*."[27] Neither side was enthusiastic about fighting a nuclear war. Nevertheless, neither side was willing to capitulate: indeed, both Kennedy and his nemesis acted in ways that increased the risk of such a war.

There were, however, those in the halls of power unwilling to risk nuclear war to prevail in Berlin. However, Senators Fulbright and Mansfield (prescient, early critics of the Indochina War) advocated compromise: a demilitarized Berlin administered under the auspices of the United Nations.[28] But Kennedy was more disposed to contingency plans proffered by military advisors. The plans, by and large, eschewed the

Dulles' doctrine of massive retaliation (as an initial response) in favor of flexible response: Herman Kahn's "ladder of escalation" became an arresting and operative metaphor. Planning was guided by a gradual escalation strategy that would inform the Cuban missile crisis the next year. But in the case of Berlin, as in the case of Cuba, the strategy did not rule out full-scale nuclear war-fighting as the last alternative. (Curiously, on occasion, policymakers ruminated as to what good would come out of this alternative.)

Evidently, the prospect of nuclear war was seriously considered. It is chilling to read the National Security Action Memorandum even after the passage of four decades:

If despite Allied use of substantial non-nuclear forces, the Soviets continue to encroach upon our vital interests, then the Allies should use nuclear weapons, staring with ... A. Selective nuclear attacks for the primary purpose of demonstrating the will to use nuclear weapons. B. Limited tactical employment of nuclear weapons.... C. General Nuclear War.[29]

The flexible response strategy was plausible in theory but highly problematic in practice, especially in the Berlin confrontation. The Soviets enjoyed overwhelming conventional superiority due to their proximity to West Berlin and the strength of the Red Army. Tactical nuclear war-fighting in Berlin or in the forests of Germany would destroy much of the country. And, even if a first strike on the Soviet nuclear arsenal were possible, the Soviets would likely retain the capacity to retaliate by killing millions of Americans.

Once again the choice was not between fight or flight, for a crisis is a war of ambiguous words and symbolic posturing. Both sides increased military spending and preparedness and showcased the latest weapons systems. In a fateful speech Deputy Secretary of Defense Roswell Gilpatric boasted of U.S. superiority in nuclear weaponry—tens of thousands of tactical and strategic nuclear weapons above and beyond the numbers in the Soviet arsenal. And he couldn't resist the temptation to taunt the Soviets over their deteriorating relations with China. As Ronald Steel concludes: "For the Russians, the implications [of the speech] were, in Hilsman's [a Kennedy confidant and advisor] words "horrendous." What frightened them was not that we had military superiority, for they know that all along—but that *we* knew it."[30] (To reiterate, Eisenhower wisely avoided such bravado lest he exacerbate the arms race.)

Shortly thereafter, perhaps in response, in a dramatically symbolic performance, the Soviets tested the most powerful weapons ever detonated: a thirty and a fifty-eight megaton hydrogen bomb.[31] It is also plausible to suspect that, in response, Khrushchev also escalated the arms race and made plans to install Soviet nuclear missiles in Cuba. As Beschloss suggests, the speech pressured the Soviet premier "to do something spectacular to change the widespread perception of the nuclear imbalance between the Soviet Union and the United States.[32]

In what may have been a template for the resolution of the Cuban missile crisis, the president secretly instructed his brother to inform the Soviets that he could show flexibility if the tanks were removed within twenty-four hours. The Soviets blinked first. And, in what may have presaged the Trollope ploy, Kennedy ignored a belligerent missive from Khrushchev and responded to a more tractable message. And yet, the symbolic performances escalated. Both officials of the Kennedy administration and Khrushchev offer comparable accounts of the climax of the crisis. After considerable mutually assured bravado and posturing, Soviet and American tanks faced one another in Berlin. Both sides nudged up the ladder of escalation to credibly threaten one another and to show resolve. As Khrushchev wrote: "The tanks and troops on both sides spent the night lined up facing each other across the border. It was late October."[33]

However, unlike Eisenhower who could avoid crises and defuse confrontations without suffering charges of appeasement, Kennedy could never appease his generals. The American commander, General Lucius Clay, informed the president that the Soviet tanks were probably just for show. Kennedy reassured the general that he was confident that the military hadn't lost its nerve. Clay's rejoinder is telling: "Mr. President, we're not worried about our nerves. We're worrying about those of you people in Washington."[34]

The Soviets remedied the "border control" issue by constructing the infamous Berlin Wall. When there was no American response to stringing a barbed wire barrier, the East Germans quickly reinforced the barrier with stone and cement. Khrushchev admits that—to understate the case—the wall was not popular with Berliners: "There were illegal attempts to cross over to the West, resulting in some incidents along the border, some of them with an unpleasant outcome."[35] While the wall didn't win friends and influence people for the Soviets, it did stop migration to the West. While the wall was certainly preferable to warfare—especially nuclear warfare—it was widely construed as a humiliation for the West in general and for Kennedy in particular.

Campaigning for chancellor, Willy Brandt excoriated the Western generals on the scene: "You let Ulbricht kick you in the rear.... The entire East is going to laugh from Pankow to Vladivostok." And commenting on Kennedy's role on the world stage, Brandt remarked, "The curtain went up, and the stage was empty."[36]

Urging that the wall violated the Potsdam Agreement, to say nothing of the vaunted courage and resolve of the New Frontiersmen, allies accused the president of perpetrating a second Munich. (Such historical metaphors are a stock in trade in such rhetoric.) Later Kennedy appeared in Berlin to demonstrate American resolve. He chose the oft quoted phrase *Ich bin ein Berliner;* some thought *Ich bin ein Munchener* would have been more appropriate. But words did not suffice to cast off metaphors drawn from Chamberlain's ill fated attempts at appeasement. Fate would bestow one more chance to be remembered as a legendry profile in courage. Due to adroit posthumous impression management of the Cuban missile crisis, Kennedy would be remembered in terms of metaphors drawn from Churchill and his lonely struggles.

Kennedy's humiliation in Berlin led to a fateful decision that would become a key factor in Kennedy's bravura crisis: the deployment of American Jupiter missiles in Turkey. Apparently, the decision was governed by impression management, not strategic exigencies. As a study ordered by Bundy concluded, the missiles should be installed as planned "primarily on the view that, in the aftermath of Khrushchev's hard posture at Vienna, cancellation . . . might be a sign of weakness."[37]

As we shall see shortly, columnist James Reston revealed the mixed metaphors that bedeviled Kennedy's decision-making when he offered a telling gloss on the Cuban missile crisis: "Kennedy talked like Churchill and acted like Chamberlain."[38]

CONFRONTATIONS INVOLVING THE MIDDLE EAST

> Dulles was Secretary of State to a President who was passionately opposed to war in the way only an experienced military man can be. Eisenhower was not interested in the nuances of the balance of power; even if a long-range danger to the global equilibrium did exist in the Middle East. . . . To Eisenhower, the Suez crisis was not sufficiently threatening to merit the use of force. His friendly grin notwithstanding, he had a very strong personality and a not very pleasant one when crossed.
>
> —Kissinger[39]

The Suez Episode

> You have attacked Egypt knowing that it is considerably weaker than you are, that it does not have much of an army, and that it does not have many weapons. But there are other countries which are entirely capable of coming to Egypt's defense.
>
> —Khrushchev's warning to the British, French, and Israeli invaders of Egypt.[40]

Kissinger is right. Eisenhower had little enthusiasm for war. He was more concerned with avoiding the reality of warfare—especially nuclear warfare—than parsing metaphors about the balance of power and global equilibrium. The unusual, if not unique, features of this episode are note-worthy:

- It marks the first time the Soviets ventured beyond their usual sphere of influence.
- It marks the first instance of Soviet saber-rattling in a crisis—a veiled nuclear threat against three American allies.
- It offers a rare, and perhaps hopeful, example of an American president reject-ing historical metaphors and trying to conceptualize an event in its own right.
- It is a remarkable instance when the United States sided with the Soviets against American allies by endorsing a United Nations resolution. Even more signifi-cant: Eisenhower made veiled threats—some would call it an ultimatum—to withdraw from NATO unless the British, French, and Israelis retreated.

Both Khrushchev and Kissinger narrate similar details to set the epi-sode in context. Emboldened, apparently, by their burgeoning nuclear arsenal, the Soviets become involved in the Middle East for the first time. Khrushchev explains: "Our economy, our armed forces, and the weight of our influence all increased mightily.... We were able to step in and assist President Nasser and the Arab peoples."[41] Both authors agree that that newfound Kremlin atomic diplomacy was based upon both deterrence and compellence. Khrushchev and American commentators suggest that it was believed that a robust Soviet arsenal would deter the United States from interfering with Soviet moves in the Middle East. And turning to the Suez incident, apparently it was believed that credible Soviet nuclear threats would compel the British, French, and Israelis to abandon their efforts to seize the Suez Canal and to depose Gamal Nasser.

There is little controversy regarding the salient facts. The Soviets gave military and economic aid to the Nasser regime. After the Americans reneged on their offer to finance the Aswan Dam, the Soviets agreed to help. Not surprisingly, both authors assign noble motives to their respec-tive politics and sinister motives to the adversaries. Khrushchev claims the Soviets aimed to create a better life for the Egyptian people by supporting their struggle to free themselves of Western (mainly British) imperialism. Kissinger sees Soviet actions as a failure of deterrence to contain perfidious Soviet ambitions. As he explains: "America was drawn into the Middle East by the containment theory which required opposition to Soviet expansion in every region."[42] He likened containment to a zero-sum game. Critics suggested a more apt game-theoretic metaphor: Prisoners' Dilemma, in which mutual cooperation is both rational and prudent. In any case, why containment is *"required"* is not spelled out; presumably it is obvious to all who share Kissinger's Cold War cosmology. In any case, in addition to safeguarding the Middle East from communism, America, according to Kissinger, offered foreign aid, and assistance with modernization.

The first offer to finance the Aswan Dam came from Anglo-American leaders in 1955. Despite professions of noble intent, Kissinger seems to suggest that this offer had more to do with playing politics than with assisting the Egyptian people: American officials hoped that a sizable grant would make Nasser more tractable, or at least more dependent on the West.[43] Both Khrushchev and Kissinger agree—there were strings attached: renouncing Soviet aid, mediating the Israeli/Palestine dispute, and joining an anti-communist alliance fashioned by the West, the Baghdad Pact.

In a direct rebuke to the United States, Nasser withdrew recognition from Chiang Kai-shek and established diplomatic relations with the People's Republic of China (known as "Red China" prior to Nixon/Kissinger Triangle Diplomacy). Nasser's actions hardly affected the security of the American homeland. Nevertheless, his symbolic defiance of containment policy angered and humiliated high American officials such as Dulles. The American government abruptly cut off aid to Egypt; the Egyptians turned to the Soviets, and—in a bold move—nationalized the Suez Canal.

To this day, Kissinger displays a remarkable lack of empathy for the Egyptian position, namely nationalizing the Suez Canal. The canal, after all, is not the Thames or the Mississippi—it bisects Egypt. It is understandable that due to a mixture of national interest and nationalist pride Nasser resented the demands of the Western powers.

Thus far there is nothing remarkable about the episode: The superpowers played politics in the Third World, endured successes and failures, and promoted symbolic performances. However, at this point, the British, French, and Israelis alienated their American ally by invading Egypt to overthrow Nasser and to seize the canal.

Khrushchev proposed a joint American/Soviet effort to stop the invasion, and Dulles proposed a conference to somehow bring the canal under international control. Both proposals were rejected as the American allies marched on Egypt. The Soviets marshalled veiled nuclear threats against the allies. Khrushchev queried the British as to how they would react to being attacked by a much more powerful nation, a nation "for instance [with] rocket weapons?"[44]

In what would become an obligatory metaphorical construction of any enemy—real or imagined—both the British and the French likened Nasser to Hitler or Mussolini. The French Prime Minister, Guy Mollet, asserted that: "Just as Hitler's policy [was] written down in *Mein Kampf*, Nasser [has] the ambition to recreate the conquests of Islam."[45] Likewise, the British Prime Minister, Anthony Eden, cabled Eisenhower: "There is no doubt in our minds that Nasser ... is now effectively in Russian hands, just as Mussolini was in Hitler's. It would be as ineffective to show weakness to Nasser ... as it was to show weakness to Mussolini."[46]

Such facile and misleading historical metaphors, as Kissinger realizes, are performative: There can be no negotiation and compromise when dealing with the likes of Hitler and Mussolini—only total victory. Much to his credit, Eisenhower resisted these metaphors. He told Eden that he had some familiarity with Hitler, and that Nasser was no Hitler—just a new leader of a weak nation with nationalist sensitivities and ambitions.

However, Eisenhower construed the situation as a crisis due to Soviet nuclear threats and the risk of a Middle Eastern war that could readily get out of control. Even apart from such apprehension, Eisenhower wisely decided that (in Kissinger's words) "military action against Nasser would so inflame Arab nationalism that Western influence would be ruined for a generation—a far darker scenario than losing control over the Canal."[47] (Were Eisenhower alive today, would he express the same apprehension about the Bush administration's invasion of Iraq?)

This apprehension is shared by a British official, R.H.S. Crossman, writing about the episode eight year after the crisis. According to Crossman an Allied victory in seizing the canal and deposing Nasser would have been worse than a Pyrrhic victory:

Victory in the Canal [dispute] would commit Britain and France to an occupation of Egypt from which it would have been impossible to withdraw, except after military defeat.... By turning on their allies and forcing a withdrawal, Eisenhower and Dulles dragged us from the edge of catastrophe.[48]

Indeed, it appears that in this situation Eisenhower found many of Kissinger's metaphors irrelevant. Ruminations about calibrating the balance of power and containing Soviet ambitions were not immediate concerns. The most pressing concern was avoiding war. In an unprecedented move, Eisenhower instituted oil and financial sanctions against the American allies, and strongly hinted (some say it was an ultimatum) that the United State would withdraw from NATO unless the British, French, and Israelis stopped their aggression. As Crossman explains: "It took Eisenhower exactly three days of oil and financial sanctions to bring the British and French governments to heel." Crossman adds that the confrontation with the United States humbled the British and French and disabused them of the notion that they were still world class, imperial powers.[49]

And, in Kissinger's words:

Eisenhower went so far as to imply that unilateral British action would risk America's willingness to sustain NATO and ... leave America's allies at the mercy of Moscow.... I could assure you that this [the invasion of Egypt] could grow to such intensity as to have the most far-reaching consequences.[50]

The British, French, and Israelis got the message and withdrew—much to Kissinger's chagrin. He speculates that Eisenhower's aversion to war inspired a euphoric Khrushchev to foment future crises in Berlin and Cuba.[51] What is not speculative, however, is that Eisenhower had no appetite for competition in risk-taking—he had seen enough of war.

The Yom Kippur War

> Moscow sent an urgent message to Washington.... [It] proposed joint superpower intervention to reinstitute the ceasefire they had arranged, and threatened to consider unilateral action if the United States refused to participate. Within an hour a meeting of the Washington Special Action Group (WSAG), *with the president absent* [italics mine] convened in the White House Situation Room.
>
> —Richard Betts's gloss on the initiation of the crisis.[52]

Contrary to the post-Watergate mythology, Nixon was not consumed with managing foreign policy; he was obsessed with managing Nixon. He was more attuned to vacationing—or a good night's sleep—than to foreign affairs that did rattle him personally.[53] For Nixon a crisis was an imbroglio, not an international challenge. Understandably, in the fall of 1973, Nixon wanted a good night's sleep more than ever for, at the time, he was embroiled in *the* defining Nixon crisis—Watergate.

According to Kissinger, Nixon was too distraught to participate in the 1973 episode. He was "as agitated and emotional as I had ever seen him." Kissinger goes on to explain that the president was not upset by the threat of nuclear war fomented by yet another October crisis with the Soviets; on the contrary, he was exercised by the "Saturday night massacre": firing the Watergate prosecutor followed by embarrassing resignations within his administration.[54]

Due to his strict instructions not to be awakened, he did not initially participate in the harrowing incident that threatened to escalate into a superpower nuclear confrontation—the 1973 Yom Kippur War. As in the Cienfuegos incident, Kissinger, not Nixon, was the principal actor.

There is little controversy about the sequence of events. Apparently, attempting to catch the Israelis off guard, Egypt and Syria attacked Israel on Yom Kippur. The Arab forces were repulsed by a powerful, Israeli counterattack. Brezhnev (the Soviet premier) and Kissinger brokered a ceasefire. However, the Israelis violated the ceasefire and threatened to decimate the Egyptian Third Army. The Soviets once again proposed joint Soviet and American efforts to enforce the ceasefire, and once again the Americans rejected the proposal.

American officials commenting upon the episode do not fully explain why Soviet proposals for cooperative U.S./Soviet efforts were automatically rejected. Apparently, such cooperation was simply unthinkable during the chill of the Cold War climate. One can only speculate about other reasons. Such cooperation: would not play well domestically in the United States; it would show the world that the two superpowers have equal stature; it might draw Egypt back into the Soviet sphere of influence, and it might increase Soviet prestige in their ongoing conflict with China (a conflict Kissinger was trying to exploit).

In any event, once again the Soviets threatened to intervene unilaterally. The Soviet premier insisted, "If you find it impossible to act jointly with us in this matter, we should be faced with the necessity urgently to consider the question of taking appropriate steps unilaterally."[55]

In response, American officials began to ascend Kahn's ladder of escalation. Kissinger spoke of the peril of nuclear war-fighting at a press conference. U.S. forces went to a higher state of alert and orchestrated symbolic performances by redeploying American intercontinental bombers and aircraft carriers. Kissinger also persuaded the Israelis to abide by the ceasefire and also sent Brezhnev a conciliatory communiqué which remains classified.[56] In the final analysis, commentators such as Betts and Bundy suggest that Kissinger brokered a ceasefire that saved the Egyptian army. There is reason to believe that behind-the-scenes diplomacy, not veiled nuclear threats, resolved the crisis.[57]

Nixon, of course, tried to take credit for the successful resolution of the episode. He exaggerated the threat, portrayed himself as a lonely—albeit decisive—statesman, and credited his courage and acumen with defusing a dangerous situation. At a news conference, without undue humility or allegiance to the facts, he claimed that at the moment of truth, he resolved "the most difficult crisis we have had since the Cuban missile confrontation of 1962." He proved to his adversary that "The tougher it gets, the cooler I get." In a coda he added: "Mr. Brezhnev knew that regardless of the pressures at home Nixon would do the right thing."[58]

Confrontations in Cuba

> A crisis, like all other news developments, is a creation of the language used
> to depict it; the appearance of a crisis is a political act, not recognition of a
> fact or a rare situation.
>
> —Murray Edelman[59]

Three confrontations between the United States and the Soviet Union involving Cuba are depicted as crises. And yet, these episodes were perceived differently, managed in starkly contrasting ways, and are remembered differently due to the diverse, contesting metaphors improvised to render these situations intelligible and manageable.

- The unforgettable Cuban missile crisis of 1962;
- The all-but-forgotten Cienfuegos Bay "mini-crisis" of 1970;

- And the ersatz Cuban Brigade crisis of 1979—an episode everyone would like to forget.

Each episode reveals the determinative role of primary and secondary metaphors in the construction and promotion of crises both for private and public consumption. In the first episode, all involved interpreted the deployment of Soviet missiles as a crisis. In the second case (as we've seen) Nixon ignored what he deemed a more formidable challenge than the 1962 episode. And, in the third case, Carter didn't believe that Soviet troops in Cuba presented a clear and present danger to the United States—no urgent choice between war and peace was required. In his mind there was no crisis. However, he promoted the episode as a crisis for domestic political reasons.

No account of nuclear crises would be complete without reference to the episode that, by all accounts, brought the world closest to the brink of thermonuclear warfare. Given the gravity of the threat—and the determinative role of diverse metaphorical constructions—this episode deserves special attention.

The Cuban Missile Crisis

"It's just as if we suddenly began to put a major number of MRBMs in Turkey. Now that'd be goddam dangerous, I would think." At that point McGeorge Bundy whose jaw must have dropped ... reminded him, "Well we *did* Mr. President."

—Richard Betts[60]

Kennedy's charmed life ended the day he assumed the presidency. He was not overwrought because his domestic agenda languished in Congress. He would "get the country moving again" by profiling himself in courage and by displaying "grace under pressure" in international crises. He would make a name for himself in foreign affairs. No wonder historian Garry Wills quips, "Accounts by New Frontiersmen make it sound as if the Kennedy presidency was just one crisis meeting after another."[61] According to Nixon, Kennedy confided: "It really is true that foreign affairs is the only important issue for a president to handle, isn't it? I mean who gives a shit if the minimum wage is $1.15 or $1.25, in comparison to this [the planned Bay of Pigs invasion]?"[62]

In order to appreciate why this episode was the defining moment of his life and presidency, it is essential to understand his deeply engrained, secondary crisis metaphors; how did he construe international crises? Judging from his two books, Kennedy construed crises as existential dramas in which a would-be hero reveals his true character. In this familiar, formulaic narrative, the protagonist no longer enjoys the charmed life of his youth. Fate casts him in the final and defining crisis of his life: a dark night of the soul in which he is scourged by relentless self-doubt and humiliation. Everyone is a rank amateur when it comes to this dark night of the soul.

Kennedy took certain adversarial challenges personally: They were interpreted as the climax of dramas that reveal the truth about men and events. Like other would-be heroes, he confronted what Turner calls "liminality" during his crisis sagas. Disoriented by unexpected, inchoate events (such as the Bay of Pigs fiasco and humiliation in Berlin) he was, in Turner's telling phrase, "betwixt and between metaphors."[63] Indeed, James Reston got it right: "Kennedy talked like Churchill and acted like Chamberlain." However, these historical metaphors seemed useless, even dangerous, in resolving the Cuban missile crisis. Kennedy foresaw that the Churchill script ended in nuclear holocaust while a *public* reenactment of the Chamberlain script ended in humiliation.

Khrushchev claims that the missiles deployed in Cuba were defensive weapons intended to deter another American invasion. (Who *doesn't* claim that his or her weapons are purely defensive? Judging from the rhetoric, the world must be free of offensive weapons.) In any case, Khrushchev claims that he knew of Operation Mongoose and other plans to invade Cuba and to install a regime congenial to American interests. He explained:

While I was on an official visit to Bulgaria ... one thought kept hammering away at my brain: what will happen if we lose Cuba?.... We had to establish a tangible and effective deterrent to American interference in the Caribbean. But what exactly? The logical answer was missiles.... We wanted to keep the Americans from invading Cuba. We wanted to make them think twice by confronting them with our missiles.[64]

But could it be that Khrushchev had mixed motives? Perhaps he wanted to deter another American invasion, but why deploy a provocative "deterrent" such as nuclear weapons; why not station Soviet troops as a "firebreak"? Khrushchev himself suggests that he wanted to give the Americans "a dose of their own medicine." Since the Americans surrounded their former Soviet ally with nuclear bases, didn't he have the right to reciprocate? It is also possible that his actions were designed to placate his domestic hawks and strident Chinese critics.

In any case, the stage was set for a high drama in five acts, a performance designed to search for the correct metaphor to send the right message to Khrushchev. As McNamara observed:

For twelve days I lived in the Pentagon ... because I feared that they [the military and other hawks] might not understand that this was a communication exercise, not a military operation ... [I was] trying to send a message, not start a war.

This was not a blockade, but a means of communication between Kennedy and Khrushchev.[65]

McNamara once declared, "There is no such thing as strategy, only crisis management." Based upon his observation, this declaration needs updating. His remark about his duty as chief Pentagon semiotician suggests that there is no longer crisis management—just impression management.

The first act was marked by indecision. True, Kennedy knew what he didn't want—missiles in Cuba. But the thought of immediately risking nuclear war to remove the missiles was also repugnant. Given his predicament, his limited, outdated stock of crisis metaphors (scripted in *Why England Slept*) seemed dangerous or unacceptable. In an age of assured destruction, the Churchill script portended a tragic climax; at the same time he was haunted by visions of Chamberlain slouching toward Munich. In this liminal phase between and betwixt metaphors he should be commended for resisting the belligerence of the hawks, but chastened for lacking the courage to accept the counsel of the doves.

Despite his misgivings, he could not resist the temptation to play the part of Churchill in the second act. For public consumption Kennedy scripted dramatic lines that he hoped would compel his adversary to retreat, thereby vindicating his preconceived destiny. Churchill became his public persona, his metaphorical template. Behind the scenes, however, he improvised a more conciliatory script. His October 22 speech to the nation was vintage Churchill. His plea for forbearance, heroism, and ultimate sacrifice paraphrased a legendary Churchill oath. But the prime minister's pledge to fight them on the beaches, and fight them in the fields and the streets—never surrender—was a tough act to follow in the radically transformed nuclear age. Nevertheless, it played well with an adoring and frightened public.

During the third act, while Kennedy played the part of a latter-day Churchill in public (it played well with domestic audiences, but not with his adversary) another Kennedy persona emerged behind the scenes— a man under the sway of a new metaphor. He resisted considerable pressure to match his oratory with his deeds. Just as wars enable generals to test new weapons, crises enable political actors to test new strategies. The liminality that beset Kennedy was generative: It produced a resonant metaphor (actually a replay of Kahn's ladder of escalation trope) that would influence generations of crisis managers and war-planners—gradual escalation strategy.

The strategy—an avowedly symbolic performance—responded (or so it seemed) to the exigencies of the new age. The strategy simultaneously reinforced displays of American resolve while giving an adversary the time and incentive to back down. The escalation, of course, had to be properly phrased to send the right message. A strident script might provoke needless belligerence—or worse. A weak message, of course, might convey timidity.

In a personal letter to Raymond Garthoff, former CIA Director John McCone, an Ex Comm member, summarized the context of the new strategic thinking that led to the gradual escalation strategy initiated with a blockade. (I am grateful to Garthoff for sharing this document):

> In the Ex Comm deliberations we pursued many alternative courses of action, ranging from presenting the issue to the UN ... or striking militarily .... The committee reasoned that the UN could (and would) do little ... and that military action would prompt an array of Soviet responses such as taking over Berlin and acting violently elsewhere. Also it was noted that military action would spill quantities of Soviet blood, thus causing a most serious confrontation that probably would escalate into war. It was decided ... that we should move positively, and always providing Kruschev [sic] with an opportunity to retreat. For that reason, military actions ... were set aside, and a program of a "quaranteen" [sic] of Cuba was adopted. This was the first step, but if it was ineffective then military action would follow, and Krushcev [sic] was so informed through channels that we knew he respected.[66]

In theory, such escalation was to be gradual; in practice, however, it was unnervingly rapid. In addition to the blockade, American armed forces were placed on an unprecedented state of high alert, DEFCON-2 (just short of full-scale nuclear war-fighting). General Thomas Power violated procedure and broadcast the alert in plain English so the Soviets would get the message. Apparently, however, Khrushchev didn't get the message. He ordered work on the missile installations accelerated and vowed that "American pirates" would not stop Soviet shipping. It also appears that the American Navy didn't get the message. Following routine procedures, Navy aircraft submarines dropped depth charges to make them surface.

The plot thickened as the Soviet armada approached the blockade line. Robert Kennedy allowed that "I felt we were on a precipice with no way off.... President Kennedy had initiated a course of events, but he no longer had control over them."[67] There was good news and bad news. The Americans claim that the Soviets did not challenge the blockade; the Soviets disagree. In any case, the bad news was that—as the hawks had warned—the blockade was merely a symbolic gesture that didn't remove the Cuban missiles. The missiles became operational.

The new strategic metaphor—gradual escalation—appeared to fail. Indeed, throughout the crisis, good news was almost invariably followed by unexpected bad news. The last Friday of the crisis, Khrushchev sent a seemingly conciliatory message: The missiles would be dismantled if the Americans agreed not to invade Cuba. Unknown to most of the Ex-Comm members, Robert Kennedy met secretly with Dobrynin that night and suggested his brother was ready to make concessions to resolve the confrontation.[68] Accordingly, in order to take advantage of Kennedy's newfound tractability, the following day ("Black Saturday") Khrushchev sent another communiqué demanding more concessions—namely the dismantling of the Turkish missiles. The "best and the brightest" found the *immediate* dismantling of these missiles unacceptable. The drama became a theatre of the absurd: Kennedy and his confidants preferred risking nuclear war to public humiliation.

The fourth act of the crisis was marked by desperation. Both the old metaphors and the new one failed them. It was as if they were lost and abandoned in a void, as Nietzsche might say, with no horizon, and no omens to light the dark night of the soul. If such prose seems over-wrought, consider Robert Kennedy's lamentation:

The president was not optimistic nor was I.... He had not abandoned hope, but what hope there was now rested with Khrushchev's revising his course within a few hours. It was a hope, not an expectation. The expectation was a military confrontation.[69]

Grasping for virtually any metaphor to guide them, Kennedy and his associates grasped at straws. Someone recalled Trollope's Victorian novel in which, as we've seen, an ingénue ignored a harsh message from her suitor and responded to the words she wanted to hear. Accordingly, the president ignored the Black Saturday missive and responded to the words he wanted to hear in Khrushchev's first message.

But the president and the others were distraught and impatient—they didn't wait for a reply. That night, unbeknownst to many of the Ex Comm members—as if to add high dudgeon to the drama—the president's brother also played the part of Chamberlain and Churchill by offering the Soviet ambassador both a secret deal and an ultimatum—the essence of indecision. The president would be willing to secretly remove the Turkish missiles at a future date if the Soviets would dismantle their missiles immediately while the world watched. Robert Kennedy urged the ambassador to accept the deal or the United States would attack Cuba in a matter of days.[70] The president and his confidants didn't expect Khrushchev to accept the ultimatum. In Robert Kennedy's words:

The thought that disturbed him [the president] the most, and that made the prospect of war more fearful than it would otherwise have been, was the specter of the death of the children of this country, and all the world—the young people who had no say ... but whose lives would be snuffed out like everyone else's.[71]

(At the time, I was a not-so-innocent adolescent; nevertheless, I didn't see a good reason for snuffing out my life.) Khrushchev brought down the curtain on the drama; he unexpectedly accepted the Secret Deal and withdrew the missiles. As he explained:

The two most powerful nations of the world had been squared off against each other, each with its finger on the button. You'd have thought that war was inevitable. But both sides showed that if the desire to avoid war is strong enough, even the most pressing disputes can be solved by compromise.[72]

Although McNamara and Bundy vehemently denied the existence of such a quid pro quo, the Jupiter missiles were withdrawn from Turkey in April 1963.

Kennedy's bravura crisis is indelibly etched on the national consciousness as a metaphorical template for heroic confrontation. While, to understate the case, gradual escalation proved to be a tragic metaphor for conducting the Vietnam War, the trope still guides American nuclear endeavors. Nevertheless, despite this failure of the gradual escalation strategy, the Secret Deal, and the risks hazarded to remove strategically inconsequential missiles, the Cuban missile crisis itself became an arresting metaphor. As Ted Sorensen, one of the participants warned:

Ever since the successful resolution of that crisis, I have noted among many political and military figures a Cuban-missile-crisis-syndrome, which calls for a repetition in some other conflict of "Jack Kennedy's tough stand of October 1962 when he told the Russians with their missiles either to pull out or look out!"[73]

What If They Gave a Crisis and Nobody Came?

There is no doubt that if a character is shown on stage who goes through the most ordinary actions, and is suddenly revealed to be the president of the United States, his actions immediately assume a much greater magnitude, and post the possibilities of much greater meaning than if he is the corner grocer.
                                  —Arthur Miller's gloss on Willy Loman[74]

You may be interested to know that my father owned a small [grocery] store ... and all the Nixon boys worked there while going to school.
                         —Nixon to Khrushchev during the Kitchen Debate crisis[75]

Given Nixon's indifference to the Soviet nuclear submarine base in Cuba and Soviet threats during the Yom Kippur War, it may appear that he had no passion for crises. Nothing could be further from the truth for the author of *Six Crises*. The events just mentioned simply were not Nixon-style crises.

What, then, were vintage Nixon crises? True, Nixon intimated that, like Wilson or Churchill, he was a great statesman faced with fateful decisions that would make an indelible impact on history. But his deeds—especially his crisis narratives—suggest that he was more like Willy Loman, the feckless salesman who wanted to be well-liked in the here and now. Like the fictive Willy Loman, the real Nixon endured crises when he felt cheated by life because—despite his willingness to play the game—he knew he was not "well-liked" by the powers that be. As Willy confessed to his wife, "You know, the trouble is, Linda, people don't seem to take to me."[76] Nixon had similar apprehension: "It is true that of all the Presidents in this century, it is probably true, that I have less ... supporters in the press than any other President. I'm one of the most hated."[77]

Kennedy and Nixon did not suffer from the same vulnerabilities, nor were they bedeviled by the same crisis metaphors. It probably never occurred to the glamorous, charismatic Kennedy that he was not well-liked. His popularity increased even *after* the Bay of Pigs fiasco. No matter what, it would be out of character for Kennedy to reassure the world that "I am not a crook." Even in defeat, it's difficult to imagine a self-pitying Kennedy vowing, "You won't have Kennedy to kick around anymore."

Kennedy likened crises to the world-historical struggles of leaders such as Chamberlain and Churchill. Nixon's struggles to be "well-liked" are akin to the low tragedy of Willy Loman in *Death of a Salesman*. Arthur Miller's synopsis of his play might well serve as Nixon's epitaph:

It is the tragedy of a man who did believe that he alone was not meeting the qualifications laid down for mankind by those clean-shaven [new] frontiersmen who inhabit the peaks of broadcasting and advertising offices. From those forests ... he heard the thundering command to succeed as it ricochets down the newspaper-lined canyons of his city ... not a human voice, but a wind of a voice to which no human can reply in kind, except to stare into the mirror of failure.[78]

Miller explains that he wanted his audience to respond to the Loman script as follows: "They would not wonder about 'What happens next and why?' They would be thinking, 'Oh, God, of course!'"[79] In James Barber's biography, Nixon's character is an open book; his take on Nixon begins with an "Oh, God, of course!"

All of us should have known how Richard M. Nixon would approach his work as President. He came to office after 22 years as a politician and public figure. In speeches, interviews, and especially in his book *Six Crises*, Nixon had described and analyzed and defended in extraordinary detail his feelings, his reactions to events and personalities, his life history, and his special techniques for coping with life.[80]

Not surprisingly, *Six Crises* reveals what Nixon construed as crises. However, perhaps what is *not* construed as a crisis (or barely mentioned, for that matter) is more revealing. The book explores the critical challenges

Nixon believed he faced in his public service from about 1948 to 1960. World-historical challenges did not serve as Nixon crisis metaphors. The events *not* interpreted as a crisis include:

- The Berlin Blockade, 1948
- The victory of Chinese communism, 1949
- The detonation of the first Soviet atomic bomb, 1949
- The Korean War, 1950–1953
- The defeat of the French in Indochina, 1954
- The detonation of a Soviet hydrogen bomb, 1954
- The Soviet invasion of Hungary, 1956
- The Soviet Sputnik, 1957
- The advent of the Castro regime, 1959
- The U-2 incident, 1960

Just as Willy Loman's crises were precipitated by venal, personal affronts, defining Nixon crises are sparked by a host of affronts from slights (incurred during goodwill missions to South America and the Soviet Union) to orchestrated assaults on his character (such as the campaign fund episode and Watergate scandal.) Simply put, Nixon did not make a crisis move at Cienfuegos Bay because this impersonal event simply had no semblance to the petty—or at best impurely personal—embarrassments narrated in *Six Crises*.

His crisis narratives are highly stylized. In these sagas of personal embarrassment Nixon represents himself as a victimized seeker of truth and justice, a relentless crusader against communism suffering the calumny of the liberal establishment. We learn of the Checkers Speech in which Nixon refutes charges that he had an illegal slush fund but confesses to receiving an unreported gift—a Cocker Spaniel puppy his daughter named "Checkers." We are told of an episode in Latin America in which a protestor harassed his motorcade. A Secret Service agent grabbed the "weirdo" and allowed Nixon to kick him in the shins, thereby resolving the crisis.

However, a closer look at a personal confrontation with Khrushchev during the Kitchen Debate crisis reveals a great deal about the presidential character and the nature of his crises. Nixon begins the narrative by quoting his adversary's comments on the Captive Nations Resolution passed by Congress in 1959:

"The resolution stinks. It stinks like fresh horse shit, and nothing smells worse than that!" I recalled from my briefing materials that Khrushchev had worked as a pig herder in his youth.... I replied in a conversational tone: "I am afraid that that Chairman is mistaken. There is something worse ... pig shit."[81]

The crises Nixon endured during his visit to Moscow in the summer of 1959 had a distinctly domestic air. The ceremonial visit marked by petty, often vulgar, encounters with Khrushchev precipitated personal crises. And yet, Nixon insists that "Every move in this crisis-laden struggle was important. At stake was world peace and the survival of freedom."[82] Given the stakes, Nixon dilates about his exchange of insults and one-upmanship. He narrates a series of small crises that cascaded in the American model city exhibit set up in Moscow. The exchange of insults, accusations, and threats began in Khrushchev's office, climbed the ladder of escalation in the model TV studio, continued at the model grocery store, and culminated in a defining moment in the model kitchen.

The unceremonious beginning of the ceremonial visit portended the coming crises. Not one to forget slights, real or imagined, Nixon would rail about the cool reception that was merely correct, nothing more—no pomp and circumstance. There were no bands, no anthems, and no crowds. The visit was not breaking news in the Soviet papers.[83]

As we have already seen, Nixon—according to his lights—successfully managed the Captive Nations Resolution mini-crisis; he readied himself for loftier feats. In the model television studio Khrushchev boasted that "When we catch up with you, in passing you by, we will wave to you. Then, if you wish, we can stop and say: Please follow us."[84] Defending the honor of the nation, Nixon reminded his nemesis that "You don't know everything!" To which the chairman replied, "If I don't know everything, you don't know anything about communism—except fear of it."[85] Nixon reports that he comported himself well during these exchanges; he wasn't at a loss for words. However, he allows that during the studio confrontation, it was not the time to take him on. But the moment of truth would soon dawn in a dramatic showdown—in the kitchen.

On the way to the kitchen, the pair passed the model grocery store, prompting Nixon to try to charm Khrushchev with a remark about his father's grocery. But charm, as Nixon's advisors warned, was not the vice president's strongest suit. The chairman was unmoved; still exercised by the Captive Nations Resolution he retorted, "All shopkeepers are thieves." Nixon couldn't let this pass. He reminded Khrushchev that he saw people weighing food "after they had bought it from the State [store]."[86]

Nixon recalls that the discussion in the kitchen began innocently enough as the two officials explored the merits of washing machines. Nixon, however, became agitated when Khrushchev charged that American products suffered from planned obsolescence. Nixon detailed the vast consumer choices available in his country only to be interrupted by yet another churlish Khrushchev diatribe about American washing machines. Nixon moralized that competition in washing machines was preferable to competition in rockets. Khrushchev went ballistic, so to speak: jabbing his finger into the vice presidential chest, he indicted American generals as warmongers.

A crisis was at hand; decorum unraveled. Nixon had to strike back, lest he leave the impression that "the second-highest official of the United States, and the government I represented were dealing with Khrushchev from a position of weakness."[87] Nixon didn't need the help of the Secret Service this time. Unable to conjure-up a flexible response he resorted to massive retaliation: The Vice President of the United States poked Khrushchev with *his* finger and urged that if war comes, both countries lose. But this robust response and exhortation did not resolve the crisis. The crisis escalated as arguments raged as to whether the Nixon and Khrushchev grandchildren would live under communism or capitalism. (Khrushchev's son, Sergi, is now an American citizen.) Nixon assures us that he responded to his adversary's threats and accusation in kind. He reports that Khrushchev finally relented—the crisis was resolved with words, not fisticuffs. Nixon's nemesis agreed that he too wanted peace and friendship with all nations, especially America. The crisis ended as Nixon put his hand on the chairman's shoulder and confessed, "I'm afraid I haven't been a very good host." Suddenly conciliatory, Chairman Khrushchev turned to the American guide and thanked the "housewife for letting us use her kitchen for our argument."[88]

The wire services picked up the picture of Nixon jabbing Khrushchev. In one of his more successful efforts at crisis management, Nixon got extraordinary political mileage from the image—it became a veritable Nixon icon. Had Brezhnev confronted Nixon personally in October of 1970, and poked his fingers in Nixon's ribs while the world watched, there might have been a Cienfuegos crisis.

Dr. Kissinger's Crisis Remedies

It makes no difference whether ... [a statesman's] subjects be willing or unwilling: they may rule with or without a code of laws.... It is the same with doctors. We do not assess the medical qualification of a doctor by the degree of willingness ... to submit ... to their painful treatment. Doctors are still doctors whether they work according to fixed prescriptions or without them.... We must insist that in this disinterested scientific ability we see the distinguishing mark of the true authority in medicine—and of true authority everywhere else as well.

—Plato, the *Statesman*[89]

He [the statesman] owes it to his people to strive, to create, and to resist the decay that besets all human institutions.

—Henry Kissinger[90]

Political actors such as Dr. Kissinger liken themselves to premier medical specialists well versed in diagnosing and treating afflictions of the international body politic by restoring homeostasis. Accordingly, he likened a crisis to a serious medical problem best treated by the most accomplished specialist. This metaphor originated, perhaps, with Plato and was succinctly framed by Goethe when he wrote: "All transitions are crises, and is a crisis not a sickness?"[91]

Adversaries are likened to a disease. George Kennan, for example, relied upon various physiological and psychological metaphors to diagnose the Soviet affliction and to prescribe the proper remedy to contain the disease.[92] Unlike those who take a crisis personally by likening the challenge to the ultimate test of their existential identity, those who invoke medical metaphors likened themselves to physician/statesmen responsible for treating other's afflictions, not their own. The physician/statesman remains cool, collected, and strictly professional. Likened to a serious medical affliction, the challenge is viewed with clinical detachment.

The medical genre is vintage Kissinger. Seldom accused of excessive modesty, Kissinger, conceived of himself as the "doctor of diplomacy" both knowledgeable and wise. Dr. Kissinger diagnosed crises as "symptoms of deeper problems which if allowed to fester would prove increasingly unmanageable.... [The correct] concept of our fundamental national interest would provide a ballast of restraint and assurance of continuity."[93] Confronting a crisis, Kissinger took charge, excluded amateurs (such as Nixon), diagnosed the malady, prescribed the tried-and-true treatment—dissembling diplomacy—and intervened at the right moment to restore homeostasis in the international body politic. This regimen resulted in the quiet, peaceful resolution of what could have been the most harrowing episode of the Cold War.

Just as Kennedy established the Ex Comm to manage the Cuban missile crisis, the Nixon/Kissinger administration established the Washington Strategic Action Group (WSAG) to manage crises. Kissinger convened the group in response to Soviet moves at Cienfuegos Bay. Curiously, although the perceived threat was more harrowing than the perceived threat in 1962, the WSAG response was surprisingly conciliatory. No hawks demanded an immediate air strike and invasion. And no one proposed public confrontations, blockades, and ultimatums. Only different species of doves inhabited the WSAG aviary.

Nixon offered impromptu suggestions about putting missiles back in Turkey or a submarine base in the Black Sea. But Kissinger rejected such "amateurish" prescriptions as a waste of time. Nixon became indifferent even as Soviet fighters harassed American reconnaissance planes. "Nixon," in Kissinger's words, "urged me to play it all down."[94]

Certain members of the WSAG likened the Soviet base to a chronic problem to be resolved in due course, not a medical emergency. Secretary of State Rogers suggested a summit meeting or secret talks at a future date. Secretary of Defense Melvin Laird (usually regarded as a hawk) was surprisingly dovish. He urged that no crisis existed: American forces could deter any Soviet threat.[95]

Kissinger disagreed. Obviously, the American arsenal did not deter the Soviets from undermining the balance of power by violating the understanding that resolved the 1962 confrontation by secretly building a nuclear base once again in Cuba. He endorsed an assessment that the secretary of defense evidently rejected—the assessment of the secretary's own "shop." In addition to the obvious—unlike the land-based missile of 1962, submarines are mobile and virtually undetectable—the Department of Defense concluded that the Cienfuegos base would enable Soviet submarines to increase their operation time away from port. Specifically, the base would enable the submarines to enhance their capacity to operate in the Gulf of Mexico. This capacity would bring additional American territory within range of "invisible" nuclear submarines.[96]

Kissinger concluded that the American arsenal alone could not preserve international homeostasis. Worse yet, doing nothing or deferring action would send the wrong message: The Soviets might be emboldened to make provocative moves elsewhere. Pleading with an indifferent Nixon, Kissinger urged that he and Dobrynin should meet secretly to resolve the situation. Nixon denied the request and prepared for his vacation. Kissinger claims that a fortuitous event occurred a few days later: an official inadvertently briefed the press on the Soviet base. (Seymour Hersh claims that Kissinger was responsible for the leak.[97])

Kissinger persuaded Nixon that, due to the leak, a dangerous public confrontation was imminent. Accordingly, he must be permitted to settle matters quickly and quietly with Dobrynin. Nixon reluctantly agreed, but insisted that his national security advisor must accompany him to Europe lest he promote the confrontation as a crisis.

Kissinger's account of his press conference presents awesome interpretive difficulties. He is obviously proud of what he portrays as cleverly contrived dissembling and duplicity. But, given his reputation, it is difficult not to suspect that Kissinger isn't entirely candid, even about his dissembling! He conjured up a carefully crafted mixture of ambiguity, half-truth, and guile designed to quell public alarm while bestowing diplomatic leverage with Dobrynin.

Predictably, when asked whether the president was going abroad at an inauspicious time, Kissinger decided not to promote the confrontation as a crisis—at least to the public. After reiterating the informal understanding that resolved the 1962 episode, he asserted the opposite of what he believed (or so he claims): "We are not ... in a position to say exactly what they [the Soviets] mean.... [And] nothing very rapid and dramatic is likely to occur."[98] Ironically, even those who were justly suspicious of Kissinger got the right message—precisely because they were suspicious. In any event, as Kissinger would soon discover, the construction of the Soviet base stopped after the press conference.

Kissinger claims that, based upon his reputation, he hoped that the public would conclude that he was not truthful—he was concealing a momentous crisis. Nixon critics such as senators Frank Church and William Fulbright fell for the rhetorical trap—they would not be taken in, or so they thought. They convinced themselves that Kissinger was really trying to promote a crisis but they wouldn't fall for it. As Kissinger quips, "Fulbright voiced his skepticism on 'Issues and Answers,' helpfully, just as the Nixon party departed from Washington." The senator complained that "nearly every year just before we have an appropriations bill in the Senate, we get these stories."[99]

He explained to Dobrynin that his press conference pronouncement "had been carefully chosen to suggest that the United States had not yet made up its mind about the precise nature of Soviet activities in Cienfeugos."[100] He stressed that he misled the American public to give the Soviets a face-saving opportunity to dismantle the base without a public spectacle. However, in reality, American leaders viewed the situation with the "utmost gravity": the base simply could not remain. If the Soviets dismantle the base immediately, their provocation would simply be represented as a "training exercise."

Nixon and Kissinger returned in early October. Kissinger met with Dobrynin and learned—with considerable satisfaction—that the Soviets agreed to abide by the informal understanding: no submarines with operational nuclear weapons would be based in Cuba. Kissinger concludes: "Rather than a dramatic confrontation on the order of 1962, we considered that quiet diplomacy was best suited to giving the USSR an opportunity to withdraw without humiliation."[101]

It would be audacious to presuppose that we know the whole story about the Cienfuegos incident or any other crisis for that matter. As Haldeman discloses: "Most of the material relating to this incident [Cienfuegos] was deleted from my diary by the government for national security reasons."[102]

For a time Kissinger's brand of dissembling and skillful application of realpolitik successfully resolved a series of confrontations. But, as he would discover, a time would come when—given his reputation—neither friend nor foe would support his tropes. Everyone from North Vietnamese officials to Republican critics rejected his self-serving metaphors. In five years he would come to lament communist victories in Vietnam and Cambodia: "I'm the only secretary of state who has lost two countries in three weeks."[103]

The Cuban Brigade Crisis

Fighting a National Conservative Political Action Committee campaign in Idaho which branded him "soft" on . . . the Soviet Union, [Senator Frank]

Church was worried that a news leak [about a brigade of Soviet soldiers
in Cuba] would make his earlier denial of Soviet forces look either gull-
ible or irresponsible. An anti-Church commercial had shown Church and
Fidel Castro smoking cigars together.... Church decided the news [of the
brigade] had to come from him. He was fighting for his political life in the
face of a growing wave of conservatism.

—Fen Osler Hampson[104]

In 1979 as President Jimmy Carter and his party prepared for the election, satellite imagery revealed a brigade of approximately 5,000 Soviet
troops in Cuba. The significance was contested. The National Security
Agency (NSA) suspected the brigade was deployed to engage in combat
or to protect nuclear weapons installations. However, the CIA and the
Department of State did not share this assessment. In any case, due to its
size and lack of air and amphibious support, no one concluded that the
brigade presented a threat to the American homeland.[105] And no one in
the Carter administration construed the brigade as a strategic threat to
any other nation, let alone a formidable crisis. However, the president and
his associates were not indifferent to the political ramifications of appearances and symbols.

The conservative opponents of Carter and Church were eager to
exploit the NSA assessment primarily for domestic political reasons.
When it appeared that the assessment would be leaked to the press,
Church obtained permission to preempt the conservatives by publicly
denouncing the existence of the brigade. The senator and the president
concurred that this move was politically expedient. Carter invoked grave,
dramatic oratory to depict the threat and to denounce Soviet actions in
general. Despite their initial enthusiasm for SALT II (an arms reduction
treaty), Carter and his associates succumbed to political expediency and
insisted that the treaty could not be ratified while the brigade remained
in Cuba.

Outraged and incredulous, Dobrynin—still Soviet ambassador after
all these years—reminded Ambassador Ralph Earle (the principal SALT
II negotiator at the time) that, as part of the understanding forged by
Kennedy and ratified by Nixon, the United States had agreed to allow
Soviet troops in Cuba. Indeed, Dobrynin reminded Earle that Soviet troops
had been in Cuba for years. In any case, surely it was inconceivable that
5,000 troops without air or sea support threatened the United States.[106]
Further intelligence analysis corroborated Dobrynin's claim. Nevertheless,
the majority of the Senate Foreign Relations Committee argued that the
Soviets couldn't be trusted; the SALT II treaty was rejected.

Despite their efforts to liken a brigade of 5,000 soldiers to a crisis that
threatened the American homeland, Carter, Church, and other liberal dem-
ocrats lost the election. American foreign policy was subject to derision and

U.S./Soviet relations plummeted to a new low. As Hampson concludes: "The Treaty was withdrawn with enormous cost to the Carter presidency and to détente itself."[107]

Was all of this necessary? Many of the players in these crises insist that it was necessary to make crisis moves due to international exigencies and the pressures of domestic politics. What do they have in mind when they speak of such necessities?

CHAPTER 8

Necessity: The Mother of Mayhem

[Political actors] speak their lines and suffer their fate in accordance with the text conceived in terms of them but not by them.

—Isaiah Berlin[1]

I remember a spring day in Berkeley: hills green as Ireland, air pungent with eucalyptus. An alumnus, Robert McNamara, reflected upon his role in the Cuban missile crisis before a small group assembled in a shaded glen. Unlike his successors in the Reagan administration, the former secretary of defense spoke not of a "nuclear springtime" in which the U.S. would "survive and prevail" in a nuclear war due to clever strategy and advanced weaponry. No. He lamented about how close the world came to unparalleled catastrophe. The Soviets, it seems, were not expected to obey Kennedy's ultimatum: Withdraw the missiles from Cuba within 48 hours or suffer an American attack. The expected outcome was full-scale, thermonuclear war between the United States and the Soviet Union. According to Theodore Sorensen (editor of Robert Kennedy's memoir on the crisis) the president's brother ruminated about the morality of risking such a conflagration:

It was Senator Kennedy's intention to add a discussion of the basic ethical question involved: what, if any circumstances or justification gives this government or any government the moral right to bring its people and possibly all people under the shadow of nuclear destruction?[2]

That such a question could be asked is profoundly disturbing. In any case, during his retrospective, McNamara reiterated what he asserted time and again in his texts and during the secretly recorded Ex Comm deliberations: Had the Soviets failed to comply with the ultimatum, it would have been *necessary* for him to order an attack on Soviet bases in Cuba—there was no choice. Specifically, had the Soviets responded as expected it would have been *necessary* for him to order a nuclear attack on the Soviet homeland resulting in full-scale nuclear war between the superpowers.

McNamara was neither the first nor the last to represent certain actions as somehow "necessary." In Thucydides' *Melian Dialogue* we learn that the Athenian generals insisted that conquest was necessary, a "necessity of nature."[3] Thucydides agrees. His narratives—afforded canonical status by many contemporary political realists as we've seen—are sagas of historical inevitability: certain choices are simply unavoidable in particular situations. Given this hard determinism, discussions of morality are futile. As Michael Walzer avers in his gloss on Thucydides: "One could no more criticize the Athenians for their wartime policies than one could criticize a stone for falling downwards."[4]

Subsequent disasters, episodes of cruelty and folly, are almost always depicted as forlorn necessities, the result of inexorable powers somehow operating beyond the will and behind the backs of decision-makers. Hebrew zealots had to immolate themselves, Christian crusaders had no choice but to liberate the Holy Land, and surely the cruel machinations of the Medicis were inevitable.

Such talk about necessity, of course, is no relic of the dim past. During World War I the Germans claimed they had no choice: neutral Belgium had to be invaded. As Chancellor von Bethmann Hollweg explained to the Reichstag: "Gentlemen, we are now in a state of necessity, and necessity knows no law. Our troops have already entered Belgium territory."[5]

And, to be sure, American adversaries are not the only ones who justify breaking treaties and civilized mores in the name of necessity. The strategic terror bombing, culminating in the destruction of Hiroshima and Nagasaki, was depicted as a necessity. Henry Stimson, Truman's secretary of war, offered a justification that became received wisdom: "No man, in our position and subject to our responsibilities, holding in his hand a weapon of such possibilities for ... saving those lives could have failed to use it."[6] McGeorge Bundy (Stimson's subordinate at the time) echoed this rationale in his retrospective:

Historically almost predestined, by the manner of its birth and its development, made doubly dramatic by the fateful coincidence that it was ready just when it might be decisive, and not headed off by a carefully designed alternative ... the bomb dropped on Hiroshima surely helped to end a fearful war.[7]

To reiterate, Robert Kennedy's memoir on the crisis reveals that he and his brother agreed: compelling the Soviets to remove their missiles from Cuba was necessary—there was no other choice: "It looks really mean, doesn't it," said the president. "But then, really there was no other choice."[8]

President Lyndon Johnson urged that it was necessary to launch Operation Rolling Thunder, the massive aerial bombardment of Vietnam. It was necessary for Nixon to "stay the course," and not "cut and run" in Vietnam. And, to be sure, it was necessary for the Bush administration to invade and occupy Iraq. As Condoleezza Rice explains: "You have to look at the body of evidence and say what does this require the United States to do? Then you are compelled to act."[9] There is no need to compound examples of decision-makers invoking "necessity" to justify their decisions. Indeed, it would be difficult to think of a decision-maker who *didn't* invoke necessity to account for morally dubious or ultimately disastrous decisions. (Salutary developments, of course, are represented as a leader's autonomous and courageous choice; he could have done otherwise, but—according to the self-serving rhetoric typical of the political spectacle—he had the intelligence and fortitude to do the right thing.)

"Necessity" is one of the most overused terms in strategic discourse. It is a primary metaphor that likens scenarios and actions to compulsions foisted upon decision-makers—allegedly, they have no choice. However, unlike the invocation of the preceding primary metaphors, decision-makers seldom invoke secondary metaphors to explain the meaning of necessity. (As we've seen, the balance of power is likened to an antique laboratory scale or biologic homeostasis; deterrence is likened to unfriendly persuasion through reason or terror; and crises are likened to existential tests or medical emergencies.) But apparently, the necessity of a situation just *is*—you either recognize the inevitability of an action or you don't.

This realization raises the problem discussed in the remainder of this chapter: *What do decision-makers mean, what do they have in mind, when they invoke "necessity" to explain their actions?* They aren't saying. What then are decision-makers talking about when they invoke "necessity"; what's the point? The short answer is "I'm not sure!" Accessing the mindset of others, to understate the case, is replete with daunting philosophic difficulties. Starting with the obvious, decision-makers are not routinely asked what they mean when they invoke "necessity": Don't ask, don't tell! Just as well. If pressed, a leader probably couldn't explain. Governing elites (or their speechwriters) don't have philosophers in mind when they craft their discourse: they are inattentive to the needs of those of us trying to get a handle on nuclear strategy. It would be considerate if they added codas to their discourse by avowing that they would not be enchanted by language, and that, accordingly, they would move from the abstract to the concrete by offering clear and distinct definitions. Invoking, perhaps, B. F. Skinner, they might argue for hard determinism—or soften it a bit with the perspective of William James's "soft determinism," the notion that individual volition, rather than external forces, can—in favorable circumstances—be the cause of action.

Turning to real possibilities, could it be that "necessity" is simply a rhetorical device, an argument-stopping appellation? The notion could simply be part and parcel of the rhetorical arsenal designed to stop questioning, let alone argumentation. Consider the available rhetorical weaponry. Proposals are quashed by indicting them as unrealistic, or worse yet, un-American, soft on terrorism, or extremist. The more sophisticated can be quieted with statistical claims that stop inquiry because "everybody knows" the virtues of Americanism, moderation, or the incontrovertible power of numbers. Likewise, "everybody knows" that, as Rice declares, sometimes you are compelled to act; you have no choice—"Ya gotta do what ya gotta do!"

Now I usually resist the temptation to claim that governing elites are compulsive truth-tellers. Nevertheless, it's entirely possible that, on occasion, decision-makers sincerely believe that they had no choice—their actions were somehow necessary. If decision-makers sincerely believe that their actions were somehow "necessary," how do we gain access to their mindsets, to their imaginative universe of meanings? This remains a vexing problem indeed, particularly because strategizing is scaffolded upon presuppositions regarding the mentality of those who manage the American arsenal and their foes. If it's often difficult to understand what's going on with your colleagues down the hall—or even within your own life-dramas, how then can we gain access to the consciousness and sensibility of those far removed from our personal and professional lives? To reiterate, decision-makers themselves are not helpful: They merely assert that an action was necessary—end of story. These elites may truly believe that they had no choice, and yet, they aren't entirely clear as to why this was so. Could it be that sincere decision-makers (if this is not an oxymoron) mean what they say but don't say what they mean because they are not mindful as to what they have in mind? Or could it be that the necessity of an action is so transparent, so self-evident, that it requires no explanation? Through a process of elimination perhaps we can get some clue as to what decision-makers have in mind. Accordingly, I begin rather confidently by outlining what decision-makers *don't* have in mind. Next I turn to Walzer's efforts to explicate the concept of necessity in a variety of contexts. I find his argument that genuine necessity refers to a supreme emergency useful yet problematic: He bases his account of a real supreme emergency on his reading of the "moral law." Since I have doubts about the existence of such a law, I suggest that the notion of necessity is part and parcel of a tacit, preconscious script in which one scenario follows another.

WHAT "NECESSITY" IS NOT

"History," harmless history, when everything unexpected in its own time is chronicled on the page as inevitable. The terror of the unforeseen is what the science of history hides, turning a disaster into an epic.

—Philip Roth[10]

It is fairly clear what elites do *not* have in mind when they absolve themselves of blame and guilt for their scenarios and improvisations by invoking necessity:

• Elites do not enter the metaphysical fray by urging that freedom of the will is illusory. Modern governing elites don't claim that their thoughts and actions are predetermined by God, genetics, or operant conditioning. Curiously, their determinism is conveniently selective. It is worth reiterating that "necessity" is invoked to account for decisions that are morally dubious, if not disastrous. But salutary developments are not represented as the outcome of inevitable processes. On the contrary, presidents take credit for peace and prosperity, lower rates of crime, fewer sun spots, and less tooth decay. But they shun responsibility for detonating nuclear weapons or risking nuclear war. Evidently, only dubious or disastrous decisions just can't be helped. What are they talking about?

• Again, it is clear what leaders are *not* talking about—logical necessity. Even a cursory glance at their promises and deeds reveals that they are not obsessed with logical consistency—a valid syllogism is not something to die for. True, McNamara's jeremiad can be represented as a *modus ponens* argument:

  • If American troops are attacked in Cuba, nuclear retaliation is necessary.
  • American troops *are* attacked.
  • Therefore, nuclear retaliation is necessary.

Had a nuclear exchange occurred, would we excuse McNamara if he explained that his actions logically followed from his premise? The premise, of course, begs the question: *Why* is retaliation necessary? No answer is given. Finally, as those of us who teach logic lament, no inexorable force acts upon students that compels them to accept, let alone to act upon, the implications of their premises. Surely we would forgive leaders who valued life over logic. Let's hope there is a choice between the logic of annihilation and human survival.

• When governing elites invoke "necessity" I doubt that they have the causal-mechanical necessity of classical physics in mind. They don't represent themselves as preprogrammed mechanisms—something akin to billiard balls acted upon by forces beyond their control. To drop yet another philosophic name, Kierkegaard was right: "Life is lived forward but thought backward." The actual process of decision-making within and between individuals at critical junctures is usually agonizing and acrimonious: What is necessary or inevitable is far from obvious. "Necessity" is imposed ex post facto to give clarity and consistency to the process.[11] In any case, as Hume taught, attributing causal necessity to events is a product of habituated imagination, not observation.

- By psychological necessity I understand abject coercion—do or die! However, no one held a gun to the heads of Truman, McNamara, Kennedy, or Rice. They would not have perished had they acted otherwise. True, it might have been a bad career move not to use nuclear weapons against Japan or not to coerce the Soviets to remove their Cuban missiles (indeed, in recently declassified tapes we learn that LBJ decided that escalating the Vietnam War was a good career move). Nevertheless, these leaders would have survived and prospered even if their grandiose ambitions had been thwarted.

- Are governing elites bound by moral necessity? Such necessity involves obligations such as promise keeping. Of course, as we learn in the opening pages of the *Republic,* promise keeping is not always—to mix metaphors—kosher. Further, it is not overly cynical to suggest that politicians do not suffer an insurmountable compulsion to keep promises. True, JKF promised to compel the Soviets to remove the missiles. However, had the Cuban missile crisis been resolved with nuclear war rather than with dissembling words, any survivor would find little comfort in knowing that Kennedy kept his word. And, had the crisis ended disastrously (as the "best and brightest" expected), surviving historians would, no doubt, represent the outcome as somehow inevitable.

NECESSARY EVILS AS SUPREME EMERGENCIES

> He has no innocent alternatives, and he knows it, at least in the beginning. But once he *has* chosen, he pretends there was no choice; having murdered Iphigenia he forgets her.... Having killed the innocent child, he is "free" to murder the innocent children at Troy.
>
> —A gloss on Agamemnon[12]

In his influential *Just and Unjust Wars* Walzer analyzes the apparent meanings attached to the concept of necessity in diverse contexts. He argues that in many situations the concept is a disingenuous rhetorical device, a facile rationalization, for violating the usual rules of combat, if not of human decency. As he quips: "Everyone's troubles make a crisis. 'Emergency' and 'crisis' are cant words used to prepare our minds for acts of brutality."[13] However, in other limited contexts, according to Walzer, certain necessary evils are truly justified. Indeed, (as Walzer allows with considerable fear and trembling) certain situations are so threatening in the extreme that nuclear terrorism and murder of the innocent are necessary evils. (But understandably, he doesn't offer "just terrorism" and "just murder" as subtitles for his book.)

Borrowing from Churchill's wartime lexicon, he invokes a secondary metaphor—supreme emergency—to reveal the true meaning of necessity. These situations are marked by an unmistakable threat of imminent, horrific danger. Accordingly, there is no choice: both decision-makers and combatants *must* violate the usual rules and mores. As he quips rather sardonically: certain horrific threats "bring us under the rule of necessity (and necessity knows no rules)."[14] (Actually, the rule of necessity expresses the "all's fair rule": all's fair in love and war.)

Walzer cautions that—given the enormity of the consequences—determining whether a supreme emergency truly exists requires close study, the best advice, and exploration of viable alternatives. Only such careful, penetrating analysis can determine whether the unmistakable threat of catastrophe is close at hand.[15] Unfortunately, as Walzer recognizes, decision-makers seldom rely upon these diligent procedures to determine whether they actually face exigent circumstances.

Walzer's analysis is generally clear, adroit, and insightful. And yet (as is the case with many ethicists) Walzer presupposes that he is somehow privy to *the* moral law. Accordingly, he seems to hold that his approval or disapproval of certain practices is more than a personal statement. Specifically, he presupposes that his account of what is *truly* necessary has a sturdy objective foundation in the moral law. I hasten to add that given Walzer's erudition and accomplishments his prescriptions shouldn't be dismissed because—in the final analysis—they are personal statements; on the contrary, not all personal statements are created equal. Walzer's pronouncements are obviously based upon the sort of analysis he prescribes. That said, what I object to is the magisterial reification of such analysis as moral law.

Even if we grant the existence of objective moral we are beset by daunting, if not irresolvable, issues: There is no consensus as to the nature of *the* moral law and what it legislates. Both Hindus and Muslims, for example, entertain notions akin to supreme emergency. But exigent circumstances in India (to understate the case) are seldom exigent circumstances in Pakistan. Moreover the leaders of these nations and their constituents do not necessarily share the American view of what constitutes exigent circumstances. Closer to home, not all American scholars share Walzer's view as to what constitutes a supreme emergency. Walzer (as we shall see) argues that the horrific threat posed by nuclear deterrence was necessary in light of the Soviet threat. However, political theorist Henry Shue argues that the threat—real or imagined—did not constitute a supreme emergency.[16]

Indeed, Walzer goes into considerable detail to try to illustrate that those who justify odious deeds by invoking notions akin to supreme emergency are often morally suspect, if not disingenuous—despite (or because of) their allusion to transcendent principles. Looking at World War I, he refers to *Kreigsraison*: the German term for the necessities of war. He bestows his imprimatur upon killing combatants and civilians directly supporting the destructive activities of enemy combatants. As he explains: "Sometimes in conditions of extremity ... commanders must commit murder or they must order others to commit it. And then they are murderers, though in a good cause."[17]

However, it is not necessary—in his reading of the moral law—to kill civilians who merely keep soldiers alive. This notion of necessities of war (used as we've seen to justify the invasion of Belgium) was not actually about necessity, in Walzer's view. It was about cost/risk/benefit analysis: compelling the submission of the enemy with the least possible expenditure of life, time, or money.[18] Such expediency does not constitute a supreme emergency.

Turning to World War II he disputes claims that the Allied strategic bombing of German and Japanese cities was necessary. Much of this deliberate destruction of civilians occurred *after* it was apparent to Churchill and the others that Nazi plans to conquer Great Britain had failed. Walzer cites evidence that suggests this strategic bombing was designed to boost British and American morale, and to exact revenge.

Likewise, contrary to the claims of the Truman administration, and subsequent apologists, the destruction of Hiroshima and Nagasaki was unnecessary, if not gratuitous. No one believed that the Japanese were about to win the war and destroy Western civilization in the summer of 1945. Exacting an unconditional surrender, in Walzer's view, does not justify killing hundreds of thousands of civilians. (Curiously, the Japanese did not surrender unconditionally after the atomic bombing; they kept their emperor.). Finally, even if the bombing ultimately saved lives by obviating the need for an invasion of Japan, such utilitarian calculations don't justify American actions. Walzer offers a salient distinction: "Our purpose was not to avert a 'butchery' that someone else was threatening, but one that we were threatening.... What supreme emergency justified the ... attacks on Japanese cities?"[19]

What then truly constitutes a supreme emergency? In Walzer's view the Nazi threat was the archetypal supreme emergency. Understandably, he has no need to dilate about the obvious—the hideous nature of Nazism. His indictment is succinct. The triumph of Nazism represented imminent danger in the extreme, the apotheosis of evil: the ultimate threat to decency and to civilization itself: "When Churchill said that a German victory ... 'would be fatal, not only to ourselves, but to the independent life of every small country in Europe,' he was speaking the exact truth."[20] The enormity of this threat, as we've seen, prompted pacifists to devote their talents to building the atomic bomb. The threat demanded that the Allies do everything necessary to defeat the Nazis. (However, to reiterate, the strategic terror bombing in Walzer's view, was unnecessary.)

Walzer is at his best when he acknowledges the troubling difficulties and moral dilemmas inherent in his analysis. He invites the reader to consider the possibility that only one nation—say Great Britain—was at risk. He asserts that the moral law permits the British—or apparently any other community—to do what they must to preserve their identity. He acknowledges that this position causes him considerable discomfort. He believes that an individual is not permitted to kill the innocent to save himself, but a community is obliged to do so in an extreme emergency, i.e. an imminent threat to its existence. He allows that he can't account for the double standard without alluding to nonexistent occult properties of collectives. Nevertheless he struggles to justify his position by suggesting that while leaders may nobly sacrifice themselves to uphold the moral law, they have no right to sacrifice their countrymen.[21] (Apparently from time immemorial leaders have ignored the moral law or read it differently. One would be hard pressed to find instances when leaders have not enthusiastically sacrificed their countrymen for causes both noble and ignoble.)

Likewise, unlike many strategists, Walzer is not evangelical about deterrence; he is profoundly troubled. His definition is on point: deterrence avoids conflict by threatening immoral retaliation in response to an immoral attack.[22] He calls things by their right name—terrorism: "The threat produces a 'balance of terror.'"[23] He understands why some regard such terrorism as grossly immoral. Obviously, deterrence credibly threatens to murder tens of millions of innocent citizens: Surely intending to carry out such a threat—to make deterrence robust and credible—is not the highest expression of morality.

As if to corroborate Niebuhr's thesis about moral man and immoral society,[24] Walzer illustrates that acts judged heinous within a nation's border are often regarded as necessary, if not virtuous, in international affairs: "If the state should seek to prevent murder by threatening to kill the family and friends of every murderer—a domestic version of ... 'massive retaliation,' surely that would be a repugnant policy."[25] And yet, Walzer bestows his qualified acceptance upon deterrence. This acceptance, with considerable misgivings, is based upon his perception of the Soviet threat as a supreme emergency. He claims that, during the Cold War, the Soviets threatened atomic blackmail, domination by Stalinist regimes, and nuclear destruction. Supposedly, the threat posed by the American nuclear arsenal prevented such catastrophic events. (As I've argued in Chapter 6, this may well be a classic post hoc argument: perhaps these events didn't occur because—save for the American invasion of Vladivostok in 1919—there was no precedent for warfare between the Soviet Union and the United States.)

Walzer is in good company—and in bad company—in invoking the notion of supreme emergency to justify necessary evils. Supreme emergency is a cross-cultural artifact. The all's fair rule is used promiscuously in love and war. In an essay on Islamic ethics we find that the notion of necessity (*darura*) allows "Muslim commanders wide latitude on the grounds of military necessity, even if this resulted in large-scale death of noncombatants." And, to be sure, all the usual inhibitions are suspended when Muslim communities face destruction.[26] Unfortunately, certain Islamic fundamentalists interpret the meaning of such destruction broadly as any encouragement of Western values.

Contrary to the popular stereotype, not all the Buddhist sages advocate unconditional pacifism. As David Chapell reveals, there is a version of Buddhist ethics that "justifies WMD [weapons of mass destruction] as a deterrent in an extreme emergency."[27] The history of nations with large Buddhist populations, such as Japan and Vietnam, suggests that Buddhists are not always gentle advocates of nonviolence.

And, apparently the Bush administration conceives of the post-9/11 world as a realm in which all's fair. The attack on America is conceptualized as an act of war, a supreme emergency which necessitates disregarding traditional treaties and inhibitions about torture. In her article on outsourcing torture, Jane Mayer documents a practice the American intelligence community euphemistically labels "extraordinary rendition" (a term that reminds one of the latest television technology, not unbearable suffering). Suspects are sent to Egypt and other American allies to be tortured. As she writes: "After September 11th ... the program expanded beyond recognition—becoming according to a former CIA official 'an abomination.'"[28]

Two realizations emerge from this chronicle of the notion of "supreme emergency":

1. The notion is widely invoked at virtually every time and place to justify actions ranging from torturing and murdering an innocent person (in a good cause) to nuclear terrorism—the credible threat to murder hundreds of millions;
2. Those who take these actions insist they act in accord with transcendent moral principles rather than personal predilection, expediency, or bloodlust.

That there are so many diverse and conflicting interpretations of putatively objective moral principles suggest we must look elsewhere to understand the nature and meaning of necessity.

NECESSITY AS NARRATIVE

> Roles may be reified in the same manner as institutions. The sector of self-consciousness that has been objectified in the role is then apprehended as an inevitable fate, for which an individual may disclaim responsibility. This kind of reification is the statement "I have no choice in the matter. I have to act this way because of my position."
>
> —Peter Berger and Thomas Luckman[29]

Wherein lies the "necessity" that leaders invoke when they shun responsibility for morally dubious or unequivocally disastrous actions? As we've seen, they may merely be invoking argument-stopping rhetoric or they may be clueless about what they mean. I doubt, however, that they are reading—or misreading—the moral law. I suspect that, unwittingly, they are telling a story, a script couched in what Rorty calls a "final vocabulary"; it is—in the cliché of a popular quiz show—their "final answer."

The story they are telling is a subcultural narrative, a largely preconscious script they improvise to give their actions meaning, direction, and justification. Usually dismissive about breathtaking universal claims regarding culture, a variety of anthropologists engage in "outdoor hermeneutics" and conclude that introjecting and improvising cherished cultural narratives are virtually universal. As Victor Turner explains:

> If we regard narrative ... as the supreme instrument for building "values" and "goals" ... which motivate human conduct into situational "meaning," then we must concede it to be a universal cultural activity, embedded in the very center of the social drama, itself another cross-cultural and trans-temporal unit in social process.[30]

To overwork Epictetus' aphorism, it's not the world that imposes necessity, it's our scripted interpretation of the world. These scripts are discourses with a clear, sequential order that connects events in a meaningful way. A narrative is not simply a list or a chronology: it adds up to something—one thing follows another. In McNamara's tragic script, a tactical nuclear response to American invaders of Cuba *must* entail a full-scale, strategic nuclear war with the Soviets. The script brings down the curtain on civilization as we know it.

The ontological status of these strategic narratives of necessity is, to say the least, problematic. These scripts are not buried in the interstices of the unconscious, nor are they fully conscious. Turner avers that if one could penetrate the minds of social actors:

> One would undoubtedly find ... at almost any endophysical level existing between the full brightness of conscious attention and the darker strata of the unconscious a set of ideas, images, concepts ... models of what they believe they do, believe they ought to do, or would like to do.[31]

However, this is not the place to explore these interstices, a space Freud refers to as preconscious or what some call "tacit knowledge." Suffice it to suggest that certain resonant cultural narratives are so much a part and parcel of discourse that they are reified as an unquestioned second nature. If I may resort to analogies that I trust are not woefully misleading: just as leaders inside the Beltway don't give speaking English a second thought, neither do they give a second thought to certain narratives. Indeed, these narratives are the unthought lingua franca inside the Beltway.

As a variety of thinkers suggest, social actors can be totally captivated by such a script: they lose sight of the fact that they are merely improvising a narrative and come to believe that the plot is driven by forces beyond their control. Sociologist Erving Goffman refers to such mystification as "deep acting":

One finds that the performer can be fully taken in by his own act; he can be sincerely convinced that the impression of reality he states is the reality.... then, for the moment at least, only the sociologist or the socially disgruntled will have any doubts about the "realness" of what is presented.[32]

In these deeply acted scripts, one thing must follow another not because of the nature of the cosmos, but because of the sequence of the script (or scenario, in Nukespeak). In short, such necessitation is literary, not literal! Could it be, for example, that suddenly cast into total war—a scenario that scripted vanquishing combatants and civilians with every available weapon—Truman did not hesitate to follow the plot by detonating apocalyptic weapons? Perhaps, as I've suggested, Kennedy improvised the scripts authored in his books: he simultaneously performed like Churchill in public but acted like Chamberlain in private. Unfortunately, he got carried away with his public performance. Thanks to adroit, posthumous impression management, the remembered JFK is immortalized as a profile in courage. However, a less romantic take on the Kennedy administration raises disturbing questions: Why would a political actor improvise a script that ended in nuclear annihilation? Indeed, what's the story when decision-makers willingly risk the destruction of themselves and everything they cherish?

I don't know the answer. But I suspect that Kennedy and the others found themselves in a predicament they never anticipated. Astonishingly, the realpolitik of the balance of power did not deter the Soviets from doing what the U.S. had done for years—installing strategic weapons beyond its borders. The "best and the brightest" did what they deemed necessary, promoted a crisis, improvised their scripts, and pushed the planet to the brink of the abyss.

Epilogue

Anyone who looks with anguish on evils so great, so repulsive, so savage, must acknowledge the tragedy of it all; and if anyone experiences them or even looks on them without anguish, his condition is even more tragic, since he remains serene by losing his humanity.

—St. Augustine[1]

By and large, American nuclear strategists lack a sense of the tragic. This deficit may account for other liabilities. William Borden (a contemporary of Brodie) is the exception. In 1946 he predicted that atomic bombs would soon be available to America's adversaries, and that in the near future, intercontinental missiles would be armed with nuclear weapons. Unlike Brodie, Borden was not sanguine about deterrence. On the contrary, he referred to the reassuring notion of mutual nuclear deterrence as a fallacy based upon wishful thinking.[2] He prophesied that: "Unless a world government intercedes in time [a decidedly unlikely prospect in his view] an attack on the United States will surely come."[3] And he allowed that the impetus for such jeremiads was "America's happy-ending complex," a "Hollywood peace."[4]

As of this writing his prophesy has not been realized. Even if the future he foretold never comes to pass, Borden's writing provides a sorely needed corrective to the elegiac praise bestowed upon apocalyptic weapons by prevailing deterrence doctrine—a sense of the tragic.

We are the only species that contemplates its own extinction. In times past this prospect was based upon supernatural fantasy or ruminations about the remote possibility of some cosmic calamity. The nuclear age makes the ultimate tragedy—species extinction—a real possibility.

As Jonathan Schell laments, the prospect of such a tragedy can be mini-mized but never eliminated. We have, in effect, eaten the forbidden fruit and consequently our forlorn species must forever live with the real pos-sibility that nuclear weapons will:

Not only put an end to the living generations but foreclose all future generations down to the end of time. It would mark the defeat of all human strivings, all human hopes, all human ideals, past and future.[5]

The situation is doubly tragic. For, as Augustine averred long ago, to gaze upon the tragic without anguish is dehumanizing. This dehumaniza-tion is manifested in the only viable defenses we have against the nuclear threat: psychological defense mechanisms that enable us to evade and repress the unprecedented peril posed by nuclear weapons. As Robert Jay Lifton recognizes, "psychic numbing" is the very signature of these psy-chological defenses. We confront the unbearable prospect of species extinc-tion by anesthetizing ourselves.[6] We would be dysfunctional if we reacted with all-too-human emotions to the thousands of strategic weapons that remain on hair-trigger alert and to images of holocausts visited upon us by the terrorist diaspora. We can tolerate the existence of these weapons not because we have dehumanized some fictive enemy, but because we have managed to dehumanize ourselves. These psychological defenses exact a heavy toll: cold-blooded indifference toward the suffering of others and to the enormity of the threat nuclear weapons pose to ourselves.

The reasons for this dehumanizing psychic numbing are understand-able but lamentable. But strategists don't share this lamentation. They extol psychic numbing as a virtue, not a liability. They presuppose that useful, let alone respectable, inquiry must be cool, detached, and unemo-tional. Personal feelings (such as sorrowful anxiety about our nuclear predicament) impede inquiry: somehow repressing emotions facilitates the discovery of great truths. This is an unreflective bias of much aca-demic inquiry. To paraphrase Bertrand Russell—a great champion of reason—I'd rather be insane with truth than sane with lies.

Here then is a modest proposal for a humanized and humane nuclear strategizing, a literature fully attentive to the reality of our humanity and of our nuclear predicament:

1. Strategists might begin by allowing that they are pursuing literary projects, not rocket science. They would come to recognize that their carefully crafted scenarios are just that: stories—narratives scaffolded upon ancient metaphors. A strategist willing to face reality as it is would acknowledge the fictive nature of the strategic genre. In the words of James Fallows: "If every discussion about nuclear weapons began with the statement that no one really knows what he's talking about, we would have come a long way toward a more balanced

perspective on these weapons."[7] Admitting that the strategic literature *is* litera
ture is not demeaning. On the contrary, great literature enlivens the imagination
while penetrating the human condition. Dostoevsky's tormented imagination
says more about our humanity than B. F. Skinner's experiments with rats and
pigeons. Jonathan Schell is no Dostoevsky, but his impassioned *Fate of the Earth*
is preferable to Herman Kahn's glib reassurances about nuclear war-fighting.
The literary references that follow offer a glimpse at what is sorely neglected in
the strategic oeuvre: our fragile, ever-fallible humanity and the looming tragedy of learning to live with nuclear weapons.

2. Strategists should acknowledge the tragic dimensions of our nuclear predicament. Such candor would be a welcome antidote to the breathless praise
   bestowed upon nuclear weapons of mass destruction. This is not the best of
   all possible worlds. Strategists might look into themselves to better understand why their writing evades the sense of the tragic. Existentialist writers such as Teilhard de Chardin recognize what would occur if strategists
   dissolved their usual boundaries and left their everyday occupations and
   relationships:

   > For the first time in my life ... I took the lamp and, leaving the zone of
   > everyday occupation and relationships where everything seems clear,
   > I went down into my innermost self, to the deep abyss whence I feel
   > dimly that my power of action emanates. At each step of the descent a
   > new person was disclosed within me of whose name I was not longer
   > sure, who no longer obeyed me. And when I had to stop my exploration
   > because the path faded beneath my steps, I found a bottomless abyss at
   > my feet, and out of it came—arising from I know not where—the current
   > which I dare call my life.[8]

3. As authors bereft of authority strategists should recognize that they are interpreters of ambiguous texts and cryptic performances, not objective observers
   of obdurate facts. They might come to better understand why, like the nuclear
   weapons themselves, the strategic literature proliferates. They could profit
   from the insight proffered by Montaigne almost five centuries ago:

   > I know not what to say to it; but experience makes it manifest, that
   > so many interpretations dissipate the truth, and break it. Who will
   > not say that glosses augment doubts and ignorance, since there is no
   > book to be found ... which the world busies itself about, whereof the
   > difficulties are cleared by interpretation. The hundredth commenta-
   > tor passes it on to the next, still more knotty and perplexed than he
   > found it. When were we ever agreed among ourselves: "this book has
   > enough; there is no more to be said about it?" Do we find any end to
   > the need of interpreting? There is more ado to interpret interpretations
   > than to interpret things; and more books upon books than upon any
   > other subjects; we do nothing but comment upon one another. Every
   > place swarms with commentaries.... Our opinions are grafted upon
   > another; the first serves as a stock to the second, and second to the
   > third, and so forth.[9]

4. Accordingly, strategists would take their obligatory, modest prefatory remarks seriously by acknowledging their fallibility. Recognizing that their reified metaphors are mere figures of speech, they would entertain serious doubts about the stories they tell. The time is long overdue for strategists to acknowledge their warm-blooded humanity, and the dubious and heartless nature of the metaphors they construct. Camus knew this long ago:

> Of whom and of what indeed can I say: "I know that!" This heart within me I can feel, and I judge that it exists. This world I can touch, and I likewise indeed that it exists. There ends all my knowledge, and the rest is construction.[10]

Notes

INTRODUCTION

1. Ernest Becker, "The Fragile Fiction," in *The Truth About the Truth*, Walter Truett Anderson, ed. (New York: Putnam, 1995), 34–35.

2. Quoted by Gregg Herken, *Counsel of War* (New York: Oxford University Press, 1987), 10.

3. Bernard Brodie, "Influence of Mass Destruction Weapons on Strategy," delivered at Naval War College, May 3, 1956. [Reprinted in National Security Archive's "Nuclear History Project".]

4. Lawrence Freedman, *The Evolution of Nuclear Strategy* (New York: Macmillan, 1982), 395.

5. Philip Green, *Deadly Logic: The Theory of Nuclear Deterrence* (New York: Schocken Books, 1969).

6. H.D.F. Kitto, *Greek Tragedy* (London: Methuen, 1978), 182.

7. As historians such as Herken reveal, Williams Borden's pessimistic prognosis was an exception. See Herken's discussion, *Counsel of War*, 10–14. Of course, not everyone shares certain strategists' interpretations of what constitutes a happy ending. It is difficult to become ebullient about Herman Kahn's scenarios that result in "only" 20,000,000 American deaths. Finally, as we shall see, in their "retirement wisdom" a variety of strategists and science advisors such as Daniel Ellsberg and Herbert York are no longer sanguine about the final scene in worldwide nuclear endeavors.

8. See Walter Truett Anderson's discussion of the Enlightenment faith in his *The Truth About The Truth* (New York: Putnam, 1995), 4.

9. Albert Camus, *Neither Victims Nor Executioners* (Berkeley: World Without War Council, 1968), 2.

10. See, for example, James A. Aho, "The Emerging Nuclear Death Cult," in *A Shuddering Dawn*, Ira Chernus and Edward Tabor Linenthal, eds. (Albany: State University of New York Press, 1989).

11. Ibid., 67.

12. These terms are invoked by Gar Alperovitz in *Atomic Diplomacy: Hiroshima and Potsdam* (New York: Vintage, 1965); Thomas Schelling, *Arms and Influence* (New Haven: Yale University Press, 1962); and Herman Kahn, *Thinking About the Unthinkable* (New York, Avon, 1962).

13. Helen Caldicott, *Nuclear Madness: What You Can Do* (New York: Bantam Books, 1980).

14. See the studies of Jerome Frank, *Sanity and Survival* (New York: Random House, 1967); Robert Jay Lifton and Richard Falk, *Indefensible Weapons* (New York: Basic Books, 1982); and Joel Kovel, *Against the State of Nuclear Terror* (Boston: South End Press, 1981).

15. This view of nuclear endeavors is found in works such as Michael Mandelbaum, *The Nuclear Question* (Cambridge: Cambridge University Press, 1979); Albert Carnesale, Paul Doty, et al., *Living With Nuclear Weapons* (New York: Bantam Books, 1983); the rational actor account of nuclear endeavors is espoused as official policy by Caspar Weinberger in "A Rational Approach to Nuclear Disarmament," in *The Ethics of Nuclear Deterrence,* James Sterba, ed. (Belmont: Wadsworth, 1985), 106–115; and Richard Barnet takes a bureaucratic view in *Roots of War* (New York: Penguin, 1981).

16. Richard Barnet, *Roots of War* (New York: Penguin, 1981), 122.

17. Leon Wieseltier, *Nuclear War/Nuclear Peace* (New York: Holt, Rinehart & Winston, 1983), 15.

18. Richard K. Betts, *Nuclear Blackmail and Nuclear Balance* (Washington, DC: The Brookings Institution, 1987), 13.

19. Herbert York, *Making Weapons/Talking Peace* (New York: Basic Books, 1987).

20. Friedrich Durrenmatt, *The Physicists* (New York: Grove Press, 1984), 96.

21. Anthony Wallace, *Religion: An Anthropological View* (New York: Random House, 1966); in my analysis I have complemented Wallace's account by discussing other relevant characteristics.

22. Robert Jay Lifton, *The Broken Connection* (New York: Simon and Schuster, 1979), 369.

23. John Canaday, *The Nuclear Muse* (Madison: University of Wisconsin Press, 2000), 6.

24. H. R. Haldeman, *The Haldeman Diaries* (New York: Putnam, 1994).

25. Dwight D. Eisenhower, "Farewell to the Nation," *U.S. Department of State Bulletin* (February 6, 1961).

26. I am indebted to my student, Michael Bruce, for this account of narrativity.

27. Albert Camus, *Neither Victims Nor Executioners* (Berkeley: World Without War Council, 1968), 2.

28. George Kennan, *The Cloud of Danger* (Boston: Little, Brown, 1978).

29. Among those offering dark counsel *without* a happy ending were Joseph Rotblatt, Enrico Fermi, Franck Report, and Robert Oppenheimer.

30. See, for example, Robert S. McNamara, *In Retrospect: The Tragedy and Lessons of Vietnam* (New York: Vintage Books, 1996).

31. Robert McNamara and Helen Caldicott, "Still on Catastrophe's Edge," *Los Angeles Times,* April 26, 2004, 26.

32. Quoted by Jonathan Schell, *The Gift of Time* (New York: Metropolitan Books, 1998), 191–194.

33. Steven Kull, *Minds at War: Nuclear Reality and the Inner Conflicts of Defense Policy Makers* (New York: Basic Books, 1988). Kull interviewed a host of strategists and decision-makers including Secretaries of Defense, members of the National Security Counsel, Joint Chiefs of Staff, presidential advisors, members of Congress, academics at "think tanks," and military contractors. I discuss his research design in Chapter 2.

34. Ibid., 29.

35. Marcus Raskin, *The Megadeath Intellectuals*, http://www.nybooks.com/articles/13621.

36. Herken, *Counsel of War*, xiv.

37. Annette Freyberg-Inan, *What Moves Man: The Realist Theory of International Relations and Its Judgment of Human Nature* (Albany: State University of New York Press, 2004), 66.

38. Milan Kundera, *The Book of Laughter and Forgetting* (New York: Penguin, 1987), 106.

CHAPTER 1

1. Jonathan Schell, *The Unconquerable World* (New York: Metropolitan Books, 2003), 276.

2. Hans Morgenthau, *Scientific Man v. Power Politics* (Chicago: University of Chicago Press, 1946), 204.

3. Quoted by John Prados in "Woolsey and The CIA," *Bulletin of the Atomic Scientists*, Vol. 49, no. 6 (July/August 1993), 6.

4. See, for example, Helen Caldicott's *Missile Envy: The Arms Race and Nuclear War* (New York: William Morrow, 1984) and *Exposing Nuclear Phallacies*, Diana E. H. Russell, ed. (New York: Pergamon Press, 1989).

5. Jim George, *Discourses of Global Politics: Critical (Re)Introduction to International Relations* (Boulder, Col.: Lynne Rienner Publishers, 1994), 26.

6. See, for example, *Exposing Nuclear Phallacies*, Diana E. H. Russell, ed. (New York: Pergamon Press, 1989).

7. Quoted by Ole R. Holsti in Philip Tetlock, Jo Husbands, et al., "Crisis Decision Making," *Behavior, Society and Nuclear War*, Vol. 1 (New York: Oxford University Press, 1989), 16.

8. Ole R. Holsti, *Crisis Escalation War* (Montreal: McGill-Queen's University Press, 1972), 23.

9. Barbara Tuchman, *The March of Folly* (New York: Alfred Knopf, 1984).

10. Clifford Geertz, *Local Knowledge* (New York: Basic Books, 1983), 51.

11. Ernest Cassirer, *An Essay of Man* (Garden City, NY: Doubleday Anchor, 1956), 43.

12. Fred Kaplan, *The Wizards of Armageddon* (New York: Simon and Schuster, 1983), 30.

13. Ibid., 9.

14. Raymond Aron, *Peace and War: A Theory of International Relations* (Garden City, N.Y.: Doubleday, 1966), 600.

15. Victor Turner, *Dramas, Fields, and Metaphors* (Ithaca, N.Y.: Cornell University Press, 1971), 38.

16. Richard Betts, *Nuclear Blackmail and Nuclear Balance* (Washington, D.C.: The Brookings Institution, 1987), 2.

17. Mark Slouka, "A Year Later: Notes on America's Intimations of Mortality," *Harper's,* September 2002, 36.

18. Wallace Shawn, "The Foreign Policy Therapist," in *A Just Response,* Katrina Vanden Heuvel, ed. (New York: Nation Books, 2002), 296.

19. In addition to Kaplan's account of the nuclear arms race, see Lawrence Freedman, *The Price of Peace* (New York, Henry Holt, 1986); and Gregg Herken, *The Counsels of War* (New York: Oxford University Press, 1987).

20. It is widely suggested that the George W. Bush Administration is reluctant to confront a nuclear-armed North Korea but obviously more enthusiastic about having its way with Iraq.

21. In addition to Gar Alperovitz' *Atomic Diplomacy: Hiroshima and Potsdam* (New York: Vintage, 1965), Alperovitz updates his argument in "New Evidence," *The Bulletin of the Atomic Scientists,* June 1985. Also see Richard Betts, *Nuclear Blackmail and Nuclear Balance* (Washington, D.C.: The Brookings Institution, 1987).

22. Betts, Chapters 1 and 3.

23. Quoted by Jim George, *Discourses of Global Politics: Critical (Re)Introduction to International Relations* (Boulder, Col.: Lynne Rienner Publishers, 1994), 92.

24. See my discussion of these events in *What If They Gave a Crisis and Nobody Came: Interpreting International Crises* (Westport, Conn.: Praeger, 1997), Chapter 3.

25. Ibid., Chapter 5.

26. Interview with Rear Admiral Eugene Carroll, Jr., at the Center for Defense Information, Washington, D.C., December 19, 1999.

CHAPTER 2

1. Richard Neustadt and Ernest May, *Thinking in Time* (New York: The Free Press, 1986), 106.

2. Hugh Gusterson, "Tall Tales and Deceptive Discourses," *The Bulletin of the Atomic Scientists,* November/December 2001, 65.

3. Robert Jay Lifton, *The Broken Connection* (New York: Simon and Schuster, 1979).

4. H. L. Mencken, "Notes on Democracy," in *American Political Thinking,* Robert Isask, ed. (Fort Worth, Tex.: Harcourt Brace, 1994), 549.

5. John Canaday, *The Nuclear Muse* (Madison: University of Wisconsin Press, 2000), 51.

6. Philip Green, *Deadly Logic: The Theory of Nuclear Deterrence* (New York: Schocken Books, 1969), xi.

7. Herman Kahn, *Thinking About the Unthinkable in the 1980s* (New York: Simon and Schuster, 1984), 85.

8. Ibid., 56

9. Philip Green, *Deadly Logic: The Theory of Nuclear Deterrence* (New York: Schocken Books, 1969), 28.

10. Jonathan Schell, "Reflections," in the *New Yorker*, February 15, 1982, 45.

11. Edward Luttwak, *Strategy: The Logic of War and Peace* (Cambridge: Harvard University Press, 1987), 3.

12. Ibid.

13. See, for example, Karl Popper's "Science: Conjectures and Refutations," in E. D. Klemke et al., eds., *Philosophy of Science* (Amherst: Prometheus Books, 1998), 38–47.

14. C. Wright Mills, *The Causes of World War III* (New York: Ballantine, 1958), 45.

15. This is the "take-home lesson" of Albert Carnesale and Paul Doty, in *Living with Nuclear Weapons* (New York: Bantam, 1983).

16. Bernard Brodie, "Influence of Mass Destruction Weapons on Strategy," delivered at the Naval War College, May 3, 1956. [Reprinted in National Security Archive's "Nuclear History Project."]

17. Lawrence Freedman, *The Evolution of Nuclear Strategy*, 2nd ed. (New York: St. Martin's Press, 1989), xvii.

18. See Ronald Steel's discussion in "War Games," *New York Review of Books*, Vol. 6, No. 10, June 9, 1966.

19. Abolitionists such as Jonathan Schell endorse the nuclear virginity argument. He recognizes that the knowledge for building nuclear weaponry will always bedevil humanity. However, he argues that nuclear weapons can be abolished. See his *The Abolition* (New York: Knopf, 1984).

20. John Stuart Mill, *On Liberty* (Indianapolis: Hacket, 1978), 17.

21. Kahn, *Thinking About the Unthinkable*, 216.

22. Dvora Yanow, "Public Policies as Identity Stories," *Advances in Program Evaluation*, Vol. 6 (JAI Press, 1999), 30.

23. Like his colleagues, Kahn believed that deterrence works and will continue to work. But, unlike many other strategists, Kahn is noteworthy for his extensive and detailed conjectures about what could and should happen in the unlikely event that deterrence fails.

24. Quoted by Paul Chilton, "Nukespeak: Nuclear Language, Culture and Propaganda," in *The Nuclear Predicament*, Donna Gregory, ed. (New York: St. Martin's Press, 1986), 127.

25. As we shall see, "deterrence" is an elastic, ambiguous concept. Not surprisingly, deterrence is metaphorically likened to diverse, even contradictory, phenomena.

26. Lawrence Freedman, *The Price of Peace* (New York: Henry Holt, 1986), 1.

27. Richard Rorty, "Ironists and Metaphysicians," in *The Truth about the Truth*, Walter Truett Anderson, ed. (New York: Putnam, 1995), 101–102.

28. Ibid., 102.

29. John H. Herz, "Political Realism Revisited," *International Studies Quarterly*, Vol. 25, No. 2, June 1981, 183.

CHAPTER 3

1. Quoted by John Canaday, *The Nuclear Muse* (Madison: University of Wisconsin Press, 2000), 222.

2. Quoted by Greg Herken, *The Counsels of War* (New York: Oxford University Press, 1987), 27.

3. Paul Chilton, "Nukespeak," in *Undercurrents*, 48: 12–14.

4. Peter Moss, "Rhetoric of Defense in the United States: Language, Myth, and Ideology," in *Language and the Nuclear Arms Debate: Nukespeak Today*, Paul Chilton, ed. (London: Frances Pinter, 1983), 46.

5. Roger Fowler and Tim Marshall, "The War Against Peacemongering: Language and Ideology," in *Language and the Nuclear Arms Debate: Nukespeak Today* Paul Chilton, ed. (London: Frances Pinter, 1983), 46.

6. Friedrich Nietzsche, "On Truth and Lies in a Nonmoral Sense," in *Philosophy and Truth: Selections from Nietzsche's Notebooks of the Early 1870s*, Daniel Breazealse, ed. (Atlantic Highlands: Humanities Press, 84.

7. Kahn's caveats about uncertainty and caution seldom temper his writing. He begins the study by enunciating 24 propositions he deems almost certainly true. Carol Kahn (no relation) edited and completed the work after his death. She stresses that Kahn was unfamiliar with studies that conclude a nuclear conflagration would usher in "nuclear winter." However, she reassures us that Kahn "surely would have taken any new factors into account." [Kahn, *On Escalation: Metaphors and Scenarios* (New York: Praeger, 1965), 30]

8. Susan Neiman, *Evil in Modern Thought* (Princeton: Princeton University Press, 2002).

9. I am indebted to linguist Paul Chilton for this telling term.

10. Carol Cohn, "Nuclear Language and How We Learned to Pat the Bomb," in Francesca M. Cancian and James William Gibson, eds., *Making War/Making Peace* (Belmont: Wadsworth, 1990), 111.

11. This phrase is the title of Jonathan Schell's influential *The Fate of the Earth* (New York: Knopf, 1982). This work was roundly criticized by Kahn for being needlessly alarmist.

12. Bruce Blair, "Post Cold War Nuclear Strategies," http://twilight.dsi. unimi/it/uspid./Atti/Blair.html (accessed September 2004).

13. Paraphrased and quoted by J. Peter Euben in his *The Tragedy of Political Theory* (Princeton, N.J.: Princeton University Press, 1990), 6.

14. Richard Rorty, "Ironists and Metaphysicians," in *The Truth about the Truth*, Walter Truett Anderson, ed. (New York: Putnam, 1995), 100.

15. George Lakoff and Mark Johnson, *Metaphors We Live By* (Chicago: University of Chicago Press, 1980), 158.

16. Ibid., 5. To indulge in a pessimistic moment, perhaps a study of strategic metaphors should be entitled, "Metaphors We Die By."

17. Murray Edelman, *Politics as Symbolic Action: Mass Arousal and Quiescence* (Chicago: Markham, 1971), 68.

18. Cohn, "Nuclear Language," 115.

19. Ibid., 119.

20. Paul Chilton, "Nukespeak: Nuclear Language, Culture and Propaganda," in *The Nuclear Predicament*, Donna Gregory, ed. (New York: St. Martin's Press, 1986), 131.

21. See, for example, Victor Turner's discussion in his *Dramas, Fields, Metaphors* (Ithaca, N.Y.: Cornell University Press, 1974).

22. John Canaday, *The Nuclear Muse* (Madison: University of Wisconsin Press, 2000), 180–181.

23. Ibid., 209.

CHAPTER 4

1. David Lilienthal, *Change, Hope & The Bomb* (Princeton, N.J.: Princeton University Press, 1963), 18–19.

2. Quoted by Ira Chernus in *Dr. Strangegod: On the Symbolic Meaning of Nuclear Weapons* (Columbia: University of South Carolina Press, 1986), 12–13.

3. Quoted by Peter Pringle and James Siegelman, *The Nuclear Barons* (New York: Holt, Rinehart, and Winston, 1981), 28.

4. Sigmund Freud, *Group Psychology* (New York: W. W. Norton, 1959), 12.

5. General Thomas Farrell's oft quoted firsthand account of the Trinity Test cited by John Canaday, *The Nuclear Muse* (Madison: University of Wisconsin Press, 2000), 213.

6. Spencer R. Weart, *Nuclear Fear* (Cambridge, Mass.: Harvard University Press, 1988), 47.

7. Quoted by Daniel Ford in "The Cult of the Atom" in *The New Yorker*, 25, October 1987, 197.

8. In discussing these early discoveries and experiments I am indebted to Bernard O'Keefe, *Nuclear Hostages* (Boston: Houghton Mifflin, 1983), Chapter 1.

9. Perhaps Newton's equation is emblematic of the democratization of warfare: Unlike medieval chivalrous battles, military forces were exerted by mobilizing mass armies of ordinary citizens. Einstein's fabled equation reveals the "countervalue" strategy of annihilating the masses.

10. Quoted by Ronald W. Clark, *The Greatest Power on Earth* (New York: Harper and Row, 1980), 17.

11. Weart, *Nuclear Fear*, 15.

12. Ibid., 27–28.

13. Ibid., 26.

14. Quoted by Ronald W. Clark, *The Greatest Power on Earth* (New York: Harper and Row, 1980), 24.

15. Ibid., 15–16.

16. Weart, *Nuclear Fear*, Preface.

17. John Canaday, *The Nuclear Muse* (Madison: University of Wisconsin Press, 2000), 91; see 87–197 for a detailed, nuanced discussion of the play.

18. Ibid., 191.

19. Ibid., 137.

20. See, for example, the account of the relationship between Oppenheimer and Groves in Peter Pringle and William Spigelman, *The Nuclear Barons* (New York: Avon, 1981), 18–22.

21. Victor Weisskopf, "Looking Back at Los Alamos," in *Assessing the Nuclear Age*, Len Ackland and Steve McGuire, eds. (Chicago: University of Chicago Press, 1986), 23.

22. Haakon Chevalier, *The Man Who Would Be God* (New York: Putnam, 1959), 272–73.

23. Mircea Eliade, *The Sacred and the Profane* (New York: Harcourt, 1987), 10.

24. Ibid., 7.

25. Stewart Alsop and Ralph E. Lapp, "The Strange Death of Louis Slotkin," in *Man against Nature*, C. Neider, ed. (New York: Harper, 1954).

26. Alvin Weinberger, "Sacrifice," *The Bulletin of the Atomic Scientists*, June 1985, 28.

27. Alvin Weinberger, "Can Technology Replace Social Engineering?" in *Technology and the Future*, Albert Teich, ed. (New York: St. Martin's Press, 1986), 24.

28. Ernest Becker, *The Structure of Evil* (New York: The Free Press, 1975), 99.

29. Canaday, *The Nuclear Muse*, 19–20.

30. Richard Rhodes, *The Making of the Atomic Bomb* (New York: Simon & Schuster, 1988), 354–355.

31. Quoted by James A. Aho, "The Emerging Nuclear Death Cult," in *A Shuddering Dawn*, Ira Chernus and Edward Tabor Linethal, eds. (Albany: State University of New York Press, 1989), 55.

32. Canaday, 202.

33. Ibid., 198.

34. Ibid., 200.

35. Gregg Herken, *Counsels of War* (New York: Oxford University Press, 1987), xiv.

CHAPTER 5

1. Quoted by Fred Kaplan, *The Wizards of Armageddon* (New York: Simon and Schuster, 1983), 33.

2. Quoted by Sidney Lens, *The Day Before Doomsday* (Boston: Beacon Press, 1977), 28.

3. Quoted by Peter Pringle and James Spigelman, *The Nuclear Barons* (New York: Holt, Rinehart, and Winston, 1981), 51.

4. Quoted by Gregg Herken, *The Winning Weapon* (New York: Vintage, 1982), 4.

5. Richard Barnet, *Roots of War* (New York: Penguin, 1981), 48.

6. Joseph Rotblat, "Leaving the Bomb Project," in *Assessing the Nuclear Age*, Harrison Brown, ed. (Chicago: The Bulletin of the Atomic Scientists, 1986), 21.

7. Quoted by Peter Pringle and William Spigelman, *The Nuclear Barons* (Holt, Rinehart, and Winston, 1981), 49.

8. Douglas MacArthur, "Nuclear War: 'A Frankenstein'," in *Rumors of War*, C. A. Ceseratti and J. T. Vitale, eds. (New York: Seabury Press, 1982), 13.

9. Ibid., 46.

10. See Edgar Bottomore's account of the episode in his *The Balance of Terror* (Boston: Beacon Press, 1971), 6–7.

11. Quoted by Peter Pringle, in *The Nuclear Barons* (Holt, Rinehart, and Winston, 1981), 49.

12. Ibid., 89.

13. Ibid., 115–116.

14. Quoted by Gregg Herken, *Counsels of War* (New York: Oxford University Press, 1982), 50.

15. Quoted by Inis L. Claude, Jr., *Power and International Relations* (New York: Random House, 1962), 44.

16. Gregory Crane, "Thucydides and the Ancient Simplicity," http://texts. cdlib.org/dynamax SML?docld (accessed September 2004), (University of California Press, Internet Scholarship Editions), 1.

17. Ibid., 49.

18. Quoted by Michio Kaku and Daniel Axelrod, *To Win a Nuclear War* (Boston: South End Press, 1987), 214.

19. Ibid., 22; Claude quotes Vernon Van Dyke in *International Politics* (New York: Appleton-Century-Crofts, 1957), 219.

20. Ibid., 37.

21. While Claude is sympathetic to Richard Cobden's gloss on the balance of power literature, Claude believes the terms can be intelligibly discussed in systematic approaches to the distribution of interstate power. In addition to his reference to Cobden on page 13, see his clarification on pages 42–43.

22. Interview with Rear Admiral Eugene Carroll, Jr., Center for Defense Information, Washington, D.C., March 18, 1999.

23. Inis L. Claude, Jr., *Power and International Relations* (New York: Random House, 1962), 37.

24. Ibid., See Claude's discussion of Wilson, 75–88.

25. Henry A. Kissinger, *American Foreign Policy* (New York: W. W. Norton, 1979), 59–60.

26. Ibid., 60.

27. Ibid., 61.

28. Victor Turner, "Dewey, Dilthey, and Drama," in *Anthropology of Experience*, Victor Turner and Edward M. Bruner, eds. (Urbana: University of Illinois Press, 1986), 41.

29. See Richard K. Betts' discussion of SALT in *Nuclear Blackmail and Nuclear Balance* (Washington: The Brookings Institution, 1987), 186–187.

30. Quoted by Michael Mandelbaum, *The Nuclear Question* (Cambridge: Cambridge University Press, 1979), 89.

31. Fred Kaplan, *The Wizards of Armageddon* (New York: Simon and Schuster, 1983), 87.

32. Ibid., 110.

33. Albert Wohlstetter, "The Delicate Balance of Terror," *Foreign Affairs*, Vol. 37, No. 2, January 1959, 211–234.

34. Ibid., 214.

35. Ibid., 222.

36. Ibid., 216.

37. Kenneth N. Waltz, "More May Be Better" in Scott D. Sagan and Kenneth N. Waltz, *The Spread of Nuclear Weapons: A Debate* (New York: W. W. Norton, 1995), 45.

38. Gregg Herken, *Counsels of War* (New York: Oxford University Press, 1987), 146.

39. David. W. Gregg, *Worker Protection Alternatives for a Nuclear Attack with 30 Minutes (or Less) Warning* (Washington, D.C.: National Technical Information Service, 1984), 17.

40. See Philip Green's critique of Kahn's analysis of civil defense in his *Deadly Logic: The Theory of Nuclear Deterrence* (New York: Schocken Books, 1969), 23–75.

41. Quoted by Green, Ibid., 33.

42. Quoted by Green, Ibid., 31.

43. Herman Kahn, *Thinking About the Unthinkable in the 1980s* (New York: Simon and Schuster, 1984), 93.

44. "America's Doomsday Project," *U.S. News & World Report*, August 7, 1989, 6–17.

45. Ibid., 1.

46. Ibid.

47. Ibid., 6.

48. Ibid., 17.

49. David W. Gregg, "Memorandum to All Concerned LLNL Employees," October 26, 1984, 3.

50. Ibid., 4.

51. Ibid.

CHAPTER 6

1. General K.D. Johnson, "The Morality of Nuclear Deterrence," in *The Nuclear Crisis Reader*, Gwyn Prins, ed. (New York: Vintage, 1984), 144–145.

2. Quoted by Admiral Eugene Carroll, "Nuclear Weapons and Deterrence," in *The Nuclear Crisis Reader*, Gwyn Prins, ed. (New York: Vintage, 1984), 3.

3. Quoted by Robert W. Malcolmson, *Nuclear Fallacies* (Kingston and Montreal: McGill University Press, 1985), 70.

4. Quoted by Malcolmson, Ibid., 70.

5. See, for example, Richard Betts, *Nuclear Blackmail and Nuclear Balance* (Washington, D.C.: Brookings Institution, 1987).

6. Caspar Weinberger, "A Rational Approach to Disarmament," in *The Ethics of Nuclear Deterrence*, James Sterba, ed. (Belmont, CA: Wadsworth, 1985), 58.

7. Michael Mandelbaum, *The Nuclear Question* (Cambridge: Cambridge University Press, 1979), vii.

8. Lawrence Freedman, *The Price of Peace* (New York: Henry Holt, 1986), 1.

9. Lawrence Eagleburger, "The New Security Challenges and the Future Role of the Alliance," a lecture presented to the Eurogroup Conference, Washington, D.C., June 25, 1991.

10. Manfred Worner, *The Atlantic Alliance in the New Era*," *NATO Review*, Vol. 39, No. 1, February 1991, 3–9. He reiterated this view at the Atlantic Council Meeting in Washington, D.C., June 25, 1991.

11. Kenneth N. Waltz, "More May Be Better" in Scott D. Sagan and Kenneth N. Waltz, *The Spread of Nuclear Weapons: A Debate* (New York: W. W. Norton, 1995), 45.

12. Scott D. Sagan and Kenneth N. Waltz, *The Spread of Nuclear Weapons: A Debate* (New York: W. W. Norton, 1995), 58.

13. Ibid., 47.

14. Ibid., 86–87.

15. Michel Foucault, "The Order of Discourse" in *Language and Politics*, Michael Shapiro, ed. (New York: New York University Press, 1989), 7.

16. Bernard Brodie, *The Absolute Weapon: Atomic Power and World Order* (New York: Harcourt, 1946), 76.

17 See Lawrence Freedman's discussion in his *The Evolution of Nuclear Strategy,* 2nd ed. (New York: St. Martin's Press, 1989), 277–279.

18. Ibid., 2.

19. Gregg Herken, *Counsels of War* (New York: Oxford University Press, 1987), 175.

20. Ibid., 428–429.

21. Ibid., xvii.

22. I use the term "deterrence doctrine" rather than "deterrence theory" because the doctrine does not share the characteristics of well established scientific theories such as Newtonian Mechanics or Thermodynamics.

23. Philip Green, *Deadly Logic: The Theory of Nuclear Deterrence* (New York: Schocken Books, 1969), 7. Virtually any attempt to clearly define deterrence, even in the broadest sense, is problematic: As Green realizes, Herman Kahn claims his war-fighting doctrines are a "deterrent."

24. See Philip Green's discussion in his *Deadly Logic: The Theory of Nuclear Deterrence* (New York: Schocken Books, 1969), 119–123.

25. Ibid., 124.

26. Herman Kahn, *On Escalation: Metaphors and Scenarios* (New York: Praeger, 1965), 281.

27. Fyodor Dostoevsky, *Notes from Underground.* Walter Kaufman, ed. (New York: Penguin, 1963), 69–70.

28. Herman Kahn, *On Escalation: Metaphors and Scenarios* (New York: Praeger, 1965), 275–284.

29. See Richard K. Betts's discussion in his *Nuclear Blackmail and Nuclear Balance* (Washington: The Brookings Institution, 1987), 30.

30. See Gregg Herken's account of Ellsberg's thinking in *Counsels of War* (New York: Oxford University Press, 1987), 143–144.

31. See McGeorge Bundy's discussion in his *Danger and Survival* (New York: Random House, 1987), 381–382.

32. See Louis Beres's discussion of this episode in *Apocalypse* (Chicago: University of Chicago Press, 1980), 68–70.

33. Quoted by Philip Green in his *Deadly Logic: The Theory of Nuclear Deterrence* (New York: Schocken Books, 1969), 144.

34. Thomas C. Schelling, "War without Pain and Other Models," *World Politics,* XV (April, 1963), 486.

35. Those who claim that weapons system such as the MX missiles are deterrents argued that in the event of a *limited* Soviet first strike, the remaining missiles would deter a Soviet second strike.

36. General K. D. Johnson, "The Morality of Nuclear Deterrence," in *The Nuclear Crisis Reader,* Gwyn Prins, ed. (New York: Vintage, 1984), 146.

37. Solly Zuckerman, "Nuclear Fantasies" in *The New York Review of Books,* June 14, 1984, 28.

38. For an account of these episodes see Gregg Herken, "The Earthly Origin of Star Wars," *The Bulletin of the Atomic Scientists,* October, 1987, 114.

39. Quoted by Theodore Draper in "An Open Letter to Weinberger" in *The New York Review of Books,* Vol. xxix, No. 17, 48.

40. Ibid.

41. Herman Kahn, *Thinking About the Unthinkable* (New York: Avon, 1962), 282.

42. Ibid., 174.

43. Herman Kahn, *On Thermonuclear War* (Princeton: Princeton University Press, 1960), 21.

44. Philip Green, *Deadly Logic: The Theory of Nuclear Deterrence* (New York: Schocken Books, 1969), 75.

45. Ibid., 124.

46. Eugene Carroll, "Nuclear Weapons and Deterrence" in *The Nuclear Crisis Reader,* Gwyn Prins, ed. (New York: Vintage, 1984), 3.

47. Philip Green, *Deadly Logic: The Theory of Nuclear Deterrence* (New York: Schocken Books, 1969), 36.

48. Quoted by Greg Herken, *Counsels of War* (New York: Oxford University Press, 1987), 349.

49. Quoted by Greg Herken, "The Earthly Origin of Star Wars," 116.

50. Thomas C. Schelling, *The Strategy of Conflict* (New York: Oxford University Press, 1963), 207–209.

51. E.P. Thompson, "The Logic of Exterminism," *New Left Review,* No. 121, 1983, 15.

52. Quoted by Graham Allison, *Essence of Decision* (Boston: Little, Brown, 1971), 1.

53. Ron Hirschbein, *What If They Gave a Crisis and Nobody Came?* (Westport, Conn.: Praeger, 1997), Chapter 3.

54. Quoted by Herbert York in his *Race to Oblivion* (New York: Simon and Schuster, 1970), 168.

55. According to Rear Admiral Eugene Carroll (whose last assignment was nuclear war planning) modern submarines are quieter and therefore even less detectable than before. Moreover, even if antimissile defense proposals lived up to all their promises, such a system would be ineffectual against stealth-coated cruise missiles and short-arc ballistic missiles long deployed on submarines. (Interview in Chico, California; November 16, 1988).

56. Henry A. Kissinger, *Years of Upheaval* (Boston: Little, Brown 1982), 257.

57. Theodore Draper, "An Open Letter to Weinberger," *The New York Review of Books*, Vol. xxix, No. 17, 49.

58. Quoted by Daniel Axelrod and Michio Kaku, *To Win a Nuclear War* (Boston: South End Press, 1987), 101.

59. "The Creation of SIOP-62: More Evidence on the Origins of Overkill," William Burr, ed., The National Security Archive Electronic Briefing Book #130, http://www.gwu.edu/-nsaarchiv/NSAEBB/NSAEBB130/index.htm, 8.

60. Daniel Axelrod and Michio Kaku, *To Win a Nuclear War* (Boston: South End Press, 1987), 2.

61. Ibid., 191.

62. Colin Gray, "Victory is Possible," *Foreign Policy,* Summer, 1980, 21.

63. Daniel Ellsberg, "A Call to Mutiny" in E. P. Thompson and Dan Smith, eds., *Protest and Survive* (New York and London: Monthly Review Press, 1981). I am indebted to Ellsberg for sending his unpublished "The Construction of Instability: U.S. First-use Threat and the Risk of Nuclear War," December 1986.

64. Betts, *Nuclear Blackmail*, 13.

65. Eugene Carroll, "Nuclear Weapons and Deterrence," in *The Nuclear Crisis Reader,* Gwyn Prins, ed. (New York: Vintage, 1984), 4.

66. See Michael Mandelbaum's *The Nuclear Question* (Cambridge: Cambridge University Press, 1979), vii.

CHAPTER 7

1. Milan Kundera, *The Book of Laughter and Forgetting* (New York: Penguin, 1978), 106. This chapter, in part, revises the analysis offered in my *What if They Gave a Crisis and Nobody Came: Interpreting International Crises* (Westport: Praeger, 1997).

2. Perhaps because the crisis was not constructed and managed in accord with the cherished crisis metaphors of our culture, the material on the 1970 episode is scant. Curiously, the successful—albeit undramatic—resolution of the episode is of little interest to international relations specialists. Participants briefly discuss the episode in Richard M. Nixon, *The Memoirs of Richard Nixon* (Boston: Grosset & Dunlap, 1978); Henry A. Kissinger, *The White House Years* (Boston: Little, Brown, 1979); Henry A. Kissinger, *Years of Upheaval* (Boston: Little, Brown, 1982); H. R. Haldeman, *The Haldeman Diaries* (New York: Putnam, 1994); and Anatoly Dobrynin, *In Confidence* (New York: Times Books, 1995). Secondary sources include Steven E. Ambrose, *Nixon,* vol. 2, (New York: Simon and Schuster, 1989); Seymour Hersh, *The Price of Power* (New York: Summit Books, 1983); and Tom Wicker, *One of Us: Richard Nixon and the American Dream* (New York: Random House, 1992).

3. Clifford Geertz, *Local Knowledge* (New York: Basic Books, 1983), 69.

4. Ernest Becker, *The Denial of Death* (New York: The Free Press, 1973), x.

5. Richard Clark, *Against All Enemies: Inside America's War on Terror* (New York: Free Press, 2004), 24.

6. Since the concept of deterrence is bedeviled by ambiguity, there is considerable controversy as to what constitutes a failure of deterrence. True, most would agree that a full-scale Soviet attack on the United States would be such a failure, but what of the North Korean attack on the South or the Vietnamese resistance to the U.S. invasion?

7. Randolph Starn, "Historians and Crisis" *Past and Present,* 52 (Fall 1971), 3.

8. See Herman Kahn's *On Escalation: Metaphors and Scenarios* (New York: Praeger, 1965), 9–15 and Chapters IV and V.

9. Ibid., 69.

10. Dwight D. Eisenhower, "Farewell to the Nation," *U.S. Department of State Bulletin* (February 6, 1961), 44.

11. See Richard K. Betts's discussion in his *Nuclear Blackmail and Nuclear Balance* (Washington: The Brookings Institution, 1987), 138–141.

12. Quoted by Michael Beschloss, *The Crisis Years* (New York: HarperCollins, 1991), 225.

13. Khrushchev's account of this and other confrontations involving Berlin is found in *Khrushchev Remembers,* Edward Crankshaw, ed. (New York: Bantam, 1971), 500–510. Many of Crankshaw's glosses on Khrushchev's commentaries seem inappropriate, if not patronizing, as he reminds the reader of the American position and Khrushchev's "true" motives.

14. Betts offer a succinct account of the episode in his *Nuclear Blackmail and Nuclear Balance* (Washington: The Brookings Institution, 1987), 23–30.

15. Ibid.

16. Ibid.

17. Khrushchev, *Khrushchev Remembers,* 500.

18. McGeorge Bundy, *Danger and Survival* (New York: Random House, 1988), 363.

19. Ibid., 359.

20. Khrushchev, *Khrushchev Remembers*, 502.

21. Ibid., 503.

22. An anonymous source quoted by Gerald S. Strober and Deborah H. Strober, *"Let Us Begin Anew": An Oral History of the Kennedy Presidency* (New York: HarperCollins, 1993), 334–335.

23. Khrushchev, *Khrushchev Remembers*, 507.

24. Laurence Change and Peter Kornbluh, eds., *The Cuban Missile Crisis* (New York: New Press, 1992), 11–12. This volume contains documents declassified by the authors' organization, the National Security Archive, Washington. D.C.

25. See Richard K. Betts's discussion, *Nuclear Blackmail*, 92–109.

26. This confrontation is quoted and discussed by Michael Beschloss, *The Crisis Years* (New York: HarperCollins, 1991), 223–224.

27. Theodore Sorensen, *Kennedy* (New York: Harper & Row, 1965), 587.

28. See Betts's discussion, *Nuclear Blackmail*, 94–95.

29. Quoted by Betts, *Nuclear Blackmail*, 96–97.

30. Ronald Steel, "Lessons of the Cuban Missile Crisis," in *The Cuban Missile Crisis*, Robert Divine, ed. (Chicago: Quadrangle Books, 1971), 229–230.

31. See Betts' discussion, *Nuclear Blackmail*, 105.

32. Beschloss, *The Crisis Years*, 332.

33. Khrushchev, *Khrushchev Remembers*, 509.

34. Quoted by Beschloss, *The Crisis Years*, 334.

35. Khrushchev, *Khrushchev Remembers*, 504.

36. Quoted by Khrushchev, Ibid., 273–274.

37. Quoted by Chang and Kornbluh, *The Cuban Missile Crisis*, 15.

38. Quoted by Patrick Glynn in his *Closing Pandora's Box* (New York: Basic Books, 1992), 179.

39. Kissinger, *Years of Upheaval* (Boston: Little and Brown & Co., 1982), 538.

40. Khrushchev, *Khrushchev Remembers*, 481.

41. Ibid., 475.

42. Kissinger, *Years of Upheaval*, 525.

43. Ibid., 528–529.

44. See Kissinger's discussion of these threats, *Years of Upheaval*, 542–543.

45. Quoted by Betts, *Nuclear Blackmail*, 62.

46. Quoted by Betts, Ibid., 531 and 537.

47. Ibid., 532.

48. R.H.S. Crossman, "The Suez Question," *New York Review of Books*, Vol. 2, No. 8, May 28, 1964, http://www.nybooks.com/articles/4943, 2–3.

49. Ibid., 2.

50. Quoted by Crossman, Ibid., 534.

51. Ibid., 548.

52. Betts, *The Cuban Missile Crisis*, 123.

53. Joan Hoff-Wilson, "Richard M. Nixon: The Corporate President" in *Leadership in the Modern Presidency*, Fred I Greenstein, ed. (Cambridge: Harvard University Press, 1988), 168.

54. McGeorge Bundy's discussion in his *Danger and Survival* (New York: Random House, 1987), 519.

55. Quoted by Bundy, Ibid., 518.

56. Ibid., 521.

57. See Betts's conclusion, *The Cuban Missile Crisis*, 129; and Bundy's *Danger and Survival*, 524–525.

58. Quoted by Bundy, *Danger and Survival*, 524.

59. Murray Edelman, *Constructing the Political Spectacle* (Chicago: University of Chicago Press, 1988), 31.

60. Betts, *Nuclear Survival*, 113.

61. Garry Wills, *The Kennedy Imprisonment* (Boston: Little, Brown, 1981), 218.

62. Quoted by Richard M. Nixon, in his *RN: The Memoirs of Richard Nixon* (New York: Grosset & Dunlap, 1978), 235.

63. See Victor Turner's discussion of the social dramas known as crises, and the liminal nature of these episodes, in his *Dramas, Fields, and Metaphors* (Ithaca, N.Y.: Cornell University Press, 1974).

64. Khrushchev, *Khrushchev Remembers*, 546.

65. Quoted by James G. Blight and David Welch, eds., *On The Brink: Americans and Soviets Reexamine the Cuban Missile Crisis* (New York: Hill and Wang, 1989), 63–64.

66. Personal letter from John A. McCone to Raymond L. Garthoff, September 22, 1987. In the letter, McCone claims that they didn't institute a blockade since they would have been charged with an act of war. Clearly the blockade was called a "quarantine" to avoid this charge.

67. Robert F. Kennedy, *Thirteen Days: A Memoir on the Cuban Missile Crisis* (New York: W. W. Norton, 1969), 70–71.

68. Interview with Raymond Garthoff at the Brookings Institution, August 1989. Garthoff, charged with compiling Cuban missile crisis documents for the Kennedy Library, claims that Robert Kennedy's calendar documenting these meetings was excised from the body of the documents. Anatoly Dobrynin corroborates Garthoff's claims about the secret meetings with Kennedy in his *In Confidence* (New York: Times Books, 1995), 84–88.

69. Kennedy, *Thirteen Days*, 109.

70. Garthoff interview.

71. Ibid.

72. Khrushchev, *Khrushchev Remembers*, 555.

73. Theodore Sorensen, *The Kennedy Legacy* (New York: Macmillan, 1969), 187.

74. Arthur Miller, "Introduction to Collected Plays" in *Willy Loman*, Harold Bloom, ed. (New York: Chelsea House, 1991), 39.

75. Richard M. Nixon, *Six Crises* (New York: Simon and Schuster, 1990), 254.

76. Arthur Miller, *Death of a Salesman* (New York: Viking Press, 1949), 36.

77. Quoted by Marvin Kalb, *The Nixon Memo* (Chicago: University of Chicago Press, 1994, 14.

78. Miller, "Introduction to Collected Plays," 2.

79. Ibid., 33–34.

80. James David Barber, *The Presidential Character*, 2nd ed. (Englewood Cliffs: Prentice Hall, 1977), 347.

81. Richard M. Nixon, *Leaders* (New York: Warner Books, 1982), 174.

82. Nixon, *Six Crises*, 205.

83. Ibid., 246.

84. Quoted by Nixon, Ibid., 253.

85. Ibid., 254.

86. Ibid., 255.

87. Ibid., 256–257.

88. Quoted by Nixon, Ibid., 258.

89. Plato, "Statesman," in *The Collected Dialogues of Plato,* Edith Hamilton and Huntington Cairns, eds. (New York: Pantheon Books, 1961), 1062.

90. Kissinger, *White House Years,* 55.

91. Randolph Starn, "Historians and Crisis," *Past and Present* , 52 (Fall 1971), 7.

92. "Mr. X" essay in *Foreign Affairs* attributed to George Kennan; see his discussion of this article in his *The Cloud of Danger* (Boston: Little, Brown, 1978).

93. Kissinger, *Years of Upheaval,* 65.

94. Ibid., 642–643.

95. Ibid. 645.

96. Ibid., 640.

97. See Hersh's discussion in *The Price of Power* (New York: Summit Books, 1983), Chapter 20.

98. Kissinger, *Years of Upheaval,* 646.

99. Ibid., 648.

100. Ibid., 647.

101. Ibid., 651.

102. H. R. Haldeman, *The Haldeman Diaries* (New York: Putnam, 1994), 197.

103. Quoted by Walter Isaacson in *Kissinger* (New York: Simon and Schuster, 1992), 647.

104. Fred Osler Hampson, "The Divided Decision-Maker: American Domestic Politics and the Cuban Crises," in *The Domestic Sources of Foreign Policy,* Charles W. Kegley, Jr. and Eugene Wittkopf, eds. (New York: St. Martin's Press, 1988), 244–245.

105. Ibid., 242–246.

106. Interview with Ambassador Ralph Earle; Chico, California; November 16, 1990.

107. Hampson, "The Divided Decision-Maker," 343.

CHAPTER 8

1. Isaiah Berlin, *Four Essays on Liberty* (Oxford, England: Oxford University Press, 1969), 54.

2. Robert F. Kennedy, *Thirteen Days: A Memoir on the Cuban Missile Crisis* (New York: W. W. Norton, 1969), 128.

3. See Michael Walzer's discussion of this *Dialogue* in his *Just and Unjust Wars* (New York: Basic Books, 1992), 5.

4. Ibid., 7.

5. Quoted by Walzer, Ibid., 240.

6. Quoted by Walzer, Ibid., 267.

7. McGeorge Bundy, *Danger and Survival* (New York: Random House, 1988), 97.

8. Kennedy, *Thirteen Days,* 67.

9. Quoted in the *San Francisco Chronicle,* July 23, 2003, D10.

10. Philip Roth, *The Plot Against America* (Boston: Houghton Mifflin, 2004), 114.

11. See my account of crisis decision-making in *What if They Gave a Crisis and Nobody Came: Interpreting International Crises* (Westport, Conn.: Praeger, 1997).

12. J. Peter Euben, *The Tragedy of Political Theory* (Princeton, N.J.: Princeton University Press, 1990), 36.

13. Walzer, *Just and Unjust Wars*, 251.

14. Ibid., 254.

15. Ibid., 260.

16. Walzer and Shue debate this topic in *Ethics and Weapons of Mass Destruction*, Sohail H. Hashmi and Steven P. Lee, eds. (Cambridge, England: Cambridge University Press, 2004), 139–167.

17. Walzer, *Just and Unjust Wars*, 323.

18. Ibid., 144.

19. Ibid., 267.

20. Ibid., 254.

21. Ibid.

22. Ibid., 269

23. Ibid., 270.

24. Reinhold Niebuhr, *Moral Man and Immoral Society* (New York: Scribners, 1932).

25. Ibid., 272.

26. Sohail H. Hashmi, "Islamic Ethics: An Argument for Nonproliferation," in Hasmi and Lee, *Ethics and Weapons*, 330.

27. David W. Chapell, "Buddhist Perspectives," in Ibid., 232.

28. Jane Mayer, "Outsourcing Torture, " in *The New Yorker*, February 14, 2005, 106–107.

29. Peter Berger and Thomas Luckman, "The Dehumanized World," in *The Truth About the Truth*, Walter Truett Anderson, ed. (New York: Putnam, 1995), 38.

30. Victor Turner, "Social Dramas and Stories About Them," *Critical Inquiry* 7 (1980), 141.

31. Victor Turner, "Dewey, Dilthey, and Drama" in *Anthropology of Experience*, Victor Turner and Edward M. Bruner, eds. (Urbana: University of Illinois Press, 1986), 36.

32. Erving Goffman, *The Presentation of Self in Everyday Life* (Garden City, N.Y.: Doubleday, 1959), 17.

EPILOGUE

1. Quoted by Garry Wills, "What is a Just War?," in *New York Review of Books*, Vol. LI, No. 14, November 18, 2004, 34.

2. See Gregg Herken's account of the debate between Borden and Brodie in Herken's *Counsels of War* (New York: Oxford University Press, 1987), 10–14.

3. William Borden, *There Will Be No Time: The Revolution in Strategy* (New York: Macmillan, 1946), 41.

4. Quoted by Herken, *Counsels of War*, 13.

5. Jonathan Schell, *The Abolition* (New York: Alfred A. Knopf, 1984), 21.

6. Robert Jay Lifton and Richard Falk, *Indefensible Weapons* (New York: Basic Books, 1983), Chapter 10.

7. James Fallows, *National Defense* (New York: Vintage, 1981), 176.

8. Pierre Teilhard de Chardin, *The Divine Milieu* (New York: Harper & Row, 1960), 6.

9. Michel de Montaigne, *The Complete Essays*, M.A. Screech, trans. (London: Penguin, 1987), 312.

10. Albert Camus, "The Absurdity of Human Existence," in *The Meaning of Life*, E.D. Klemke, ed. (New York: Oxford University Press, 2000), 98.

Bibliography

Aho, James A. "The Emerging Nuclear Death Cult." In *A Shuddering Dawn*, edited by Ira Chernus and Edward Tabor Linethal. Albany: State University of New York Press, 1989.

Allison, Graham. *The Essence of Decision: Explaining the Cuban Missile Crisis.* Boston: Little, Brown, 1971.

Alperovitz, Gar. *Atomic Diplomacy: Hiroshima and Potsdam.* New York: Vintage, 1965.

———. "New Evidence." *Bulletin of the Atomic Scientists,* June 1985.

Alsop, Stewart and Ralph E. Lapp. "The Strange Death of Louis Slotkin." In *Man Against Nature,* edited by C. Neider. New York: Harper, 1954.

Ambrose, Steven E. *Nixon,* vol. 2. New York: Simon and Schuster, 1989.

Aron, Raymond. *Peace and War: A Theory of International Relations.* Garden City, N.Y.: Doubleday,, 1966.

Axelrod, Daniel and Michio Kaku. *To Win a Nuclear War.* Boston: South End Press, 1987.

Barber, James David. *The Presidential Character.* 2nd ed. Englewood Cliffs, N.J.: Prentice Hall, 1977.

Barnet, Richard. *Roots of War.* New York: Penguin, 1981.

Becker, Ernest. *The Denial Of Death.* New York: The Free Press, 1973.

———. *The Structure of Evil.* New York: The Free Press, 1975.

———. "The Fragile Fiction." In *The Truth About the Truth,* edited by Walter Truett Anderson. New York: Putnam, 1995.

Beres, Louis. *Apocalypse.* Chicago: University of Chicago Press, 1980.

Berger, Peter and Thomas Luckman. "The Dehumanized World." In *The Truth About the Truth,* edited by Walter Truett Anderson. New York: Putnam, 1995.

Berlin, Isaiah. *Four Essays on Liberty*. Oxford, England: Oxford University Press, 1969.

Betts, Richard K. *Nuclear Blackmail and Nuclear Balance*. Washington, D.C.: The Brookings Institution, Washington, D.C., 1987.

Blair, Bruce. "Post Cold War Nuclear Strategies." http://twilight.dsi.unimi/it/uspid./Atti/Blair.html (accessed September 2004).

Blight, James G. and David Welch. *On The Brink: Americans and Soviets Reexamine the Cuban Missile Crisis*. New York: Hill and Wang, 1989.

Borden, William. *There Will Be No Time: The Revolution in Strategy*. New York: Macmillan, 1946.

Bottomore, Edgar. *The Balance of Terror*. Boston: Beacon Press, 1971.

Brodie, Bernard. *The Absolute Weapon: Atomic Power and World Order*. New York: Harcourt, 1946.

———. "Influence of Mass Destruction Weapons on Strategy" delivered at the Naval War College, May 3, 1956. [Reprinted in National Security Archive's "Nuclear History Project."]

Bueno de Mesquita, Bruce and William H. Riker. "An Assessment of the Merits of Selective Nuclear Proliferation." *Journal of Conflict Resolution* 26, no.2 (June 1982).

Bundy, McGeorge. *Danger and Survival*. New York: Random House, 1988.

Burr, William. "The Creation of SIOP-62: More Evidence on the Origins of Over-kill." In The National Security Archive Electronic Briefing Book #130, http://www.gwu.edu/-nsaarchiv/NSAEBB/NSAEBB130/index.htm.

Caldicott, Helen. *Nuclear Madness: What You Can Do*. New York: Bantam Books, 1980.

———. *Missile Envy: The Arms Race and Nuclear War*. New York: William Morrow, 1984.

Camus, Albert. "The Absurdity of Human Existence." In *The Meaning of Life*, edited by E. D. Klemke. New York: Oxford University Press, 2000.

———. *Neither Victims Nor Executioners*. Berkeley: World Without War Council, 1968.

Canaday, John. *The Nuclear Muse*. Madison: University of Wisconsin Press, 2000.

Carnesale, Albert, and Paul Doty et al. *Living With Nuclear Weapons*. New York: Bantam Books, 1983.

Carroll, Eugene Jr. "Nuclear Weapons and Deterrence." In *The Nuclear Crisis Reader*, edited by Gwyn Prins. New York: Vintage, 1984.

———. Interview in Chico, California, November 16, 1988.

———. Interview at the Center for Defense Information, Washington, D.C., December 19, 1999.

———. Interview at the Center for Defense Information, Washington, D.C., March 18, 1999.

Cassirer, Ernest. *An Essay of Man*. Garden City, N.Y.: Doubleday Anchor, 1956.

Change, Laurence and Peter Kornbluh. *The Cuban Missile Crisis*. New York: New Press, 1992.

Chardin, Pierre Teilhard de. *The Divine Milieu*. New York: Harper & Row, 1960.

Chernus, Ira. *Dr. Strangegod: On the Symbolic Meaning of Nuclear Weapons*. Columbia: University of South Carolina Press, 1986.

Chevalier, Haakon. *The Man Who Would Be God*. New York: Putnam, 1959.

Chilton, Paul. "Nukespeak: Nuclear Language, Culture and Propaganda." In *The Nuclear Predicament*, edited by Donna Gregory. New York: St. Martin's Press, 1986.

Clark, Richard. *Against All Enemies: Inside America's War on Terror.* New York: Free Press, 2004.

Clark, Ronald W. *The Greatest Power on Earth.* New York: Harper and Row, 1980.

Claude, Inis. L. Jr. *Power and International Relations.* New York: Random House, 1962.

Cohn, Carol. "Nuclear Language and How We Learned to Pat the Bomb." In *Making War/Making Peace,* edited by Francesca M. Cancian and James William Gibson. Belmont, CA: Wadsworth, 1990.

Crane, Gregory. "Thucydides and the Ancient Simplicity." http://texts.cdlib.org/dynamaxSML?docld (accessed September 2004). (University of California Press, Internet Scholarship Editions.)

Crossman, R.H.S. "The Suez Question." *New York Review of Books.* Vol. 2, No. 8 (May 28, 1964), http://www.nybooks.com/articles/13343.

Dobrynin, Anatoly. *In Confidence.* New York: Times Books, 1995.

Dostoevsky, Fyodor. "Notes from Underground." In *Fyodor Dostoevsky,* edited by Walter Kaufman. New York: Penguin, 1963.

Draper, Theodore. "An Open Letter to Weinberger." *The New York Review of Books,* Vol. xxix, No. 17.

Durrenmatt, Friedrich. *The Physicists.* New York: Grove Press, 1984.

Eagleburger, Lawrence. "The New Security Challenges and the Future Role of the Alliance," a lecture presented to the Eurogroup Conference, Washington, D.C., June 25, 1991.

Earle, Ambassador Ralph. Lecture in Chico, California, November 16, 1990.

Edelman, Murray. *Constructing the Political Spectacle.* Chicago: University of Chicago Press, 1988.

———. *Politics as Symbolic Action: Mass Arousal and Quiescence.* Chicago: Markham, 1971.

Eisenhower, Dwight D. "Farewell to the Nation." *U.S. Department of State Bulletin.* February 6, 1961.

Eliade, Mircea. *The Sacred and the Profane.* New York: Harcourt, 1987.

Ellsberg, Daniel. "A Call to Mutiny." In *Protest and Survive,* edited by E. P. Thompson and Dan Smith. New York and London: Monthly Review Press, 1981.

Euben, J. Peter. *The Tragedy of Political Theory.* Princeton, N.J.: Princeton University Press, 1990.

Fallows, James. *National Defense.* New York: Vintage, 1981.

Ford, Daniel. "The Cult of the Atom." *The New Yorker.* 25, October, 1987.

Foucault, Michel. "The Order of Discourse." In *Language and Politics,* edited by Michael Shapiro. New York: New York University Press, 1989.

Frank, Jerome. *Sanity and Survival.* New York: Random House, 1967.

Freedman, Lawrence. *The Evolution of Nuclear Strategy.* 2nd ed. New York: St. Martin's Press, 1989.

———. *The Price of Peace.* New York, Henry Holt, 1986.

Freud, Sigmund. *Group Psychology.* New York: W. W. Norton, 1959.

Freyberg-Inan, Annette. *What Moves Man: The Realist Theory of International Relations and its Judgment of Human Nature.* Albany: State University of New York Press, 2004.

Garthoff, Raymond. Interview at the Brookings Institution, Washington, D.C., August 1989.

Geertz, Clifford. *Local Knowledge.* New York: Basic Books, 1983.

George, Jim. *Discourses of Global Politics: Critical (Re)Introduction to International Relations.* Boulder, Col.: Lynne Rienner Publishers, 1994.

Glynn, Patrick. *Closing Pandora's Box.* New York: Basic Books, 1992.

Goffman, Erving. *The Presentation of Self in Everyday Life.* Garden City, N.Y.: Doubleday, 1959.

Gray, Colin. "Victory is Possible." *Foreign Policy.* Summer, 1980.

Green, Philip. *Deadly Logic: The Theory of Nuclear Deterrence.* New York: Schocken Books, 1969.

Gregg, David. W. *Worker Protection Alternatives for a Nuclear Attack with 30 Minutes (or Less) Warning.* Washington, D.C.: National Technical Information Service, 1984.

———. "Memorandum to All Concerned LLNL Employees." Oct. 26, 1984, 3.

Gusterson, Hugh. "Tall Tales and Deceptive Discourses." *Bulletin of the Atomic Scientists.* Nov/Dec. 2001.

Haldeman, H. R. *The Haldeman Diaries.* New York: Putnam, 1994.

Hampson, Fred Osler. "The Divided Decision-Maker: American Domestic Politics and the Cuban Crises." In *The Domestic Sources of Foreign Policy,* edited by Charles W. Kegley, Jr. and Eugene Wittkopf. New York: St. Martin's Press, 1988.

Herken, Gregg. *Counsels of War.* New York: Oxford University Press, 1987.

———. "The Earthly Origin of Star Wars." *The Bulletin of the Atomic Scientists.* October, 1987.

———. *The Winning Weapon.* New York: Vintage, 1982.

Hersh, Seymour. *The Price of Power.* New York: Summit Books, 1983.

Herz, John H. "Political Realism Revisited." *International Studies Quarterly.* Vol. 25, No. 2 (June 1981).

Hirschbein, Ron. *What if They Gave a Crisis and Nobody Came: Interpreting International Crises.* Westport, Conn.: Praeger, 1997.

Hoff-Wilson, Joan. "Richard M. Nixon: The Corporate President." In *Leadership in the Modern Presidency,* edited by Fred I Greenstein. Cambridge, Mass.: Harvard University Press, 1988.

Holsti, Ole R. "Crisis Decision Making." In *Behavior, Society and Nuclear War,* Vol. 1, edited by Philip Tetlock, Jo Husbands, et al. New York: Oxford University Press, 1989.

———. *Crisis Escalation War.* Montreal: McGill-Queen's University Press, 1972.

Isaacson, Walter. *Kissinger.* New York: Simon and Schuster, 1992.

Johnson, General K. D. "The Morality of Nuclear Deterrence." In *The Nuclear Crisis Reader,* edited by Gwyn Prins. New York: Vintage, 1984.

Kahn, Herman. *On Escalation: Metaphors and Scenarios.* New York: Praeger, 1965.

———. *On Thermonuclear War.* Princeton, N.J.: Princeton University Press, 1960.

———. *Thinking About the Unthinkable.* New York: Avon, 1962.

Kalb, Marvin. *The Nixon Memo.* Chicago: University of Chicago Press, 1994.

Kaplan, Fred. *The Wizards of Armageddon.* New York: Simon and Schuster, 1983.

Kennan, George. *Cloud of Danger.* Boston: Little, Brown, 1978.

Kennedy, Robert. *Thirteen Days: A Memoir of the Cuban Missile Crisis.* New York: W. W. Norton, 1969.

Khrushchev, Nikita. *Khrushchev Remembers*, edited by Edward Crankshaw. New York: Bantam, 1971.

Kissinger, Henry A. *American Foreign Policy*. New York: W.W. Norton, 1979.

———. *The White House Years*. Boston: Little, Brown, 1979.

———. *Years of Upheaval*. Boston: Little and Brown & Co., 1982.

Kitto, H.D.F. *Greek Tragedy*. London: Methuen & Co., 1978.

Kovel, Joel. *Against the State of Nuclear Terror*. Boston: South End Press, 1981.

Kull, Steven. *Minds at War: Nuclear Reality and the Inner Conflicts of Defense Policy Makers*. New York: Basic Books, 1988.

Kundera, Milan. *The Book of Laughter and Forgetting*. New York: Penguin, 1987.

Lakoff, George and Mark Johnson. *Metaphors We Live By*. Chicago: University of Chicago Press, 1980.

Lens, Sidney. *The Day Before Doomsday*. Boston: Beacon Press, 1977.

Lifton, Robert Jay. *The Broken Connection*. New York: Simon and Schuster, 1979.

Lifton, Robert Jay and Richard Falk. *Indefensible Weapons*. New York: Basic Books, 1982.

Lilienthal, David. *Change, Hope & The Bomb*. Princeton, N.J.: Princeton University Press, 1963.

Luttwak, Edward. *Strategy: The Logic of War and Peace*. Cambridge, Mass.: Harvard University Press, 1987.

MacArthur, Douglas. "Nuclear War: 'A Frankenstein.'" In *Rumors of War*, edited by C.A. Ceseratti and J.T. Vitale. New York: Seabury Press, 1982.

Malcolmson, Robert W. *Nuclear Fallacies*. Kingston and Montreal: McGill University Press, 1985.

McCone, John A. Personal letter from John A. McCone to Raymond L. Garhoff, September 22, 1987.

McNamara, Robert S. *In Retrospect: The Tragedy and Lessons of Vietnam*. New York: Vintage, 1996.

McNamara, Robert and Helen Caldicott. "Still on Catastrophe's Edge." *Los Angeles Times*, April 26, 2004.

Mandelbaum, Michael. *The Nuclear Question*. Cambridge, England: Cambridge University Press, 1979.

Mencken, H.L. "Notes on Democracy." In *American Political Thinking*, edited by Robert Isask. Fort Worth, Tex.: Harcourt Brace, 1994.

Mill, John Stuart. *On Liberty*. Indianapolis, Ind.: Hacket, 1978.

Miller, Arthur. "Introduction to Collected Plays." In *Willy Loman*, edited by Harold Bloom. New York: Chelsea House, 1991.

———. *Death of a Salesman*. New York: Viking Press, 1949.

Mills, C. Wright. *The Causes of World War III*. New York: Ballantine, 1958.

Montaigne, Michel de. *The Complete Essays*. Translated by M.A. Screech. London: Penguin, 1987.

Morgenthau, Hans. *Scientific Man v. Power Politics*. Chicago: University of Chicago Press, 1946.

Moss, Peter. "Rhetoric of Defense in the United States: Language, Myth, and Ideology." In *Language and the Nuclear Arms Debate: Nukespeak Today*, edited by Paul Chilton. London: Frances Pinter, 1983.

Neiman, Susan. *Evil in Modern Thought*. Princeton, N.J.: Princeton University Press, 2002.

Neustadt, Richard and Ernest May. *Thinking in Time*. New York: The Free Press, 1986.

Nixon, Richard M. *Leaders*. New York: Warner Books, 1982.

———. *The Memoirs of Richard Nixon*. Boston: Grosset & Dunlap, 1978.

———. *Six Crises*. New York: Simon and Schuster, 1990.

O'Keefe, Bernard, *Nuclear Hostages*. Boston: Houghton Mifflin, 1983.

Plato. "Statesman." In *The Collected Dialogues of Plato*, edited by Edith Hamilton and Huntington Cairns. New York: Pantheon Books, 1961.

Popper, Karl. "Science: Conjectures and Refutations." In *Philosophy of Science*, edited by E. D. Klemke et. al. Amherst, Mass.: Prometheus Books, 1998.

Prados, John in "Woolsey and the CIA." In *Bulletin of the Atomic Scientists*, Vol. 49, no. 6 July/August 1993.

Raskin, Marcus. *The Metadeath Intellectuals*. http://www.nybooks.com/articles/13621.

Rhodes, Richard. *The Making of the Atomic Bomb*. New York: Simon & Schuster, 1988.

Rorty, Richard. "Ironists and Metaphysicians." In *The Truth about the Truth*, edited by Walter Truett Anderson. New York: Putnam, 1995.

Rotblat, Joseph. "Leaving the Bomb Project." In *Assessing the Nuclear Age*, edited by Harrison Brown. Chicago: The Bulletin of the Atomic Scientists, 1986.

Russell, Diana E.H., ed. *Exposing Nuclear Phallacies*. New York: Pergamon Press, 1989.

Sagan, Scott D. and Kenneth N. Waltz. *The Spread of Nuclear Weapons: A Debate*. New York: W. W. Norton, 1995.

Schell, Jonathan, *The Abolition*. New York: Knopf, 1984.

———. *The Gift of Time*. New York: Metropolitan Books, 1998.

———. *The Unconquerable World*. New York: Metropolitan Books, 2003.

———. "Reflections." *The New Yorker*. Feb. 15, 1982.

Schelling, Thomas C. *Arms and Influence*. New Haven, Conn.: Yale University Press, 1962.

———. *The Strategy of Conflict*. New York: Oxford University Press, 1963.

———. "War without Pain and Other Models." *World Politics*. XV April, 1963.

Slouka, Mark. "A Year Later: Notes on America's Intimations of Mortality." *Harper's*. September 2002.

Sorensen, Theodore. *Kennedy*. New York: Harper & Row, 1965.

———. *The Kennedy Legacy*. New York: Macmillan, 1969.

Starn, Randolph. "Historians and Crisis." *Past and Present*. 52 (Fall 1971).

Steel, Ronald. "Lessons of the Cuban Missile Crisis." In *The Cuban Missile Crisis*, edited by Robert Divine. Chicago: Quadrangle Books, 1971.

———. "War Games," *New York Review of Books*, Vol. 6, #10 (June 9, 1966).

Strober, Gerald S. and Deborah H. Strober. *"Let Us Begin Anew": An Oral History of the Kennedy Presidency*. New York: HarperCollins, 1993.

Thompson, E. P. "The Logic of Exterminism." *New Left Review*, #121.

Tuchman, Barbara. *The March of Folly*. New York: Alfred Knopf, 1984.

Turner, Victor. *Dramas, Fields, and Metaphors*. Ithaca, N.Y.: Cornell University Press, 1971.

———. "Dewey, Dilthey, and Drama." In *Anthropology of Experience*, edited by Victor Turner and Edward M. Bruner. Urbana: University of Illinois Press, 1986.

———. "Social Dramas and Stories About Them." *Critical Inquiry* 7 (1980).

Wallace, Anthony *Religion: An Anthropological View*. New York: Random House, 1966.

Walzer, Michael. "Dialogue." *Just and Unjust Wars*. New York: Basic Books, 1992.

Weart, Spencer R. *Nuclear Fear*. Cambridge, Mass.: Harvard University Press, 1988.

Weinberger, Alvin. "Can Technology Replace Social Engineering?" In *Technology and the Future*, edited by Albert Teich. New York: St. Martin's Press, 1986.

———. "Sacrifice." *The Bulletin of the Atomic Scientists*, June 1985.

Weinberger, Caspar. "A Rational Approach to Nuclear Disarmament." In *The Ethics of Nuclear Deterrence*, edited by James Sterba. Belmont, CA: Wadsworth, 1985.

Weisskopf, Victor. "Looking Back at Los Alamos." In *Assessing the Nuclear Age*, edited by Len Ackland and Steve McGuire. Chicago: University of Chicago Press, 1986.

Wicker, Tom. *One of Us: Richard Nixon and the American Dream*. New York: Random House, 1992.

Wieseltier, Leon. *Nuclear War/Nuclear Peace*. New York: Holt, Rinehart & Winston, 1983.

Wills, Garry. *The Kennedy Imprisonment*. Boston: Little, Brown, 1981.

———. "What is a Just War?" *New York Review of Books*, Vo. LI, #14 (Nov. 18, 2004).

Wohlstetter, Albert. "The Delicate Balance of Terror." *Foreign Affairs*, Vol. 37, #2, (Jan. 1959).

Worner, Manfred. "The Atlantic Alliance in the New Era." *NATO Review*, Vol. 39, #1 (Feb. 1991).

Yanow, Dvora, "Public Policies as Identity Stories." *Advances in Program Evaluation*, JAI Press, Vol. 6 (1999).

York, Herbert. *Making Weapons/Talking Peace*. New York: Basic Books, 1987.

———. *Race to Oblivion*. New York: Simon and Schuster, 1970.

Zuckerman, Solly. "Nuclear Fantasies." *New York Review of Books*, June 14, 1984.

Index

About the Author

RON HIRSCHBEIN is Professor of Philosophy and Director of the Peace Institute at California State University, Chico. Hirschbein has served as a visiting professor at University of California campuses in peace and conflict studies at Berkeley and San Diego, and at the United Nations University in Austria. He also served as President, Concerned Philosophers for Peace. He is the author of numerous articles and books offering a humanistic approach to a variety of foreign and domestic controversies.